THE MIND OF THE
EUROPEAN ROMANTICS

300-3
51

Also by H. G. Schenk

THE AFTERMATH OF THE NAPOLEONIC WARS (1947)
DIE KULTURKRITIK DER EUROPÄISCHEN ROMANTIK (1956)

Delacroix (self-portrait)

THE MIND
OF THE
EUROPEAN ROMANTICS

AN ESSAY
IN CULTURAL HISTORY

by
H. G. SCHENK

With a Preface by
Isaiah Berlin

Oxford New York Toronto Melbourne
OXFORD UNIVERSITY PRESS
1979

Oxford University Press, Walton Street, Oxford OX2 6DP

OXFORD LONDON GLASGOW
NEW YORK TORONTO MELBOURNE WELLINGTON
KUALA LUMPUR SINGAPORE JAKARTA HONG KONG TOKYO
DELHI BOMBAY CALCUTTA MADRAS KARACHI
IBADAN NAIROBI DAR ES SALAAM CAPE TOWN

British Library Cataloguing in Publication Data

Schenk, Hans Georg
The mind of the European Romantics.
1. Romanticism – Europe
I. Title
700′.94   PN751   78–41047

ISBN 0–19–285083–0

Printed in Great Britain by
Lowe & Brydone Printers Limited, Thetford, Norfolk.

To my Wife

and to the memory of my Brother Wilhelm

Acknowledgements

MY work on this subject would have been impossible without the resources of the Bodleian Library and of the Taylor Institution at Oxford, as well as of the British Museum and the London Library. Owing to the generous hospitality of my friends Charles and Kitty Crawley I was also able to pay frequent visits to the Cambridge University Library. My thanks are due to the staffs of all these libraries. Travel grants from the Modern History and Social Studies Faculties of Oxford University enabled me to consult important foreign libraries, notably in Paris, Basle, Heidelberg and Tübingen, and to establish invaluable personal contacts with foreign scholars working in the same field, among them Pierre Moreau, and the late Walter Muschg, Paul Kluckhohn and Fritz Strich. I am also indebted to the Nietzsche-Stiftung in Switzerland, who invited me to spend some time at the Nietzsche-Haus in Sils-Maria, the ideal setting for reflections on the Epilogue to this book. In England I received much encouragement from Basil Willey at Cambridge and from the late Helen Darbishire, whom I had the privilege to meet on one of my frequent visits to Grasmere.

Special thanks are due to my friends Margaret Toynbee, John Walsh, Kenneth Ballhatchet and Harry Booth, who at various stages carefully scrutinized the manuscript, and to Mrs. Anna Winternitz who produced an impeccable typescript. My late brother Wilhelm always took a deep interest in my work and was a fruitful source of inspiration to me in the conception of this book. To my mother, who died shortly before the completion of the manuscript, I owe the early development of my taste in Romanticism and the many opportunities to discuss my work as it grew. Words are inadequate to express my indebtedness to my wife, without whose unfailing support and encouragement this book could never have been written.

H. G. S.

Oxford, 1966

Contents

Contents

Part Four:

ROMANTIC ENCHANTMENT

Illustrations

The portraits of Delacroix, Schlegel, Goya, George Sand,
Beethoven and Wagner are reproduced by courtesy of The
Mansell Collection; those of Manzoni, Lenau, Lamennais,
Lermontov, Schelling, Liszt and Nietzsche by courtesy of The
Radio Times Hulton Picture Library.

Preface

by

ISAIAH BERLIN

INTELLECTUAL history is a field in which English writers, in general, have taken less interest than those of other countries. There are notable exceptions to this rule; but they are few. The history of English thought, even in the nineteenth century when it had greater influence than that of any other country, still remains to be written.

The controversy about the relation of ideas to action is, perhaps for this reason, an issue, but not a live issue, in the writings of British historians, philosophers and critics. The examination of the interplay of ideas with social, economic and technological development has (especially in the last two hundred years) largely been left to writers of other nations; and even then more attention has been paid in England to their conclusions than to their methods. It may be that the particular pattern of social and political development in the British Isles has served to concentrate the attention of modern British historians—those of the eighteenth century and after—on the causes and effects of the great social upheavals: the Industrial Revolution, the French Revolution and their consequences; and has led to a relative neglect on their part of the other great movement, contemporary with these, which, no less than the Renaissance, the Reformation and the rise of the natural sciences and technology has altered ways of thinking and behaviour in the West. Perhaps it should not be described as a movement—which implies some degree of organization—so much as a set of attitudes, a way of thinking and acting that is loosely described as Romantic. This topic is usually left to the history of literature and the arts. Yet it is a wider force which for two hundred years has deeply, and indeed decisively, affected European life. The word Romanticism is vague, and like most terms of its kind, tends to be too general to be of use. "It is impossible to think seriously with words such as Classicism, Romanticism, Humanism or Realism," said a famous French poet and critic in the early years of the twentieth century. "One cannot get drunk or quench one's thirst with labels on a bottle." Yet it is scarcely deniable that during the period that begins in the late Renaissance and ends with the full development of industrial capitalism, a vast transformation of ideas, language, attitudes, ways of thinking and acting took place. Any student of the eighteenth century is bound to notice that towards its end the beliefs of two millenniums were, if not destroyed, at any rate challenged on an ever-widening scale; and that many of them were undermined.

Since the Greeks, and perhaps long before them, men had believed that to the central questions about the nature and purpose of their lives and of the world in which they lived, true, objective, universal and eternal answers could be found. If the answers could not be discovered by me, then perhaps by someone more expert or wiser than I; if not in the circumstances in which I found myself, then in others more propitious: in an innocent and happy past— a Garden of Eden from which our ancestors had for their sins been expelled, or perhaps in a Golden Age that still lay in the future, which posterity (perhaps after much labour and suffering) would, or at any rate could, one day reach. It was assumed that all the truly central problems were soluble in principle even if not in practice. Somewhere true answers to all genuine questions must exist, if not in the minds of men, then in the mind of an omniscient being—real or imaginary, material or ideal, a personal Deity, or the universe come to full consciousness of itself. The presupposition that underlies most classical and Christian thought, orthodox and heretical, scientific and religious, was connected with the belief that, whether men knew it or not, the whole of life on earth was in some sense bound up with the search for answers to the great, tormenting questions of fact and of conduct; of what there is, was, will be, can be; of what to do, what to live by, what to seek, hope for, admire, fear, avoid; whether the end of life was happiness or justice or virtue or self-fulfilment or grace and salvation. Individuals, schools of thought, entire civilizations differed about what the answers were, about the proper method of discovering them, about the nature and place of moral or spiritual or scientific authority—that is to say, how to identify the experts who are qualified to discover and communicate the answers; they argued about what constitutes such qualifications and justifies such claims to authority. But there was no doubt that the truth lay somewhere; that it could in principle be found. Conflicting beliefs were held about the central questions: whether the truth was to be found in reason or in faith, in the Church or the laboratory, in the insights of the uniquely privileged individual—a prophet, a mystic, an alchemist, a metaphysician; or in the collective consciousness of a body of men—the society of the faithful, the traditions of a tribe, a race, a nation, a social class, an academy of experts, an *élite* of uniquely endowed or trained beings; or, on the contrary, in the mind or heart of any man, anywhere, at any time, provided that he remained innocent and uncorrupted by false doctrines. What was common to all these views—incompatible enough for wars of extermination to have been fought in their name—was the assumption that there existed a reality, a structure of things, a *rerum natura*, which the qualified inquirer could see, study and, in principle, get right. Men were violently divided about the nature and identity of the wise—those who understood the nature of things—but not about the proposition that such wise men existed or could be conceived, and that they would know that which would enable them to deduce correctly what men should believe, how they should act, what they should live by and for.

This was the great foundation of belief which Romanticism attacked and weakened. Whatever the differences between the leading Romantic thinkers—the early Schiller and the later Fichte, Schelling and Jacobi, Tieck and the Schlegels when they were young, Chateaubriand and Byron, Coleridge and Carlyle, Kierkegaard, Stirner, Nietzsche, Baudelaire—there runs through their writings a common notion, held with varying degrees of consciousness and depth, that truth is not an objective structure, independent of those who seek it, the hidden treasure waiting to be found but is itself in all its guises created by the seeker. It is not to be brought into being necessarily by the finite individual: according to some it is created by a greater power, a universal spirit, personal or impersonal, in which the individual is an element, or of which he is an aspect, an emanation, an imperfect reflection. But the common assumption of the Romantics that runs counter to the *philosophia perennis* is that the answers to the great questions are not to be discovered so much as to be invented. They are not something found, they are something literally made. In its extreme Idealistic form it is a vision of the entire world. In its more familiar form, it confines itself to the realm of values, ideals, rules of conduct, aesthetic, religious, social, moral, political, not of a natural or supernatural order capable of being investigated, described and explained by the appropriate method—rational examination or some more mysterious procedure—but of something that man creates, as he creates works of art; not by imitating, or even obtaining illumination from pre-existent models or truths, or by applying pre-existent truths or rules, that are objective, universal, eternal, unalterable; but by an act of creation, the introduction into the world of something literally novel—the unique expression of an individual and therefore unique, creative activity, natural or supernatural, human or in part divine, owing nothing to anything outside it (in some versions because nothing can be conceived as being outside it) self-subsistent, self-justified, self-fulfilling. Hence that new emphasis on the subjective and ideal rather than the objective and the real, on the process of creation rather than its effects, on motives rather than consequences; and, as a necessary corollary of this, on the quality of the vision—the state of mind or soul of the acting agent—purity of heart, innocence of intention—sincerity of purpose rather than getting the answer right—accurate correspondence to the 'given'. Hence the emphasis on activity, movement, that cannot be reduced to static segments, the flow that cannot be arrested, frozen, analysed without being thereby fatally distorted; hence the constant protest against the reduction of 'life' to dead fragments of organism, to 'mere' mechanical or uniform units; and the corresponding tendency towards similes and metaphors drawn from 'dynamic' sciences—biology, physiology, introspective psychology—and the worship of music, which, of all the arts, appears to have the least relation to universally observable, uniform natural order. Hence, too, celebration of all forms of defiance directed against the 'given'—the impersonal, the 'brute fact' in morals or in politics or against the static and the accepted, and the value placed on minorities and martyrs as such, no matter what the ideal for which they suffer. This, too, is the thought of the doctrine that work is sacred as such, not because of its social function, but because it is the imposition of the individual or collective personality, that is, activity, upon inert stuff. The activity, the struggle is all, the victory nothing: in Fichte's words, "Frey seyn ist nichts; frey werden ist der Himmel." (To be free is nothing; to become free is very Heaven.) Failure is nobler than success. Self-immolation for a cause is the thing, not the validity of the cause itself, for it is the sacrifice undertaken for its sake that sanctifies the cause, not some intrinsic property of it. These are the symptoms of the Romantic attitude. Hence the worship of the artist, whether in sound, or word, or colour, as the highest manifestation of the ever-active spirit, and the popular image of the artist in his garret, wild-eyed, wild-haired, poor, solitary, mocked-at; but independent, free, spiritually superior to his Philistine tormentors. This attitude has a darker side too: worship not merely of the painter or the composer or the poet, but of that more sinister artist whose materials are men—the destroyer of old societies and the creator of new ones—no matter at what human cost: the superhuman leader who tortures and destroys in order to build on new foundations—Napoleon in his most revolutionary aspect. It is this embodiment of the Romantic ideal that took more and more hysterical forms and in its extreme ended in violent irrationalism and Fascism. Yet this same outlook also bred respect for individuality, for the creative impulse, for the unique, the independent, for freedom to live and act in the light of personal, undictated beliefs and principles, of undistorted emotional needs, for the value of private life, of personal relationships, of the individual conscience, of human rights. The positive and negative heritage of Romanticism—on the one hand contempt for opportunism, regard for individual variety, scepticism of oppressive general formulae and final solutions, and on the other self-prostration before superior beings and the exaltation of arbitrary power, passion and cruelty—these tendencies all at once reflected and promoted by Romantic doctrines have done more to mould both the events of our century and the concepts in terms of which they are viewed and explained than is commonly recognized in most histories of our time.

I do not, of course, wish to suggest that Dr. Schenk is committed to accepting the view that I have tried to express; nor does he seek to deal with all the problems posed by Romanticists. The reader of his book will see that Dr. Schenk traces this movement in large measure to the waning of Christian orthodoxy and the despairing quest for means of escaping the spiritual devastation that was created, and suggests that this at times led to nihilism, at other times to a return to Christianity—and especially the Roman Church—at times to an agonized oscillation between the two. No doubt this often was the case; and while it seems to me that this interpretation does not exhaust the issues—intellectual, emotional, social and historical—any more than other explanations that concentrate on a single factor, knowledge of the successive phases of the beliefs of Novalis, Friedrich Schlegel or Nietzsche is indispensable to any account of the Romanticists.

Dr. Schenk's wide learning and skill in conveying the ideas and the psychological characteristics of some among the leading Romantic thinkers and artists of the last two centuries is therefore to be warmly welcomed. If self-understanding is one of the goals—perhaps the central goal—of mental activity, Dr. Schenk deserves well of his English readers. For to most of them the world of which he writes (and by which their own outlook has been more profoundly affected than most of them suspect) remains largely unknown. This book constitutes a notable addition to the minimum of information needed by anyone who wants to understand how men in the West came to be what they are. It is to be hoped that Dr. Schenk's devoted labour will stimulate others to explore further this still underdeveloped, rich and critically important field.

Dramatis Personae

Atterbom, Swedish poet and scholar (1790–1855)
Baader, German Catholic philosopher (1765–1841)
Beethoven, German composer (1770–1827)
Berlioz, French composer (1803–69)
Byron, Lord, English poet and Philhellene (1788–1824)
Carlyle, Scottish historian and essayist (1795–1881)
Carus, German physician and philosopher (1789–1869)
Chateaubriand, French author and statesman (1768–1848)
Coleridge, English poet and philosopher (1772–1834)
Delacroix, French painter (1798–1863)
Eichendorff, German poet (1788–1857)
Fichte, German philosopher (1762–1814)
Fröbel, German educationist (1782–1852)
Garrett, Portuguese historical novelist (1799–1854)
Géricault, French painter (1791–1824)
Girodet-Trioson, French painter (1767–1824)
Görres, German historian and publicist (1776–1848)
Goya, Spanish painter and lithographer (1746–1828)
Hoffmann, German writer and musician (1776–1822)
Hugo, French poet and dramatist (1802–85)
Keats, English poet (1795–1821)
Kollár, Slovak scholar (1793–1852)
Krasiński, Polish poet and dramatist (1812–59)
Lamartine, French author and statesman (1790–1869)
Lamennais, French religious thinker and political publicist (1782–
    1854)
Lenau, Austrian poet and dramatist (1802–50)
Leopardi, Italian poet (1798–1837)
Lermontov, Russian poet and novelist (1814–47)
Liszt, Hungarian composer (1811–86)
Ludwig II, King of Bavaria (1845–86)
Manzoni, Italian poet and historical novelist (1785–1873)

Dramatis Personae

Michelet, French historian (1798–1874)

Mickiewicz, Polish poet and scholar (1798–1855)

Morphy, American chessmaster (1837–84)

Musset, French poet (1810–57)

Nerval, French poet (1808–55)

Nietzsche, German philosopher (1844–1900)

Nodier, French writer and scholar (1780–1844)

Novalis, German poet and philosopher (1772–1801)

Oehlenschläger, Danish poet (1779–1850)

Pugin, English architect (1812–52)

Rosmini-Serbati, Italian religious thinker (1797–1855)

Sand, George, French novelist (1804–76)

Schelling, German philosopher (1775–1854)

Schlegel, August Wilhelm, German poet and scholar (1767–1853)

Schlegel, Friedrich, German Catholic philosopher and critic (1772–1829)

Schleiermacher, German Protestant theologian (1768–1834)

Schopenhauer, German philosopher (1788–1860)

Schubert, Franz, Austrian composer (1797–1828)

Schubert, Gotthilf Heinrich, German scientist (1780–1860)

Schumann, German composer (1810–56)

Scott, Sir Walter, Scottish historical novelist (1771–1832)

Senancour, French essayist (1770–1846)

Shelley, English poet (1792–1822)

Sismondi, Swiss historian and economist (1773–1842)

Southey, English poet (1774–1843)

Staël, Baroness de, French writer (1766–1817)

Thierry, French historian (1795–1856)

Thoreau, American writer (1817–62)

Turner, English painter (1775–1851)

Vigny, French poet and historical novelist (1797–1863)

Wagner, German composer (1813–83)

Wergeland, Norwegian poet (1808–45)

Wordsworth, English poet (1770–1850)

Introduction

ROMANTICISM, that complex phenomenon which flourished in the first half of the nineteenth century, is still the most recent European-wide spiritual and intellectual movement. After about 1850 it came to be replaced by a host of other movements, less universal or less profound, and some of these—Symbolism, for example—continued to be strongly influenced by Romantic concepts.

In its territorial extent Romanticism not only affected all parts of Europe, with the exception of Turkey, but to a lesser extent even the Americas. Its scope was the widest imaginable. Far from being confined to literature in general, or poetry in particular, it manifested itself also in varying degrees in music and the visual arts, historiography and social thought, and in man's general outlook on life in this world and the next. The balance between man's rational and intuitive faculties, the approach to nature, the method of tackling medical and other sciences, and even the style of playing the time-honoured game of chess—all these and many other things besides came to be transformed by that all-embracing movement. Not that the epoch in question was entirely lacking in other intellectual currents. Moreover, even where Romanticism prevailed, we must be prepared to detect variations of each *leit-motiv* as it affected Romanticism in different countries and generations. As for the latter, the men or women of 1800, in whatever country, naturally differed in their outlook in many respects from the first Romantic generation born round about 1770. Nor must we expect each characteristic feature of the movement to be found in every single Romantic. Schopenhauer's disdain for the Middle Ages, for instance, is not sufficient evidence to disqualify him as a typical Romantic philosopher. Yet despite these variations it is my firm conviction that there exists a main theme, and thus my concern in the pages to follow is to trace the unity of the movement without disregarding its complexity. It is not for the sake of coining a paradox that I hasten to add that the unity in question can perhaps best be characterized as contradictoriness, dissonance and inner conflict of the Romantic mind.[1] Utopian dreams for the future side by side with nostalgia for the past; a marked nihilistic mood accompanied by a fervent yearning for a faith; serious attempts to bring about a Christian revival followed, in an admittedly marginal case, by the very abandonment of faith on the part of the former apologist; the tug-of-war between the old religion and the new ideologies—these are some of the unresolved contradictions which lie at the core of the movement. No shorter formula can be devised to define the essence of Romanticism. All short-cut definitions that have been put forward—well over a hundred—are unsatisfactory.[2] For Romanticism, as one of its earliest critics, Kierkegaard, noted in 1836, implies overflowing all boundaries.[3] As for the positive characteristics of the Romantic mind, the spirit of seeking and of adventure has rightly been singled out.[4]

Synoptic studies of European Romanticism, though few in number, are not altogether lacking. Already in the 1870s and 1880s, the Danish writer Georg Morris Cohen Brandes attempted something of this kind in his *Main Currents in Nineteenth-Century Literature*, based on a course of lectures at Copenhagen University. More recently, the important French series 'L'Evolution de l'Humanité' brought out three separate volumes devoted to different aspects of the Romantic era, namely *Le romantisme dans la littérature européenne* (1948) by Paul van Tieghem, *Les arts plastiques* (1949) by Louis Réau, and finally, *Le romantisme dans la musique européenne* (1955) by Jean Chantavoine and Jean Gaudefroy-Demombynes. The only attempts made at integrating all three studies consist in the brilliant prefaces written for each of the volumes by Henri Berr, general editor of the series, and a brief introductory essay entitled 'La place du romantisme dans l'esprit humain', by Paul Chalus, included in the final volume. Although van Tieghem confining himself almost exclusively to Romantic literature, studiously avoided the more general approach of the intellectual or cultural historian, his achievement marks a significant advance. Nevertheless, the Rumanian historian B. Munteano, in a constructive review of the book, is justified in his criticism that

Introduction

van Tieghem relies too much on the 'horizontal' approach and too little on a deeper searching 'vertical' synthesis.[5]

Two synoptic studies of a more circumscribed character remain to be mentioned, both of them by Italian scholars. In *La Carne, la Morte e il Diavolo nella Letteratura Romantica*, published in English under the title *The Romantic Agony* (1933), Mario Praz isolates, as he himself admits, "one particular aspect, fundamental though it may be, of Romantic literature . . . that is the education of sensibility and more especially erotic sensibility". Unless this deliberate limitation is borne in mind, the reader is in danger of getting too onesided a picture of the morbid side of Romanticism.

Arturo Farinelli's *Il Romanticismo nel mondo latino* (1927) is mainly based on Italian, French and Iberian sources, but this limitation is to some extent offset by the impressive range of Farinelli's subject matter. More important still, his is the first systematic treatment of the subject, or at any rate of important parts of it.

My own aim has been to study the development of Romantic ideas and sentiments seen in the larger context of history. Literature and philosophy, in the widest sense of those terms, as far as they reflect the deeper issues of cultural history, provide part of the documentary evidence which is also furnished by music, paintings and the like. Details of literary style or poetic diction, however, do not fall within my scope, for I believe that Chateaubriand was right when he declared on a famous occasion: "Ideas can be, and are, cosmopolitan, but not style, which has a soil, a sky, and sun all its own."[6]

In England, cultural history in general, and the history of ideas in particular, are only gradually coming into their own. It should be remembered, however, that Henry Thomas Buckle, over a hundred years ago, embarked on his ambitious *Introduction to the History of Civilization in England* (1857–61), and that towards the end of the nineteenth century the legal historian Frederick William Maitland urged his fellow historians to investigate not only "what men have done and said, but what men have thought in bygone ages". In a like vein the German historian Leopold von Ranke, as early as 1830, envisaged an "inward history of our civilization". This aim, as was later shown by his compatriot Wilhelm Dilthey,

historians can hope to achieve only if they encompass in their scope
the development of religious sentiment and thought. In the present
case such an approach is especially called for since the Romantic
attitude to religion has never as yet been treated on a European
scale.

Anyone who is working in the field of cultural history must
acknowledge his debt to Jacob Burckhardt who, both in his
Civilization of the Renaissance in Italy as well as in the posthumously published *Griechische Kulturgeschichte*, attempted to portray
a bygone age in all its facets. This kind of approach was later
successfully used by Ricarda Huch in her study of German
Romanticism.[7] There appears to be no compelling reason why it
should not be tried in a wider European study. Paul Hazard's
synoptic survey of the Enlightenment,[8] concluded at about the
time I was setting out on my task, provided yet another inspiring
example.

The method of presentation which I have used is not entirely
uniform. In Part One, the Romantic revolt against the dominant
ideas of the eighteenth century is outlined in a more general way.
On the other hand, the three remaining parts as well as the Epilogue
consist of chapters in which a particular Romantic idea or sentiment is illustrated in the form of pen-portraits or character-
sketches of individual Romantics.[9] Human beings and their intellectual life have always been closely related, but perhaps never
more so than during the Romantic era.

Again it was Burckhardt who pointed out that the principle of
selection of what the historian considers memorable or highly
significant data cannot but be a subjective one. Consequently, "to
each eye, perhaps, the outlines of a given cultural epoch present a
different picture".[10] Historians and their readers alike do well to
be mindful of Burckhardt's proviso. I, for one, am highly conscious
of it.

PART ONE

The Revolt against the Eighteenth Century

CHAPTER ONE

The Reaction against Rationalism

THE outbreak of the French Revolution and the advent of Romanticism, which took place in the very last years of the eighteenth century, were almost contemporaneous. Before venturing to construe a causal connexion, it may be pertinent to point out that these two events shared one essential characteristic: namely, the eruption of the irrational. This is true of the French Revolution, despite the well-known fact that many contemporaries believed it would usher in the longed-for Age of Reason. Kant, Condorcet, Godwin and Hegel are notable examples of this attitude. However, as the Revolution unfolded, other contemporaries hailed it on precisely opposite grounds. What that great event had inaugurated, it was claimed, was the establishment of human life on a basis of pure feeling. Nor could it be denied that strong irrational forces, hitherto kept in check by a traditionalist and hierarchic society, had been unleashed by the Revolution, a turn of events which the Romantics regarded as highly auspicious. In a sense it might be said that the explosion of irrational, or subconscious impulses that characterized so many aspects of the Revolution was the signal for the Romantic battle against Reason. The Revolution thus helped to launch the Romantic Movement. But this is as far as we can take the surmise of a causal connexion. It is hardly more than a surmise, for it might equally be argued that the great reaction against rationalism would have happened even without the Revolution, though in that case it would presumably have taken longer to gather momentum. Although each historical situation is in some ways unique, a comparison of similar attacks on rationalism, in other civilizations, or in earlier periods in our own, may yet throw light on this problem. Perhaps L. F. Cazamian is right in suspecting that there exists a psychological rhythm between Classicism (in the widest sense of that term) and some opposing tendencies. At any rate, the onslaught on the ancient Greek Enlightenment, in the fifth century B.C., would appear to bear some resemblance to the phenomenon studied in this chapter.[1]

During the Romantic period the over-valuation of the rational side of man was attacked in many different ways and on various grounds. The battle against Reason as 'the prime Enchantress' was fought all over Europe, or, at any rate, in all those parts of Europe which had previously come under the influence of rationalist Enlightenment. While Espronceda, the Spanish Romantic, in his poem *Estudiante de Salamanca*, cursed the torment of Reason, the leading Polish Romantic, Mickiewicz, in a poem entitled *Romanticism*, declared that feeling and faith had more appeal for him than the eye and the magnifying glass of the wise man, and the Italian Leopardi placed the highest qualities of the heart above those of Reason.[2] In England, Coleridge—whom Basil Willey regards as the leading representative of the European reaction against the eighteenth century[3]—maintained that deep thinking was attainable only by a man of deep feeling. It should be noted that when the Romantics used the term 'feeling' they meant what psychologists nowadays would call 'sensation' or 'sensibility', the distinction between 'feeling' (a rational function according to C. G. Jung) and 'sensation' or 'sensibility' (an irrational one) being unknown at the time.

As with so many other Romantic attitudes, the reaction against the cool and detached objectivity of rationalist thinkers had been anticipated by Jean-Jacques Rousseau. "La froide raison n'a jamais rien fait d'illustre",[4] he had written in *Julie ou la Nouvelle Héloïse*. In the famous letter to de Franquières (1769), he proclaimed a kind of supremacy of the heart: "La raison prend à la longue le pli que le cœur lui donne."[5] More striking still was the thought expressed in his *Lettres Morales*: "Exister, pour nous, c'est sentir; et notre sensibilité est incontestablement antérieure à notre raison."[6] The contrast to Descartes' rationalist motto, 'Cogito ergo sum', could not have been put more sharply. The debt owed by the Romantics to Rousseau, to which we will return in subsequent chapters of this study, would by itself require a monograph in which that thinker's paradoxical double role as one of the chief exponents but also earliest and most decisive

4

critics of the Enlightenment would have to be analysed more fully.

Closely linked with the cult of the emotions was the Romantic exaltation of the imagination over reason. In Shelley's words: "Reason is to the imagination as the instrument to the agent; as the body to the spirit; as the shadow to the substance." [7] The poet's emphasis on the supreme importance of the imagination was shared by musicians and painters. Franz Schubert, in an effusive entry in his diary, exclaims:

> Oh imagination, thou supreme jewel of mankind, thou in-exhaustible source from which artists and scholars drink! Oh, rest with us—despite the fact that thou art recognized only by a few—so as to preserve us from that so-called Enlightenment, that ugly skeleton without flesh or blood! [8]

Among visual artists, Géricault and Delacroix rejected all fetters to the exercise of the imagination. Since this facet of Romanticism is well known, no more examples need be adduced. However, an important motive for the Romantic emphasis on imagination must be noted in this context, namely the idea that imagination, and imagination alone, can help the artist or poet to do justice to the uniqueness or peculiarity of the particular object he has chosen to portray. [9]

If one accepts Jung's fourfold classification of basic psychological functions, i.e. thinking, feeling, sensation and intuition, and the resulting psychological typology, many Romantics would clearly fall into the third category which Jung, in the original German, calls 'Empfindungstypus' (sensational type). This type, in contradistinction to the first two, is an irrational one, but so is the fourth type, the intuitive, which Jung defines as a person whose general attitude is orientated by the principle of intuition, i.e. perception by way of the unconscious. [10] Again it is obvious that several Romantics may be found in this category. Novalis in Germany, Charles Nodier in France and Carlyle in Britain—to name but three exponents—all placed intuition, as a source of man's insight, above reason. Remarkably, this applied also to chess, for it was a characteristic of the Romantic chess-master, e.g. Deschapelles and de la Bourdonnais in France, the Irishman

McDonnell, the American Paul Morphy, and to a lesser extent the German Anderssen, to rely for the conduct of the game rather on intuition than on reasoned calculation. Of Morphy in particular it was claimed that he played some of his best moves by intuition, as it was impossible for the human brain to have analysed thoroughly all the ramifications in so short a time.

Although intuition is not strictly confined to a particular age group, there seems to be some kind of correlation between intuitive perception and youth, which may account for the fact that the Romantic era was the era of youth *par excellence*. The reliance on an intuitive process of creation on the part of so many Romantics may also help to explain the phenomenon that their creative period was often as short as it was brilliant. Morphy's meteoric career provides an especially striking example. Born in New Orleans in 1837, of mixed Irish, Spanish and Creole descent, he had started as a chess prodigy and at the age of twelve, without any previous knowledge of the openings, is reported to have made his moves as if by inspiration. By 1857 he had established himself as the leading American master, and in the course of his subsequent visit to Europe (1858-9), between the ages of twenty-one and twenty-two, he showed himself superior to all other famous chess-masters of his time,[12] only to sink into relative obscurity soon after his return to the States. Several more instances will be referred to in later chapters. The fact that so great a part of Romantic art, literature and philosophy has remained a torso, can also be explained in this way. The three examples that spring to mind—they could easily be multiplied—are Keats's *Hyperion*, Schelling's *Weltalter* and Schubert's *Unfinished Symphony*.

At times the Romantic assault on rationalism led to attacks on Reason itself, and in this respect Kant was justified in apprehending the most disastrous political consequences.[13] In the present century, the contempt for Reason in favour of the instincts (usually of the lowest type) or of 'race' or 'blood', however remote from original Romantic concepts, has not been entirely unrelated to them.[14] More often, however, rationalism was attacked by the Romantics not on the grounds that the intellectual results yielded by it were false, but rather on the grounds that they were inadequate, or in other words that an essential part of human nature was being starved. This is why Joseph von Eichendorff, with his great interest in metaphysical problems, could not accept the teachings of Kant's rationalist disciples. These philosophers, as he put it, were discarding the mysterious and inscrutable, which, to his mind, pervaded the whole of human existence, as a disturbing and superfluous element.[15] The Romantics in their turn tried to encompass the whole of existence, an attitude well illustrated in one of Coleridge's letters:

> I have known some who have been rationally educated, as it is styled. They were marked by a microscopic acuteness, but when they looked at great things, all became blank and they saw nothing, and denied (very illogically) that anything could be seen . . . and called the want of imagination judgment and the never being moved to rapture philosophy.[16]

Of all rationalist philosophers, Locke seemed to Coleridge to have contributed most to the destruction of 'metaphysical science'. The macroscopic metaphysical approach, or, in Jung's terminology, "the attempt to reach the most complete perception of the whole universe",[17] characterizes a great deal of Romantic irrationalism. It may be understood as a corollary of the Romantic quest for infinitude which was able to take on the most varied shapes.

The Romantics' irrationalist bent also enabled them to divine, and even to explore, the unconscious regions of the mind. Schopenhauer, in particular, was among the first to realize that man's consciousness was but a thin crust, and that underneath it there existed a whole world of unconscious non-rational urges (to which Schopenhauer gave the name Will)—to all intents and purposes an anticipation of Freud's theory of the 'Id'. This conception was later elaborated by Goethe's friend Carl Gustav Carus, himself a physician, painter and philosopher, especially in his book *Psyche*, where he looked for the key to the conscious life of the soul in the unconscious. Wordsworth's use, in *The Prelude*, of words such as 'undersoul' or 'underconsciousness' points in the same direction. In pathological cases of madness or crime the unconscious layers of the mind appear, as it were, exposed in the physiognomy of the person, at least to the eye of the experienced diagnostician or of the great painter. This is why Géricault, in the winter of 1822–3, took for the subject of his portraits ten insane persons, among them a kleptomaniac, a kidnapper, a man with military megalomania, a woman gambler, and a pathologically jealous old woman ('La Folle').[18]

Finally, the world of dreams. Significantly, the eighteenth-century rationalists had not shown much interest in this shadowy and baffling aspect of human psychology. All the more its importance was stressed by pre-Romantic thinkers like Hamann and Herder. To the former, the dream signified 'eine Höllenfahrt der Selbsterkenntnis' (a journey to the Inferno of self-knowledge). At the height of the Romantic period itself, Gotthilf Heinrich Schubert, physician and exponent of Schelling's *Naturphilosophie*, brought out his *Symbolik des Traumes* (Dream Symbolism) which to some extent foreshadows Freud's interpretation of dreams. Among Romantic men of letters, E. T. A. Hoffmann in Germany and Gérard de Nerval in France penetrated most deeply into the uncanny yet fascinating region of dreams. "Les rêves sont ce qu'il y a de plus doux et peut-être de plus vrai dans la vie."[19] That remark by Charles Nodier epitomizes the provocative irrationalism of the Romantics.

CHAPTER TWO

Progress and Disenchantment

THE idea of unlimited man-made Progress towards ever-increasing happiness in this world—the last great Western heresy, as W. B. Yeats has called it—is at present largely discredited, although propagandists of all political parties still continue to pay lip-service to it. Nor can an age which has seen two World Wars, the totalitarian revolutions and, most of all, the extermination camps be expected to believe in the inevitable improvement of human nature. Indeed, disillusionment with the idea of Progress has

Chateaubriand (lithograph by Lemercier)

Coleridge (portrait by Peter Vandyke)

reached such a degree that, unfortunately, the very organ of hope seems to be seriously impaired, if not destroyed, together with the tempting illusion.

The story of the enchantment of Western man with the achievements and visions of Progress does not concern us here. Various aspects have often been described, though a comprehensive treatment is still lacking. It is well to bear in mind, though, that "belief in progress . . . came to be the world-view of Western civilization as the classical Christian orthodoxy was abandoned".[1] Our task is to examine the first stages of the disenchantment as it manifested itself in the European Romantic movement.

Even before the age of Romanticism, the prevalent eighteenth-century belief in progress was not entirely uncontested.[2] Giambattista Vico for one, who was to inspire Coleridge's outlook on history, saw man's development in terms of a perpetual cycle. The optimism of other thinkers was rudely shaken by the disastrous earthquake of Lisbon (1755) and the bloodshed of the Seven Years War. However, the strongest reaction against the idea of history as a picture of steady human progress towards perfection came from the two great harbingers of European Romanticism, Rousseau and Johann Gottfried Herder. When, in 1774, the latter came to formulate his views on the subject, he acknowledged his debt to Rousseau, whose voice, some two decades earlier, had been 'crying in the wilderness'. Rousseau was indeed the first to shatter the modern dogma that the increase of knowledge makes eventually for greater happiness.[3] Both thinkers rejected the naïve belief that the contemporary age constituted the summit of human culture, an attitude explicitly put forward, for example, in Isaak Iselin's *Philosophische Mutmassungen über die Geschichte der Menschheit* (1764). Significantly, Herder for his part went so far as to deny that an absolute yardstick could be found for the measuring of human happiness.[4] History had taught him that each period, each nation and each individual had its own relative notion of happiness. Here we already notice the clash between the rational belief in absolute standards and the Romantic concepts of relativity or singularity.

Despite these dissenting voices, the optimism of the Enlightenment was still advancing until it reached its greatest intensity in the very last years before the French Revolution and during its initial stages. Kant, in 1792, firmly believed in the inevitability of human progress towards ever increasing intellectual and moral perfection. In the following year William Godwin, in his *Inquiry Concerning Political Justice and Its Influence on Morals and Happiness*, envisaged a secular paradise which strongly resembled earlier Christian millenarian expectations, while Condorcet in France, at the height of the Terror, still clung to his belief in the indefinite moral improvement of mankind.

Initially, the first Romantic generation reacted in a like vein. Their early enthusiasm for the Revolution can be accounted for in different ways. One thing is certain, namely that both movements, Romanticism as well as the Revolution, were united in their impassioned striving for freedom. The ideal of Liberty, the most rousing of the three revolutionary war-cries, blended naturally with the subjectivist outlook that characterized early Romanticism. Hand in hand with the demand for political liberty went the quest for spontaneity in literature and the arts. Nor was this a mere coincidence. Madame de Staël was right when she maintained that social freedom was bound to lead to reform in literature.[5] A society in which political freedom was accomplished, so her argument ran, would no longer tolerate a type of literature shackled by artificial restraints. It seems probable that the French Revolution, for all its classical ancient Roman trappings, helped to break the stranglehold of classical French taste.

To return to the belief in progress: as long as the cause of Liberty seemed to be gaining ground in France, the delight on the part of the Romantics knew no bounds. Looking back from the distance of many years, Wordsworth confessed that he did not know how any generous-minded young man entering on life at the time of that great uprising could have escaped the illusion. In *The Excursion* he has left us a poetic description of that dazzling mirage. The fall of the "dread Bastille" is seen in retrospect:

> From the wreck
> A golden palace rose or seem'd to rise
> The appointed seat of equitable law
> And mild paternal sway.

Another testimony of those high-flown hopes is to be found in a
poem which Coleridge dedicated to Wordsworth:

> Amid the tremor of a realm aglow,
> Amid a mighty nation jubilant,
> When from the general heart of human kind
> Hope sprang forth like a full-born Deity.

Coleridge's earlier *Ode on the Destruction of the Bastille*, written
while he was still at Christ's Hospital, had ended on a note of
triumphant expectation that France's example would inspire the
whole world with a love of liberty.

The Terror in France (1793–4) and later the change from defensive
to aggressive French nationalism with the ensuing Armageddon in
Europe and beyond acted as eye-openers. Deep disillusionment is
expressed in *The Prelude*:

> And now, become Oppressors in their turn,
> Frenchmen had changed a war of self-defence
> For one of conquest, losing sight of all
> Which they had struggled for; and mounted up
> Openly, in the view of earth and heaven,
> The scale of Liberty.[6]

The earlier hope that the Revolution would usher in an age of
federalism and decentralization had proved an illusion. On the
contrary, the power of modern Leviathan, it was anxiously observed, increased steadily, and with it the power of the modern
State bureaucracy which some Romantics came to liken to a life-
less automaton.[7]

Whereas up to 1794, or even 1798, most of the leading European
thinkers—there were notable exceptions[8]—had expected the
French Revolution to bring about the cure of all or most of the
evils with which European civilization was afflicted, men now
began to realize that the causes of the evil lay deeper and could
not be removed by the Revolution in question. By the time it had
become clear that Robespierre's dictatorship was followed in
France by a corrupt and self-seeking administration, Wordsworth

definitely abandoned the hope that general happiness could be
brought about by sweeping political changes. A few years later
Coleridge, referring to pro-Jacobin tendencies in Britain, exclaimed:

> We have been too long
> Dupes of a deep delusion! Some, belike,
> Groaning with restless enmity, expect
> All change from change of constituted power;
> As if a Government had been a robe,
> On which our vice and wretchedness were tagged
> Like fancy-points and fringes, with the robe
> Pulled off at pleasure.[9]

Romantic disillusionment went even deeper than that. Not
only had the Revolution failed to fulfil the great expectations of
Liberty and Fraternity, but to some it even seemed to have
inaugurated a sinister new epoch. This, at any rate, was the impression of Friedrich Schlegel as he recorded it many years later:

> A phenomenon which for the first time awakened the deeper
> searching political theorists and observers of the world from
> their illusion and, as a dangerous sign of the time, filled them
> with earnest horror, was the appearance of unselfish crimes,
> arisen from a confused and erroneous idea of the fanatic and
> unruly Zeitgeist.[10]

Whether or not men whose quest for power was as unquenchable
as that of Robespierre can rightly be called unselfish, the fact
remains that the 'seagreen Incorruptible' and his disciple and
henchman, Saint-Just, lived, as it were, in a depersonalized atmosphere where evil had become separated from other individual
vices, and it was this very aspect that gave their political actions a
monstrously uncanny tinge. E. T. A. Hoffmann, who did not
possess F. Schlegel's gift for historical exposition but who possessed the truly poetic power of symbolism, created in *Klein
Zaches* the symbol for the modern dehumanized statesman.

Romantic disillusionment was, as we have seen, partly due to the
fact that Liberty and Fraternity had not kept their promise, as it

were. The middle slogan, Equality, which in effect proved the most lasting of the three, was itself hotly debated by the Romantics, and in this respect we find some of them deviate most decisively from the current ideology of secular Progress, and even from their idol Rousseau who had done so much to extol political and social equality.

The dominant interpretation of secular Progress implied the desirability of political, social and cultural levelling: an idea which met with strong and determined opposition in Romantic circles. The Romantics, or some of them at any rate, were the first to point to the danger of the vulgarization of our culture; the danger, in other words, of the gradual absorption of the educated classes by the masses—a phenomenon which, according to M. I. Rostovtsev, underlay the process of decline of the ancient Roman civilization[11].

Romantics such as F. Schlegel and Schelling in Germany, Benjamin Constant and Vigny in France, or Coleridge and Carlyle in Great Britain, all lamented the horrid prospect of a mass civilization with its progressive encroachment on individual liberty. In many ways their forebodings are borne out by Ortega y Gasset's disconcertingly true diagnosis of our age.[12]

So marked was the anti-egalitarian *leit-motiv* in the Romantic movement, at any rate before 1830, that some historians have interpreted Romanticism as the swan song of the European nobility.[13] To be sure, there is more than a grain of truth in this view. Indeed, the list of Romantic noblemen is impressive, for we can count among them Chateaubriand, Vigny and Musset in France, Manzoni and Leopardi in Italy, Novalis, Arnim and Eichendorff in Germany, Mickiewicz and Krasiński in Poland, and Byron and Pugin in Britain. George Sand was, on her mother's side, an offspring of the Royal House of Saxony. If illegitimate descent is taken into consideration, Delacroix qualifies as well, for he was almost certainly a natural son of Talleyrand. So does Richard Wagner, whose ancestry seems to have included one of the Saxe-Weimar princes.

It should, however, be realized that the sociological 'explanation' of Romanticism can at best yield some kind of approximation. Wilhelm Dilthey was undoubtedly right when he remarked that "conditions do not contain the full causal explanation of intellectual phenomena". All they do, he added cautiously, "is to confine the variability of that which originates within certain boundaries".[14]

In the present case, a complex historical reality like Romanticism does not easily fit into a sociological formula. Three modifications at least should be noted. In the first place, various middle strata of society are also represented among the Romantics. Most of the exponents of the movement in England, a fair number in Germany and some in France, too, belonged to one or the other layer of that heterogeneous class. Secondly, by no means all the Romantics who were of aristocratic origin adopted an anti-egalitarian attitude. George Sand, for one, though proud of her ancestry, certainly did not. Finally, some intellectual noblemen who were most intransigently anti-egalitarian, as for example Bonald and de Maistre, never belonged to the Romantic movement. Clearly all this goes to show—if proof were needed—that, in the last analysis, the human mind is free and undetermined.

CHAPTER THREE

The Emphasis on Singularity

IT has rightly been remarked that in the Romantic period the simple became an object of suspicion. As for the political blueprints conceived by, or in the spirit of, the 'esprits simplistes' of rationalist Enlightenment, they were now regarded as useless, or even as repulsive. The Swedish Romantic Pehr Atterbom scoffed at "that world-reforming abracadabra", while Coleridge, in *The Friend*, refuted the idea that a constitution could be devised which would be equally suitable to China and America, or to Russia and Great Britain. Recipes for such a constitution deserved in his opinion "as little respect in political as a quack's panacea in medical practice".[1] And Chateaubriand recoiled from the horror of a universal society that would make all nations uniform. His feelings were shared by Walter Scott:

> Let us remain as nature made us—Englishmen, Irishmen, Scotchmen, with something like the impress of our several countries upon each! We would not become better subjects if all resembled each other like so many smooth shillings.

The reason Scott gives for his view is so typically Romantic that it shall be quoted in full:

> The degree of national diversity between different countries is but an instance of that general variety which Nature seems to have adopted as a principle through all her works, as anxious to avoid as modern statesmen to enforce, anything like an approach to absolute uniformity.

The Romantic attitude in this respect is essentially different from the individualism expounded by rationalist minds. Whereas the latter emphasized the equality and inter-changeability of individual beings or groups, the Romantics laid the greatest stress on their peculiarity, or singularity, and therefore made more allowances for the rights of personality. This applied not only to individuals but also to communities such as provinces or nationalities.

In the opinion of the Romantics, the peculiar character of a given nationality manifested itself in its *Volksgeist* or folk-spirit, a typical will o' the wisp if viewed through rationalist spectacles. Yet, despite its notorious elusiveness, the notion in question formed undoubtedly one of the ideological cornerstones of the Romantic movement. Herder, again, blazed the trail. As early as 1767, he expressed the idea that each people had a unique character which was manifest in all its customs and institutions, its works of art and literature, and which was intrinsically valuable in itself.[2] Unlike Reason, with her universal and immutable precepts, Herder's Romantic *Weltgeist*, or Spirit of the World, was for ever developing, the historical manifestations of the various nationalities forming so many stages in that development. Nor was autonomous political existence a *conditio sine qua non* of a nationality's right to recognition. Indeed, Herder's concern for the submerged or suppressed European nationalities helped considerably to raise the latters' self-confidence. Various Slav nationalities in particular received invaluable encouragement from Herder's collection of their folk songs, as well as from the chapter on the Slavs in his main work, *Ideen zur Philosophie der Geschichte der Menschheit*[3] (Ideas towards a Philosophy of History of Mankind), where their pacific and industrious character was extolled. His emphatic prediction that the Slavs would before long awaken from their enforced slumber certainly helped to bring about that very event. Soon *Volksgeist*, the magic German formula, came to be translated into *narodnij duch*, and with it a host of Romantic associations penetrated into Slav thinking.

Herder's earliest apostle among the Slavs was the Slovak poet Jan Kollár, the founder of Panslavism. Returning, in 1819, to Prague from the University of Jena, he saw the Bohemian capital in an entirely new light, for, as he wrote in his memoirs, he had in the meantime tasted "the bitter and agonizing fruit from the tree of nationality".[4] Though himself a Slovak, he believed that there existed but one Czechoslovak language. At present almost reduced to the level of a *lingua rustica*, that tongue deserved in his opinion recognition as one of the four Slav literary languages, the three others being Russian, Polish and Illyrian (i.e. Serbo-croat).[5] However, once set in motion, the proliferation of Slav literary languages proceeded rapidly. Within the Habsburg Empire the Slovaks, unmoved by Kollár's plea, soon refused to play the role of identical twin nation to the Czechs. Nor were the Slovenes, further South, prepared to remain culturally beyond the pale.[6] Another of Herder's Slav disciples, the Slovak scholar Pavel Josef Šafařik, who had also studied at Jena, was the first to make full allowance for the distinctive character of each of the then existing Slav nationalities.[7]

In Western Europe, the Romantic impact on cultural patriotism was no less marked. In Spain and Southern France respectively, old literary languages such as Galician, Catalan, Provençal and Bask (or Eskuara), all owed their resurgence to the Romantic Movement. In the extreme North West, the indigenous population of Iceland, stimulated by Bjarni Thorarensen, Tomas Saemundsson and others,[8] was reawakened to the consciousness of forming a nation distinct from the ruling Danes, a process which took place equally vigorously in Norway. Moreover, the Norwegians even went so far as to develop two new cultural languages, the Riksmaal (or Bokmaal), championed by Wergeland, which was based on the language spoken in towns, and the Landsmaal, first propagated by the scholar Ivar Aasen, which in typically Romantic fashion went back to the folklore and dialects of the countryside.[9]

This is not the place for a complete survey of all nationalities resuscitated by Romanticism. However, brief mention must be made of the Celtic revival in Ireland. Here the old Gaelic tongue which still survived was extolled in one of Philip Fitzgibbon's Gaelic poems. Here is a characteristic passage from it, translated into English:

> The language of Erne is brilliant as gold;
> It shines with a lustre unrivalled of old,
> Even glanced at by strangers, to whom 'tis unknown,
> It dazzles their eyes with a light all its own.

Two of the stanzas envisage the final triumph of the native tongue:

> O, then shall our halls with the Gaelic resound,
> In the notes of the harp and the claoirseach half drowned,
> And the banquet be spread and the chess board all night,
> Test the skill of our Chiefs, and their power for the fight.

> The history of Eire shall shine forth in thee,
> Thou shalt sound as a horn from the lip of the free;
> And our priests in their forefathers' temples once more
> Shall through thee call on men to rejoice and adore.

To explain a phenomenon such as the emergence of cultural patriotism in purely political or sociological terms would obviously be misleading. With this proviso, however, it might be argued that the threatening standardization of Europe—a threat brought home by rationalist enlightened despots such as Joseph II and accentuated by Napoleon's attempt at building a universal State—acted as a challenge to which patriotism of a defensive and culture-sustaining kind was the timely response.[10] The Dutch historian

Johan Huizinga was right when he made a sharp distinction between patriotism and nationalism. Whereas with the former the
prevailing sentiment is one of attachment, the latter is based on
the feeling of pride which only too often leads to overweening
arrogance and aggression. It has to be admitted, however, that
patriotism and nationalism, though sometimes clearly distinguish-
able, were apt to merge into one another.

On a different plane the notion of singularity (or peculiarity) was
strongly emphasized by the Romantics in respect of individuals.
Here, too, eighteenth-century thinkers had helped to pave the
way. Indeed, none other than Rousseau was among the first to
discover in the variety of shapes that men assume the deeply concealed nature of man. The idea that all individuals are unique and
incomparable, which can be traced as far back as Leibniz and
Shaftesbury, found enthusiastic exponents in young Goethe,
Herder and the Dutch philosopher Frans Hemsterhuis. During
the Romantic period itself, it was most fully developed by the
German thinker Friedrich Ernst Daniel Schleiermacher. In his
meditations, published in 1800 under the title *Monologen*, he
described how great an uplift he had received from the realization
that each human being constitutes a unique combination of human
characteristics and thus helps to reveal mankind in a most prodigious multiplicity of facets.[11] Indeed, the number of these facets
is so vast that the total picture is one of an infinity of shapes. We
may note in passing how the Romantic *leit-motiv* of infinitude
emerges again.

The Romantic concept in question proved particularly fruitful
in the sphere of education. In his *Emile* (1762), Rousseau—precursor also in this respect—had already emphasized that each
stage in the child's development has a completeness of its own and
that the perfection of the later stage can be attained only through
the fulfilment of the earlier. He had thus revolutionized the theory
of education, though in actual practice, according to his own *Confessions* he thought fit to place all his children in a foundling hos-

pital. On the other hand, the German Friedrich Froebel, who at one time worked under Pestalozzi, showed as much interest in the creation of new educational institutions as in the ideas on which these were based. The first of his model schools was founded, in 1816, at Griesheim and soon moved to Keilhau, both of them villages in his native Thuringia. In his main work, *The Education of Man*,[12] published in 1826, Froebel laid the greatest stress on the first stage of life up to the age of seven, for his conception of harmonious development led him to attach much importance to that neglected stage. Out of this idea grew the first *Kindergarten* which he opened in 1837 at Blankenburg in the Thuringian forest. According to his intention, it was to be a school for the psychological training of little children by means of spontaneous play and productive activity.[13] In his weekly paper, *Sonntagsblatt*, he elucidated his system:

> It is for us to see that the child develops, from the first, freely and independently, as complete in himself, and yet as a harmonious part of a larger whole.

It goes without saying that the concern for the development of the small child, which had so far-reaching an impact on modern education, was also bound up with the Romantic interest in the non-rational functions of the mind that has been discussed in an earlier chapter of this study.

In the realm of literature and the arts, the significance of 'singularity' can hardly be overestimated. As early as 1800, Friedrich Schlegel, in a programmatic declaration, thus contrasted reason and poetry:

> Reason is but one and the same in all; however, just as each human being has his own nature and his own peculiar love, so each person also carries his own poetry in himself.[14]

Once it was recognized that each poet had his own distinctive peculiarities, the task of the composer who undertook to set poems to music became far more complex if also more rewarding.

Schubert's pre-eminence as a composer of *Lieder* rests precisely on the inimitable manner with which he accomplished this task. Not only is his range of keys far richer than that of any earlier or contemporary composer,[15] but, more important still, that freedom of modulation is used by him to do justice to the modulation of moods and sentiments expressed in each poem. Few among Schubert's contemporaries acknowledged his achievement in this respect, but Johann Mayrhofer—one of the poets whose verse Schubert had rendered immortal—paid him this posthumous tribute:

> If the wealth of melody he invented justly astonishes, amazement is further heightened by the clear-sightedness, the certainty and the felicity with which he penetrated into the life of the words and, I should say, into the peculiarity of each poet. How differently and yet how characteristically does he deal with Goethe, Schiller, Müller, Rückert, Schlegel, Scott, Schulze and others![16]

Romantic composers, as for example Weber, Rossini or Berlioz, also paid a great deal of attention to the particular *timbre* of each orchestral instrument. The horn, the clarinet and the *cor anglais*— to name but three of them—were made to yield entirely novel effects.

If taken to its logical conclusion, 'singularity' applied not only to each distinctive stage in a person's development, but even to much shorter units of time, and in the last analysis to each single moment in life. This was one of the reasons why the Romantics abandoned themselves wholeheartedly, or so it seemed, to the most fleeting emotions. In a world which was conceived of as being in perpetual flux, human feelings and moods were for ever changing. All that mattered was that each of those moods was genuine, however irreconcilable it might appear to be with sentiments that had immediately preceded it.[17] The resulting restlessness, a predominant feature of the Romantic mind, is portrayed in some outstanding Romantic paintings, especially in those of Géricault and Delacroix. Painting, or music for that matter, the two essentially modern arts according to Delacroix, were indeed the appropriate media for this purpose. Sculpture and architecture, on the other hand, were far less affected by Romanticism, for unbalance and continuous change are obviously more difficult to portray in those media.

In the end, the concept of singularity was bound to lead to the abandonment of the classical canons of absolute beauty, and their substitution by the Romantic theory of aesthetic relativity. The earliest proclamation of the new doctrine seems to have been made by the French painter Girodet-Trioson at a meeting of the four Académies held on 24 April 1817. The crucial passage of Girodet's "considerations on originality in relation to the arts of design" ran as follows:

> How can the artist, driven as he is by curiosity into remote regions, and seeing as he does in each one of the peoples of the world the different and peculiar idea it has of the beautiful . . . remain a firm adherent to the healthy doctrine of absolute beauty?[18]

Delacroix recopied this and related passages from Girodet's paper in one of his notebooks. Forty years later, he himself expounded the idea of the relativity of the beautiful in two important articles in the *Revue des Deux Mondes*.[19] Significantly, the conclusion reached by Delacroix is to the effect that the only valid criterion for the greatness of an artist must be seen in his singularity:

> On dit d'un homme pour le louer qu'il est un homme unique: ne peut-on, sans paradoxe, affirmer que c'est cette singularité, cette personnalité qui nous enchante chez un grand poète et chez un grand artiste, que cette face nouvelle des choses révélées par lui nous étonne autant qu'elle nous charme, qu'elle produit dans notre âme la sensation du beau, indépendamment des autres révélations du beau qui sont devenues le patrimoine des esprits de tous les temps, et qui sont consacrées par une plus longue admiration?[20]

CHAPTER FOUR

The Quest for Re-integration

TECHNOLOGICAL progress, which since Bacon's *New Atlantis* (1627) has often been identified with secular progress, was watched by some Romantics with indifference, by others not without dismay. An example of indifference mingled with a strong admixture of irony is furnished by Leopardi's poem 'Palinodia: Al Marchese Gino Capponi' (1835). In another poem, entitled 'Il Pensiero Dominante', Leopardi scornfully refers to his age as

> questa età superba
> Che di vote speranze si nutrica.[1]

Often the Romantics' sense of beauty was offended by the hideousness of the newly arisen industrial districts. In Great Britain, which was further advanced on this road than the Continent, Robert Southey, in his *Sir Thomas More, or Colloquies on the Progress and Prospects of Society* (1829), anticipated much of Ruskin's and William Morris's later campaign against the deformity of our mechanized world. Birmingham, in 1838, appeared to Alfred de Vigny like a Cyclopean cave, and Carus, who visited England and Scotland in 1844, was no less appalled by the sight of Manchester[2] than the American writer George Ticknor had been a quarter of a century earlier on his visit to Newcastle-on-Tyne and its surroundings. This is how he described it:

> At the side of every coal-pit a quantity of the finer parts that are thrown out is perpetually burning, and the effect produced by the earth, thus apparently everywhere on fire, both on the machinery used and the men busied with it, was horrible. It seemed as if I were in Dante's shadowy world.[3]

Significantly, John Martin, on a journey through the Black Country in the dead of night, was inspired to paint the background of his powerful painting 'The Great Day of His Wrath'. He told his son that he could not imagine anything more terrible even in the regions of everlasting punishment.[4]

But even those who did not take so gloomy a view of modern mechanization feared, as Oliver Goldsmith had already done, that the balance between agriculture and industry might one day be irrevocably upset, an apprehension voiced notably by Sismondi in France, Adam Müller and Baader in Germany, and Southey in Britain. We would do less than justice to these Romantics if we saw in them nothing more than *laudatores temporis acti* with a naïve hankering after the more traditional forms of economy. Their emphasis upon the crucial importance of agriculture and a contented agrarian population as the only healthy basis of economy deserves to be taken seriously, especially in Britain, which has travelled so far along the problematic road away from the land. What the Romantics recoiled from was the artificiality and soullessness of modern urbanized—and suburbanized—life, whose long-term effects are still hard to estimate. Although man had not yet embarked on building sky-scrapers, and the most populous cities contained fewer than a million inhabitants, the Romantics often compared them to great human deserts. The contrast between those cities and his beloved home at Grasmere, Wordsworth depicts in *The Recluse*:

> . . . he truly is alone,
> He of the multitude whose eyes are doomed
> To hold a vacant commerce day by day
> With objects wanting life, repelling love;
> Where pity shrinks from unremitting calls,
> Where numbers overwhelm humanity,
> And neighbourhood serves rather to divide
> Than to unite. What sighs more deep than his,
> Whose nobler will hath long been sacrificed;
> Who must inhabit, under a black sky,
> A City where, if indifference to disgust
> Yield not to scorn, or sorrow, living Men
> Are ofttimes to their fellow-men no more
> Than to the Forest Hermit are the leaves
> That hang aloft in myriads—nay, far less,

For they protect his walk from sun and shower,
Swell his devotion with their voice in storms,
And whisper while the stars twinkle among them
His lullaby. From crowded streets remote,
Far from the living and dead wilderness
Of the thronged World, Society is here
A true Community, a genuine frame
Of many into one incorporate.[5]

In a similar vein, Leopardi, writing from Rome in 1822, explained the callousness of life in a big city:

In a little town we may be bored, but after all men there have some relation to each other and to the things around them, because the sphere of these relations is small and proportionate to human nature. But in a large city a man lives without any relation at all to what surrounds him, because the sphere is so large that no individual can fill it or feel it around him and there is no point of contact between it and him.[6]

The Romantics also perceived that the worker in the highly developed industrial system would be in danger of being degraded to the role of a mere cog in the machine. Craftsmanship would thus be destroyed and with it the intelligent joy of a man in his daily work. Schleiermacher, the German theologian, aptly commented upon this phenomenon:

This whole sense of a common material progress is without value, since the work of humanity is carried out by an 'ingenious system' in which each man is forced to restrict his powers.

Clemens Brentano and Görres dealt with the same problem in their fantastic story about the watchmaker Bogs. So did Coleridge in his *Second Lay Sermon*, and Sismondi in his *Nouveaux principes d'économie politique*. Sismondi was also among the first to point out that overindustrialization and unlimited production must of necessity lead to economic crises which would give the lie, even in the material sphere itself, to the modern dogma of an uninterrupted upward movement. His outlook in economics, which is far more balanced than that of his contemporaries, Ricardo and Jean-

Baptiste Say, forms a notable aspect of Romanticism. True to the best traditions of the movement, Sismondi devoted a great deal of his time to the study of history. Unlike many economists of his time and ours, he was thus in a position to compare past and present. Moreover, in the face of strong opposition which was informed by the spirit of eighteenth-century Enlightenment, Sismondi reverted to the older tradition represented by such thinkers as Aristotle and St. Thomas Aquinas in that he refused to study economics in isolation from politics and ethics.

Coleridge, too, gave a great deal of thought to economic problems and their interdependence with problems of a social, moral and religious character. What he particularly abhorred in the teaching of the then dominant school of political economists was their exclusively economic approach to the problem of human labour. According to his son's testimony, he never ceased to condemn the system which considered men as "things, instruments, machines, property".[7] In *The Friend*, he declared explicitly:

> The economists who are willing to sacrifice men to the creation of a national wealth (which is national only in statistical tables) are forgetting that even for patriotic purposes no person should be treated as a thing.

Coleridge's strictures had in part been anticipated in Southey's remarkable *Letters from England* (1807), purported to have been written by Don Manuel Alvarez Espriella. The *Letters*, indeed, contain some of the earliest penetrating observations on the human aspect of the Industrial Revolution in its early stages. "In commerce, even more than in War," the pseudo-Spaniard states, "both men and beasts are considered merely as machines, and sacrificed with even less compunction."[8] Nothing could better characterize the Romantic rejection of the spirit of unmitigated capitalism.

Sismondi, Coleridge and other Romantic thinkers decidedly anticipated one of Karl Marx's most fundamental indictments of capitalism: namely, that it transformed human beings into things. But this was not all. No one, not even Marx himself, could expose the hollowness of economic liberalism better than these thinkers have done. Sismondi and Baader, Coleridge and Adam Müller, were all aware of the fact that the proletarian in the newly arisen industrial society had only seemingly gained liberty, but had most certainly lost whatever security he had previously possessed.[9] Consequently, it was recognized, the industrial proletariat was the Cinderella of modern society, but it would not long be satisfied with that humble role, especially since its antagonists, the rich, were getting richer all the time. In view of all this it should not occasion any surprise to learn from the posthumously published papers of Karl Marx that in his youth he had been strongly influenced by Romantic ideas. It should however be emphasized that the spirit of the Romantic movement struck at the very root of capitalism in a far more uncompromising way than did secularized Socialism or Communism. For both these last-mentioned movements are, in varying degrees, and with notable individual exceptions, imbued with the spirit of materialism and eudemonism which, to use Coleridge's definition, "places happiness as the object and the aim of man".[10]

Romanticism, that truly Protean movement, was among many other things also a protest against so prosaic and philistine an outlook on life. A few examples must suffice to prove this point. Giuseppe Mazzini in Italy and Frédéric Ozanam in France both condemned the utilitarian and eudemonist elements in the Saint-Simonian doctrine, a feeling that was shared by Lamartine as well as Alfred de Vigny. Equally marked was Hazlitt's and Carlyle's rejection of Bentham's eudemonist teaching. "Only this I know," Carlyle wrote in *Sartor Resartus*, "if what thou namest Happiness be our true aim, then we are all astray."

In a previous chapter of this study it has been suggested that the world of chess often reflects the prevailing cultural trends of the time. The brilliant sacrificial style of the Romantic chess-masters is a case in point. To quote but one example: Anderssen's Immortal Game against Kieseritzky, played in the London Tournament in 1851, where the victorious side gives up a Queen, two Rooks and a Bishop, epitomizes the Romantic longing for the supremacy of mind over matter.

Bourgeois philistinism was satirized by the Romantics with especial acerbity. In France, the fashion for exoticism, inaugurated by Delacroix and Gabriel Alexandre Decamps, but to some extent also Théophile Gautier's 'l'art pour l'art' campaign were protests against the drabness and mediocrity of bourgeois life. In Sweden, antiphilistine sentiments found vent in Atterbom's drama *Lycksálighetens Ö* (Felicity Island).[11] In Germany, Clemens Brentano, and later Heinrich Heine,[12] stood in the forefront of the campaign against the philistines whom Schopenhauer, another of their despisers, characterized as being concerned not with ideas, but only with their stomachs. Not so surprisingly, musicians too entered the fray. Robert Schumann's celebrated *Carneval* ends with a delightful piece which is meant to portray the march of the Davidsbündler, an imaginary group of young people dedicated to the eradication of Philistinism.

Was the Romantic protest made in vain? We cannot tell. The leading Portuguese Romantic, Garrett, summed up the situation in these words: "Our age is ruled by King Sancho Panza." But he added hopefully: "Later on Don Quixote will return."

The autonomy of economics, so abhorrent to the Romantics, was typical of the seventeenth- and eighteenth-century disintegration of European cultural unity. By 1800, too many spheres of life had already issued their Declarations of Independence. First politics, then science, and by now economics too, had proclaimed that they were not subject to any laws but their own. In the process, transcendental standards had been gradually eliminated and man had been made the measure of all things.[13]

Some of the leading Romantics vigorously opposed these tendencies. Statesmen and politicians, who since Machiavelli had brazenly freed themselves from the tutelage of ethics and religion, were shown in Coleridge's *Lay Sermons* the necessary interdependence of these severed spheres, and Baader, in 1815, directly approached the most powerful monarchs on the Continent and implored them to receive again, and with renewed intensity, the principles of religion, love and liberty into the realm of politics.[14] Again we can observe how the Romantic endeavour to reconcile politics and religion led to Romantic scepticism with regard to panaceas involving purely organizational political reforms as envisaged by countless champions of secular progress. We catch a glimpse of this insight in Shelley's last great poem, the unfinished *Triumph of Life*, when the poet has abandoned his earlier belief that the human spirit could be freed by destroying certain institutions. The clearest formulation of the Romantic view is to be found in the following passage from the writings of the unduly neglected Frenchman Charles Nodier:

> Le renouvellement de la société ne dépendit jamais d'une révolution purement politique, comme on a feint de le croire chez les modernes. Ce sont les religions qui renouvellent les peuples: le feu divin qui vivifie l'homme social ne peut être emprunté que du ciel, et c'est le sens véritable de la belle allégorie du Prométhée.[15]

Some Romantics, particularly of the first generation, before the French 'l'art pour l'art' attitude obscured the issue, felt that poetry and art had to have a basis in philosophy and an anchor in religion. Novalis and Friedrich Schlegel were no less convinced of this necessity than were Coleridge and Wordsworth. Among painters, the German 'Nazarenes', Johann Friedrich Overbeck, Peter von Cornelius and the brothers Olivier, sought to rebuild the bridge between art and religion which had been all but destroyed in the eighteenth century.[16]

It was also realized in Romantic circles that man's intellect might become a dangerous power if it emancipated itself from moral and religious scruples. Scholars and scientists had to be reminded of the ultimate scope of their search. Johann Michael Sailer, a Bavarian Catholic theologian and friend of Schelling, was most clearly aware of this task.[17] In a like vein, the physicians Carl Gustav Carus and Johann Nepomuk von Ringseis strongly emphasized the religious aspect of their vocation. The other danger facing the state of knowledge was excessive specialization. In this respect, too, the Romantics acted in an integrating and culture-sustaining manner. Novalis's bold attempt of planning a 'scientific bible', which, unlike the *Grande Encyclopédie* of the enlightened philosophers, would not exclude or minimize religious and metaphysical problems, was as remarkable as Coleridge's manifold attempts to reduce all knowledge into harmony. Novalis's encyclopedia remained a torso, a fact usually explained by his premature death at the age of twenty-nine. Coleridge was granted a far longer spell, and yet his work too, highly impressive though it is, appears as a torso. Perhaps this is the price that anyone has to pay who aims at complete comprehensiveness. That this was true of Coleridge, there cannot be the slightest doubt. Some critics, foremost among them René Wellek,[18] have, probably rightly, questioned Coleridge's originality in the field of metaphysical speculation, but none have refuted his claim of "having endeavoured to unite the insulated fragments of truth, and therewith to frame a perfect mirror". Side by side with literature and philosophy, his mind encompassed theology, politics, education and, to some extent, even the natural sciences. De Quincey was perhaps not far off the mark when he said of him:

> He gathered into focal concentration the largest body of objects, *apparently* disconnected, that any man ever yet, by any magic, could assemble, or having assembled, could manage.

Moreover, Coleridge took a keen interest in the interconnexion between all these branches of knowledge. As Wordsworth said of him:

> He was of that rare class of minds which cannot contemplate any one thing without becoming aware of its relation to everything else.

This, incidentally, also explains that exhaustive and cyclical mode of discoursing in which he is said to have indulged.

John Stuart Mill described Coleridge as one of the two great seminal minds of England in the early nineteenth century (the other being Bentham, the bugbear of the Romantics). At the present time, when the different branches of knowledge are again coalescing, it is safe to assume that, with the above proviso, Coleridge's stature will continue to rise. The same is true of Friedrich Schlegel, whose cast of mind bears much resemblance to that of Coleridge. Critic, poet, philosopher, historian, theologian, philologist and political publicist, all rolled into one, such was Schlegel's many-sidedness. And again, as in the case of his

English counterpart, Friedrich Schlegel appreciated the inter-dependence of these various branches of knowledge. One of his programmatic poems, entitled *Athenaeum*, proclaims the aim of the movement he had helped to launch:

> Der Bildung Strahlen all' in Eins zu fassen.
> . . . Bestrebten wir uns frei im treuen Bunde.[19]

Unlike Hegel, he never succeeded in constructing a great philo-sophical system. Indeed his characterization of Plato—"he had no system, but he had a philosophy"—might well be applied to Friedrich Schlegel himself. For, just as in Coleridge's case, his *œuvre* strikes one as unsystematic, unfinished, and, in a deeper sense, unfinishable. This may help to explain Novalis's remark that Friedrich Schlegel's work stimulated without satisfying. Perhaps this two-edged judgment might be applied to Romanticism in general, or at any rate to several of its aspects. However, in a more mellow frame of mind, one would, I think, be inclined to agree with Ricarda Huch's positive verdict when she remarked that the Romantics' greatest claim to fame consisted in the very fact that they desired to encompass all.[20]

CHAPTER FIVE

Forebodings and Nostalgia for the Past

IT was a Romantic historian, the German Ernst von Lasaulx, who was struck by the prophetic power so often found in poets and thinkers.[1] As regards the Romantics themselves, it can be shown that many of them possessed that rare gift of inspired, or intuitive, insight that manifested itself in an astonishing presentiment of things to come.[2] Clearly, the eruption of the irrational had its repercussions also in this sphere.

Two years after Waterloo, Chateaubriand declared that, trying to look a hundred years ahead, he saw a cloud too dark for human vision. One thing, however, he perceived quite clearly: the advent of military dictatorships.[3] Two decades after the end of the Napoleonic Wars, in the midst of an outwardly peaceful era of European history, Leopardi was haunted by the vision of new and unprecedented bloodshed:

> E già dal caro
> Sangue de suoi non asterrà la mano
> La génerosa stirpe; anzi coverte
> Fien di stragi l'Europa e l'altera riva
> Dell' atlantico mar.[4]

Yet it was doubtful whether the carnage of war was the worst that the coming century held in store for Europe. As early as the 1820s, Lamennais' prophetic ear discerned "the roaring of the Revolutions",[5] the most momentous of which was to break out exactly one hundred years after the publication of his profound *Essai sur l'indifférence en matière de religion* (1817). Lamennais also foresaw (although at a somewhat later date) that Communism would one day sacrifice liberty on the altar of equality.[6]

As for the final result of the impending social revolutions, none was more pessimistic than the Polish Romantic Count Zygmunt Krasiński. In his drama *Nieboska Komedia* (*Undivine Comedy*), written in 1834, one of the protagonists observing "the dancings of the rabble" sees there all the old crimes of the world dressed in new robes, whirling in a new dance, and he predicts: "But their end will be the same as it was thousands of years ago—vice, gold and blood."[7]

Even the inhuman atrocities committed during the Second World War were somehow anticipated by the Romantics. "Once the moral sense is almost extinguished," wrote Lamennais in 1825, "a kind of blind movement follows which drives these degraded beings towards everything which promises their coarse desires some sort of enjoyment. At times a grim instinct develops in them; they thirst after blood, and unheard of atrocities fill the world with horror." The religious aspect of the problem was emphasized by Chateaubriand as early as 1802 when he foresaw that one day when religion had been brushed aside as a superstition the way would be open for every kind of crime.[8] In the same vein Southey, England's Poet Laureate, predicted in 1829:

> Throughout what is called the Christian world there will be a contest between Impiety and Religion; the former is everywhere gathering strength, and wherever it breaks loose the foundations of human society are shaken.[9]

The Romantic preacher Lacordaire, Krasiński and others, all foresaw that militant and highly organized atheists would one day attempt to wipe religion off the face of the earth.

It is well known that apocalyptic visions—an ever-recurring accompaniment of transcendental Christianity—were fairly widespread in Europe during the post-Napoleonic Christian revival. However, it is not generally realized that Romantic forebodings of an impending collapse of our civilization were shared very widely. At times it was felt that the catastrophe might remain confined to Europe, as, for example, when Friedrich Schlegel, in 1820, defined European unity as "one and the same, serious and tragic *sujet* for the tragedy of the future".[10] This apprehension found a grotesque expression in the suggestion which Atterbom heard in 1818 from the Bavarian scholar Schlichtegroll. Iceland, the professor urged, should as soon as possible be used for a storehouse and archive of contemporary European culture, which, in his opinion, would soon be on its last legs.[11] F. G. Wetzel, an undeservedly forgotten friend of E. T. A. Hoffmann, in the concluding passage of his *Magischer Spiegel* (1806), envisaged the time when "the light will be taken from Europe, when Europe will be full of demolished sites, when goblins will meet each other on her deserts, and the paradise will have vanished in the great flood and the rage of fire."

Others feared that the collapse of Europe would spell disaster for the whole planet. Indeed Friedrich Schlegel himself spoke of "the drama of human history" which he suggested "may be very much nearer to its end than to its beginning".[12] And Chateaubriand, on the afore-said occasion, voiced his apprehension:

> There perhaps is the misery of our situation; perhaps we live, not only in the decrepitude of Europe, but in the decrepitude of the world.

The end, he thought, might well take the shape of a Russian domination over the entire globe, and Chateaubriand, who had already travelled so widely, was longing to see Russia so that he might better estimate "the power that threatens to overwhelm the world". Wetzel's fears pointed in the same direction:

> Although it seems as if in a great Eastern empire the spirit were stirring towards a new resurrection, this is only vain and imperfect endeavour. Thence will no single integrated human being arise.[13]

In this context it is noteworthy that the subject of the Last Man had a peculiar fascination for the Romantics: it was treated, among others, by Mary Wollstonecraft Shelley, Lord Byron, Thomas Campbell, T. L. Beddoes and the painter John Martin.

It is true that prophets of doom have existed at all times, and especially during the closing stages of the Middle Ages.[14] Yet it would seem that the spirit of foreboding had never been so widespread. Surely it is remarkable that the feeling of an approaching deluge was shared by Romantic thinkers rooted in such diverse backgrounds as the Germans F. Schlegel and Lasaulx, the Frenchmen Chateaubriand, Lamennais and Baudelaire, the half-Scot Byron, the Irishman Mangan, the Pole Krasiński, the Italian Leopardi, the Spaniard Larra, the Portuguese Garret and the Swiss Bachofen.

Those who feel apprehensive about the future will often cast a nostalgic glance back at the past and will at times even try to live in some bygone age. This is one of the most characteristic features of Romanticism. Thus August Wilhelm Schlegel could utter this significant thought:

> As a sentient being man is set as it were in time, however as a spontaneous being he carries time within him, and this means that he can live in the past and dwell in the spirit wherever he pleases.[15]

It was in the same vein that Chateaubriand reflected in 1811–12:

> The man who today is endowing France with the empire of the world only so that he may trample her underfoot, the man

whose genius I admire and whose despotism I abhor, that man surrounds me with his tyranny as it were with a new solitude; but though he may crush the present, the past defies him, and I remain free in all that precedes his glory.[16]

It would seem that the Romantic nostalgia for the past appeared in three main variations. First, the exhortation to an age of spiritual insecurity and dwindling faith to look with reverence to the example of the Christian Middle Ages. In the second place, nations could be made to look back to times when they had reached their political or cultural apogee. Finally, the passing of an age of feudalism and chivalry could be deplored by those who, like Alfred de Vigny or Joseph von Eichendorff or Adam Mickiewicz, belonged to the *élites* of the past, or even by others who had no axe to grind.

A pre-Romantic drama, Goethe's *Goetz von Berlichingen*, had already inaugurated the tradition of chivalry plays, but it was not until the Romantic era itself that the literary *genre* of the chivalric novel originated, and, owing to the imaginative gifts of Sir Walter Scott, immediately gained the widest appeal. Scott, partly Celtic by origin, ingeniously combined the patriotic and feudal nostalgias. In both his evocative efforts he was greatly helped by the fact that the age of heroic ideals he contrived to resurrect was far less remote in Scotland than in most other countries. For it was not so long ago, perhaps a mere generation before his birth in 1771, that clanship had been predominant in the border society to which his ancestors belonged. And retrospective patriotism could fasten on so comparatively recent an event as Bonnie Prince Charlie's Jacobite attempt of 1745–6 which, in Scott's first novel *Waverley*, is invested with all the glamour of a lost cause. Obviously, nostalgia for the past and sympathy for defeated causes often go hand in hand.

This is not the place to embark upon an analysis of the *œuvre* of the semi-anonymous author of the Waverley novels. All that matters in this context is that it is all imbued with Scott's fervent attachment to the past. *Redgauntlet*, another echo of the glorious failure of the Jacobites, provides a further example. Most probably it was this common keynote of Scott's novels that satisfied critics and historians for well over a century that the author in question was indubitably one of the Romantics. More recently that assumption has been questioned, independently by two such authorities as the Hungarian Georg Lukácz and, in Britain by David Daiches.[17] Lukácz in particular makes great play with the opinion of Balzac who reproved Scott for his 'conservative philistinisme'. Both critics, it would seem, are right only in so far as they point out that there were two sides to Scott, in other words that there also existed a prosaic Scott, or at any rate prosaic facets to some figments of his imagination. However, the distinguished critics surely go too far when they deny that Scott should be regarded as a Romantic. For if the last criterion is not sufficient, another more personal one exists: Abbotsford. Here in this newly-built make-believe castle, filled by Scott with historical relics of every kind and description, we have the typical Romantic-quixotic escape into the past, and therefore, seen from a hard-headed, realist point of view, into unreality. Nor were the consequences to be faced in the prosaic world of the day any less painful than those encountered by the hero of Cervantes, whose *novelas* had done so much to inspire Scott. True, Scott contrived to become a Border laird, but he was financially ruined in the process. We may note in passing that Abbotsford set a fashion which in the latter half of the century led to the erection of such mock medieval castles as the Prince Consort's Balmoral, Neuschwanstein, the extravagantly Romantic masterpiece of Ludwig II of Bavaria and the castle of Hohenzollern, built by Frederick William IV of Prussia.

The impact of Scott's work was hardly less prodigious than that of Lord Byron.[18] Manzoni, Alfred de Vigny with his *Cinq Mars* and Victor Hugo were but the most famous of his emulators, and Balzac, too, notwithstanding his criticism, admitted that he had been influenced by Scott. At the same time the originator of the modern historical novel did not long remain unsurpassed. Leaving aside the question as to the relative merit of Scott's best novels (e.g. *The Heart of Midlothian*) on the one hand, and, say, Victor Hugo's *Notre Dame de Paris* on the other, most critics would agree that Manzoni's one and only novel, *Promessi Sposi* (The Betrothed), is superior to anything Scott ever wrote. When Scott and Manzoni met in Milan in 1828, the latter—according to an anecdote—acknowledged his debt to his visitor by remarking that Scott had been responsible for the *Promessi Sposi*, to which Scott courteously yet truthfully retorted that in that case he would have to regard the Italian novel as his greatest achievement. It was also a measure of Manzoni's greatness that, having accomplished his masterpiece, he not only refrained from following it up with other and perhaps less significant creations of the same *genre*, but that he even came to recognize the hybrid, half-scientific and half-imaginary character as the inherent weakness of the historical novel as an art-form.[19] Vigny, who, in 1828, had thought that the historical novel was superior to the more traditional form of historiography, later came to share Manzoni's qualms when he stated:

> The novel, whatever it may be, belongs to the realm of Art; history, whatever form it takes, belongs to the realm of Philosophy and has nothing to do with Art.

That it was possible to emulate Scott also in a different medium from that of the historical novel is shown by the example of Mickiewicz's epic poem *Pan Tadeusz*, where the traditional and vanished life among Polish gentlefolk in Lithuania is depicted in rich and nostalgic colours. It should also be noted that Scott's novels, e.g. *Ivanhoe*, provided the inspiration for some of Delacroix's paintings.

Whereas Scott hardly ever penetrated further back than the Reformation, Romantic nostalgia was in many other cases focused on the Middle Ages. Ever since the Renaissance, the attitude of those who might be regarded as spokesmen of the Modern Age had tended to be antagonistic to the spirit of medievalism. Rabelais had already branded the Middle Ages as an era of darkness. The whole medieval period appeared, to men like Boileau and Pope, as one of retrogression or, to say the least, of sleep between the luminous civilization of Antiquity and that of the new awakening in the fourteenth to sixteenth centuries. During the Age of Enlightenment antagonism turned into violent hostility, notably but by no means exclusively on the part of Voltaire. Kant regarded the Middle Ages as an incomprehensible aberration of the human mind. Now, during the Romantic Age, the pendulum decidedly swung in the opposite direction, so that the Romantics have not unfairly been accused of an uncritical attitude to the Middle Ages.

Indeed, it was a Romantic himself, the Danish poet Adam Gottlob Oehlenschläger, who in his autobiography was among the first to criticize that tendency.[20]

The Romantic adoration of the Middle Ages was born of a variety of motives, among which the religious one seems to have been paramount. But artistic and political motives also played a considerable part. In fact, in Germany, where the idealization of the Middle Ages reached its greatest intensity, the religious motive, highly significant in itself, was greatly reinforced by patriotic political reflections, since the Middle Ages could be represented as the most illustrious period in German history. This retrospective pride helped to console many Germans at the time of Napoleon's ascendancy and especially when the *Sacrum Romanum Imperium Nationis Germanicae*, which had been moribund for so long, was at last officially dissolved. Besides, the feudal and chivalric pageant of the Middle Ages was conjured up in Germany as well as in other European countries. Another characteristic facet of the medieval political structure that appealed to the Romantics was the abundance of intermediary powers, such as municipalities, guilds and corporations which were now understood to have counteracted political overcentralization and absolutism. The municipal reforms in Prussia, introduced by Baron vom Stein in 1804, were inspired by the medieval example. But at the same time the complex and rigid medieval hierarchy was reappraised and was now understood to have provided the necessary counterweight to the ever-increasing anarchy from below; and indeed a great deal of the Romantic nostalgia for the Middle Ages may be said to have arisen from the half-conscious sense of political insecurity felt in an age which, at any rate since the French Revolution, had lost all sense of hierarchy and had consequently fallen into perpetual political turmoil. A characteristic example, Friedrich Hurter's *Geschichte Papst Innozenz III und seiner Zeitgenossen* (1832–42) by a Protestant convert to Catholicism, springs to mind. Clearly, the Romantic hankering after the Middle Ages was bound up with the deep desire for political stability. The less this could be expected of the future, the more readily it was discovered in, and projected into, the past.

Viewed from yet another angle, that Golden Age could be

revered either as the great period of the Holy Roman Emperors such as Otto the Great or Henry III, or no less justifiably as that of the equally illustrious Popes, as for example Gregory VII or Innocent III. Thus we find that the medieval struggle between Guelphs and Ghibellines had its echo in the different approaches of Romantic enthusiasts for the Middle Ages.

The profound impression made by medieval art, and architecture in particular, is a well-known feature of European Romanticism. In this context it should be noted that thanks to the initiative of the Romantics the building of Cologne Cathedral—the supreme example of Gothic architecture in Germany—was after an interval of four centuries resumed in the early 1840s and completed in 1880. In France, Prosper Mérimée's *protégé*, the architect Viollet-le-Duc, carried out numerous restorations of famous medieval buildings in Paris, Brittany, Rheims, Amiens and most notably in Carcassonne. In England the architect A. W. N. Pugin, a convert to Roman Catholicism, after giving a great deal of thought to the details and inner spirit of medieval architecture, became the finest and foremost architect in the neo-Gothic style.[21] It is well to remember that his *Principles of Pointed or Christian Architecture* (1841) came out much earlier than Ruskin's *Seven Lamps* (1849) or *Stones of Venice* (1851). Of Pugin's forceful *Contrasts* a non-Catholic, Charles L. Eastlake, has said: "To the circulation of this work—coloured though it may be by a strong theological bias—we may attribute the care and jealousy with which our ancient churches have since been protected and kept in repair."[22]

In the same vein Romantic painters, especially the so-called Lukasbund founded in Vienna in 1809—and, after their removal to Rome, known as the 'Nazarenes'—rediscovered the technically primitive but spiritually significant paintings of the Middle Ages which inspired so much of their own art and that of their *epigoni* such as the English Pre-Raphaelite Brotherhood. One of the founders of that last-mentioned group of artists, W. Holman Hunt, never ceased to regard the Middle Ages as a paradise lost. Reappraisal often went hand in hand with laborious search, especially in parts of Europe that had witnessed the Reformation and dissolution of monasteries, where medieval paintings, as far as they survived at all, had in many cases been removed from altars and side-altars and banished to odd nooks and crannies whence they had to be dug up under layers of debris and dust. But even countries or regions that had always remained Catholic had tended to disparage pre-Renaissance paintings and had often dealt with its specimens in hardly less cavalier a fashion. Thus Catholics too now had to be taught to appreciate the purity and depth of the so-called 'primitive' medieval painters. Stained glass painting, so characteristic a feature of medieval churches, which had fallen into disuse during the ages of Baroque and Rococo, came to be revived by the Romantic generation. Pugin, on a visit to Malvern, recorded his delight: "Here is a church in which the stained glass has not fallen a victim to Protestant zeal. It is truly magnificent." [23]

There can be little doubt that at the root of the Romantic nostalgia for the Middle Ages lay the feeling that modern man, gradually drifting away from Christianity, had suffered a severe and possibly irreparable loss. By contrast with the contemporary age of spiritual insecurity and doubt, the long bygone 'God-permeated'[24] epoch of faith, appeared to the Romantics in resplendent colours. A French critic of the Romantic movement has aptly commented upon this phenomenon:

> When a Benedictine studied the Middle Ages, he did not ask himself how it could be of service to him and whether people lived happier and more pious lives in the Middle Ages. As he himself stood within a continuity of faith and ecclesiastical organization, he could take up a more critical attitude to religion than a Romantic living in a century of revolution, in which all faith had been shaken and laid open to question.[25]

This is precisely why genuine admiration for the piety of medieval man so often tended to degenerate into *Schwärmerei*, as for example in Novalis's novel *Heinrich von Ofterdingen*, or in his enthusiastic essay *Die Christenheit oder Europa* (1799), or again in Görres's *Christliche Mystik* (1836–42), where historical facts and legends about the Middle Ages are inextricably interwoven. Friedrich Schlegel, a greater scholar than Görres, to some extent also idealized the Middle Ages. The interpretation of that epoch in his *Philosophie der Geschichte* (1829) has not unfairly been described as the mere inversion of the unsympathetic interpretation by the Enlightenment.[26] The darker chapters in the Church's history do not exist for him. And yet Friedrich Schlegel's picture is in essentials far nearer the truth than the caricature drawn by Voltaire, whose keen historical eye had in this respect been deceived by the distorting lens of his fanatical hatred of the Church.[27] For Friedrich Schlegel and Novalis among German writers, as Frédéric Ozanam among the French, appreciated the crucial fact that European culture during the Middle Ages owed almost everything to the Church. It was another German Romantic, Clemens Brentano, who succeeded so well in reconstructing the way in which the medieval Church had assumed particular responsibilities—centuries before the modern Welfare State—such as the care of lepers. However, the same imaginative writer, in his story entitled *Aus der Chronika eines fahrenden Schülers* also contrived to conjure up an impressionistic picture of medieval spirituality. Among eminent medievalists, Johann Friedrich Böhmer, editor of the *Regesta Imperii* and co-editor of the *Monumenta Germaniae Historica*, was inspired by Clemens Bretano.

To come back once more to Voltaire's contempt for so large a part of the European heritage, Coleridge's general comment is worth quoting:

> But assuredly the way to improve the present is not to despise the past; it is a great error to idolize it, but a still greater to hold it in contempt.[28]

It has rightly been remarked that the Romantics' essential contribution to historical scholarship lay in their realization that no historian worthy of the name could achieve anything without some effort of his imaginative powers.[29] Historiography, if it was to rise higher than the 'dry-as-dust', scissors-and-paste variety falsely known under that name, must contrive to bring the past to life, to resurrect the dead, together with all their human problems and conflicts. Manzoni, in his introductory remarks to *Promessi Sposi*, defines historiography as

> a mighty war against time, for snatching from his hands the years imprisoned, nay already slain by him, she calls them back unto life, passes them in review, and sends them once more into battle.

Manzoni (drawing by Ermini)

F. W. Schlegel
(engraving by Joseph Axmann, after Auguste von Buttlar)

This is exactly what Augustin Thierry, who was greatly indebted to Scott[30] and to *Ivanhoe* in particular, and who in his turn
influenced Manzoni, set out to do, and largely achieved in several
of his historical writings; to some extent this applies also to Michelet, who described an important aspect of his work in these words:

> I have given to many dead that assistance of which I myself
> shall be in need. . . . I have exhumed them for a second life.
> Now they live with us, and we feel ourselves to be their relation
> and friends. Thus a family is formed, a common city between
> the living and the dead.[31]

It was the immediate feeling for the past that characterized the
Romantic approach. This is how Thierry formulated the Romantic
postulate in his *Histoire de la Conquête de l'Angleterre par les
Normands* (1825):

> One must try to get through to the human beings, over the
> distance of centuries. One has to imagine them as living and
> active beings on a part of the earth where the very dust of their
> bones would not be found to-day. . . . It is 700 years since
> those people have died, that their hearts have ceased to beat in
> pride or suffering; but what difference does that make to the
> imagination? For the imagination there is no past, and the
> future itself belongs to the present.

Historiography thus conceived was, as Renan and Nietzsche
were to remark, the creation of the nineteenth century. Nor could
it have taken place without the great upsurge of man's imaginative
powers unleashed by the Romantic Movement. It was that impetus which not only intensified the historian's search but also
greatly varied its scope. New and important branches of knowledge came into being. Friedrich Schlegel's treatise *Ueber Sprache
und Weisheit der Indier* (1808) helped to launch the study of Hindu
philosophy and religion. At the Genevan Academy, in 1811–12,
Sismondi created the comparative study of literature in a course
of lectures in which he dealt synoptically with the history of
French, Italian, Spanish and Portuguese literature. In his exile
in Paris, the leading Polish Romantic Adam Mickiewicz, in the
1840s, was the first to embark upon a comparative survey of

Slavonic literature. The brothers Jakob and Wilhelm Grimm, together with the Dane Rasmus Kristian Rask and others, inaugurated Germanistic studies, and Friedrich Christian Diez the philology of the Romance languages and the study of Troubadour poetry so congenial to the Romantics. Celtic studies too, received a decisive stimulus, notably through the efforts of Franz Bopp, a native of the Rhineland. Celtic cultural origins in several regions of France found sympathetic investigators in Charles Nodier, the half-Irish baron Taylor and Alphonse de Caillaux, whose findings are recorded in their joint work entitled *Voyages pittoresques et romantiques dans l'ancienne France*. In Great Britain, the wild enthusiasm for Ossian, the mythical Gaelic bard, whose poems the pre-Romantic Scottish writer James Macpherson claimed to have discovered and translated into English—for the most part the poems were in fact Macpherson's own—also spring to mind. Nor did the cult of the Gaelic soulfulness of Ossian remain confined to this country. Thus Herder argued that if these poems were not genuine, it was "a pious swindle".

Yet another remarkable broadening of man's sense of the past resulted from a fresh approach to archaeology as well as from the newly inaugurated study of pre-historic times. To the latter, Romantic scholars like Georg Friedrich Creuzer, author of *Symbolik und Mythologie der alten Völker* (1810–12), and the Swiss Johann Jakob Bachofen made significant contributions. Here again the ambiguity of the Romantic mind is clearly revealed. Their highly developed sophistication makes the Romantics encompass pre-history in their retrospective search,[32] but their feeling of nostalgia for that remotest past is accentuated by the profound weariness of sophistication which is so marked a feature of Romanticism. In this respect, too, Rousseau, with his emphasis on the noble savage, and Herder had proved to be harbingers of the Romantic Movement. Taken all in all, Lord Acton was not exaggerating when he remarked that the Romantic writers had "doubled the horizon of Europe",[33] and indeed that "romanticism had brought into action the whole inheritance of man". This, as he noted, "was then attempted for the first time".[34]

The remarkable deepening of historical appreciation brought about by the Romantic Movement is also borne out by the fact that

Romantic philosophers of history, notably Friedrich Schlegel,[35] fully reckoned with a human phenomenon so often ignored in the enlightened approach to history, namely the problem of evil. Among the other Romantics who were equally alive to that problem, Coleridge and Victor Hugo—especially the latter in his Preface to *Cromwell*—spring to mind. Hence there was but one step towards the Romantic re-discovery of the tragic element in history which in our time has been so much emphasized in Arnold Toynbee's *Study of History*. Indeed, Novalis went so far as to suggest that history should be written in the form of a tragedy.[36] Hence also Thierry's emphasis on "the victims of history", such as the Highland Scots, the Irish and the Gauls. From the sphere of painting, Gabriel Alexandre Decamps' moving *Defeat of the Cimbri* (1833) might be mentioned in this context.

In his *Ideen zur Philosophie der Geschichte*, written between 1784 and 1791, Herder had already looked upon history as the development of all diverse potentialities inherent in human nature. Friedrich Schlegel, who gave much thought to the philosophical foundations of historiography, adopted this idea but gave it a typically Romantic, subjectivist touch. According to him the historian's search is primarily a manifestation of man's quest for self-knowledge in order that all the potentialities of human character and existence might be fathomed. At the beginning of the twentieth century, this conception was to form the core of Wilhelm Dilthey's profound analysis of the historical consciousness. One thing is certain: the Romantic re-interpretation of history has proved as lasting an achievement as Romantic music, to which indeed it bears resemblance by its imaginative reading of what might be called the richly orchestrated score of the past.

Yet the Romantic approach to history was certainly not free from its own peculiar dangers. In the first place we must note the often bewildering tendency to confuse the three disciplines of history, philosophy of history and theology of history, and to engage, as Michelet and Carlyle sometimes did, in lofty imaginative flights. Historical scholarship suffers hardly less from a strong overdose of imagination than from its deficiency.

Secondly, there is the somewhat morbid Romantic peculiarity of the worship of ruins. The very fact that a medieval building was lying in ruins considerably heightened its appeal for the Romantics. The Landgraf of Kassel even conceived the grotesque idea of erecting an artificial ruined castle, the Löwenburg, on the Wilhelmshöhe outside his city. Nor was this an isolated example. There was indeed a European-wide fashion of building artificial ruins.[37] How are we to explain the strange spell cast by crumbling stone and ruins on Romantic admirers? According to Achim von Arnim, a ruined edifice "creates the peculiar sensation of transience so welcome to many a melancholy soul weary of the present".[38] Two motives are thus intertwined: the desire for withdrawal from the *malaise* of the present age, and a vague, semi-religious sense of timelessness beyond. However, so complex was the Romantic soul that a third and subconscious motive may equally have been at work. For the nihilist tendencies latent in the Romantic Movement may have proved a contributory factor. It almost seems as though some Romantics preferred churches in ruins to new ones or those in good repair. A significant pictorial illustration is provided by Caspar David Friedrich's oil painting entitled 'Abbey under the Oak Tree' now in Berlin. It shows the ruined Cistercian Abbey of Eldena, near Greifswald, built by Danish monks in about 1200. Friedrich often reverted to this motif. In one of his letters he likened the Church shaken by the Reformation to a ruin. An English parallel would be Turner's water colour of Tintern Abbey, the ruin that stimulated Wordsworth to compose one of his profoundest poems. Other English painters, like Thomas Girtin or Thomas Cole, also showed great interest in medieval abbeys and castles, especially if they were ruined.

Thirdly, the Romantic appreciation of every standpoint—a postulate formulated by August Wilhelm Schlegel as early as 1791 [39]—may, as Lord Acton has pointed out, lead to the rehabilitation of every standpoint, and consequently to the gradual weakening of moral standards hitherto held to be absolute. Friedrich Schlegel, it is true, showed himself far-sighted enough to perceive this danger when, in a review of the seventh and eighth collection of Herder's *Humanitätsbriefe*, he argued that such a method would in the end produce no other result but that everything must be what it is and what it has been. Yet, in spite of that timely warning, the Romantic approach to history undoubtedly served to intensify the sense of the relativity of all moral values.

However, the most ominous aspect of the Romantic attitude to the past must be seen in the half-conscious tendency to use history as a substitute for religion. Once recollection was regarded, in Jean Paul's words, as "the only paradise from which we cannot be expelled",[40] the danger became imminent that man's mind would be focused too much on the solace of the past and too little on the hope of attaining heavenly bliss in the hereafter. At the same time the Christian transcendental concept of the human soul would be replaced by the idea of a purely 'terrestrial immortality',[41] based on posterity's memory of its past. Leopardi's thought, expressed in his *Dialogo della Natura e di un'anima*, clearly points in this direction. Later on the same idea was to be elaborated by Auguste Comte, whose system of thought, though intended to be intransigently positivistic, shows remarkable traces of Romantic influence. With Friedrich Nietzsche the theme of History as *ersatz*-religion occurs once more in a new and striking variation. In an aphorism entitled 'The historian's happiness', he voices his own joy at harbouring within himself not one immortal soul but, instead, several mortal souls.[42] Nietzsche, however, though in many ways a late Romantic *malgré lui*, lies outside the scope of this chapter.

PART TWO

Nihilism and Yearning
for a Faith

CHAPTER SIX

The Romantic Malady of the Soul

IT is understandable that the strong forebodings outlined above produced in some Romantic thinkers a feeling which Leopardi, the supreme exponent of the Romantic malady of the soul, described in his *Dialogue between Timander and Eleander* as "complete and incessant despair". But Romantic *Weltschmerz* or *mal de siècle* (synonyms for the 'malady of the soul') were far more complex phenomena than is generally realized. Only by studying the unmistakable nihilistic trends in Romanticism can we hope to fathom those symptoms. Indeed many Romantics passed, often more than once, through a stage which, following Nietzsche's terminology, we have become accustomed to define as nihilism; but already in contemporary usage 'Nihiliste' meant, according to L. S. Mercier's *Néologie* of 1801: "Un homme qui ne croit à rien." The new term first appeared in 1796.[1] In German, 'Nihilismus' was used in the same sense for the first time, apparently by Novalis.

Were some Romantics in danger of believing nothing? The answer can only be in the affirmative. We have already seen how some of their leading thinkers had lost, or never even acquired, the eighteenth-century faith in indefinite secular progress. Chateaubriand, in his exile in London in 1795, refuted the idea of progress and human perfectibility in his *Essai sur les Révolutions anciennes et modernes*. In this context, too, Leopardi's satirical poem *Palinodia. Al Marchese Gino Capponi* (1835) springs to mind. And yet at that stage the same Romantics had no faith in Christianity either; this applies to Leopardi at any time after 1821 no less than to the Chateaubriand of the middle 1790s, before he discovered the delights, if not the depths, of Christianity. Among the German Romantics, Clemens Brentano and Ludwig Tieck seem at times to have suffered most from that frame of mind which, through an overdose of scepticism, makes all ideals evaporate in thin air. An extreme expression of this nihilistic mood is furnished by the savage satire entitled *Die Nachtwachen* (1804); the author, who had been hiding under the pseudonym Bonaventura, is now belived to have been Clemens Brentano or Friedrich Georg Wetzel.[2]

Taken at their face value, the Romantics would appear to have been far too preoccupied with their own self for us to define them as nihilists. There were indeed periods in their lives when they abandoned or were about to abandon Christianity; they might even pour scorn on the rival idea of man-made Progress; but they firmly believed in themselves. Or did they? It is this question we have to examine before we can tackle the problem of the Romantic malady of the soul.

The loosening of the bonds of allegiance and belief resulted in an emancipation of the self comparable to, but far in excess of, a similar movement in the Renaissance. The process then begun, accentuated during the Enlightenment, and again during the *Sturm und Drang* period in Germany, now reached its peak. When all ideas and ideals were once again in the melting pot, it was not unnatural that the individual self might seem to be the only firm anchor. At no other period in history would Johann Gottlieb Fichte's uncompromising subjectivism have commanded such enthusiastic support. Fichte's philosophy not only impressed, but deeply influenced the early German Romantics. Young Friedrich Schlegel even went so far as to declare that the principal exposition of Fichte's philosophy, his *Grundlage der gesamten Wissenschaftslehre* of 1794, ranked as an event of similar magnitude as the French Revolution. Indirectly, the impact of Fichte's thought extended far beyond Germany. Nor was his approach applicable only to epistemological questions. Problems of moral philosophy too assumed an entirely novel appearance, for in Fichte's system virtue and vice henceforward existed only in so far as the individual's conscience conceived them. Well might Madame de Staël, for once critical of German thought, liken Fichte's concept of the self to Baron von Münchhausen's action when, in danger of drowning, he seizes his own sleeve and swings himself across the river.

In Romantic poetry the individual's defiant gesture of self-reliance was never expressed more vigorously than by the greatest Austro-Hungarian Romantic, Nikolaus Lenau. In his dramatic poem *Faust* (1835) the hero, rejecting God and Nature, clings on to his Ego, and to his Ego alone, with dogged pertinacity:

> Behaupten will ich fest mein starres Ich.
> Mir selbst genug und unerschütterlich.
> Niemanden hörig mehr und untertan
> Verfolg' ich in mich einwärts meine Bahn.[3]

The crucial words rest in the self-assurance: 'Mir selbst genug' ('sufficient to myself'). Later on, however, Faust (in whom we have very good reason to recognize Lenau himself) deplores his self-delusion in these stirring lines:

> Ich habe Gottes mich entschlagen
> Und der Natur in stolzem Hassen,
> Mich in mir selbst wollt' ich zusammenfassen;
> O Wahn! ich kann es nicht ertragen.
> Mein Ich, das hohle, finstre, karge,
> Umschauert mich gleich einem Sarge.[4]

Other Romantics, faced by the same dilemma, stressed rather a different aspect. Instead of lamenting over the burden that could not be sustained by the individual alone without hope of supernatural help, they deplored the vacancy and emptiness which surrounded those who held no beliefs. Clemens Brentano's stirring poem 'An den Engel in der Wüste' and the Count in Krasiński's *Undivine Comedy* who discovers a hole in his heart, deep and hollow as a grave, are two examples of this melancholy frame of mind.

The exploration of this mentality was carried a stage further. A subjectivist attitude bordering on nihilism constituted, as some Romantics clearly realized, an ideal breeding ground for moral and mental aberrations of all kinds. Thus the message contained in Alfred de Musset's great poem *Rolla* proclaims that, once all faith in religious and other ideals is gone, man must fall a prey to degrading passions and vices following almost irresistibly upon that 'curiosité du mal' which Musset, anticipating Baudelaire, so vividly described. Essentially the same moral can be drawn from Ludwig Tieck's remarkable novel *Geschichte des Herrn William Lovell* as well as from Jean Paul's *chef d'œuvre Titan* where it is exemplified in the character of Roquairol.

A variety of mental aberrations produced, or at any rate accentuated, by nihilistic subjectivism are equally well illustrated in Romantic literature, but not only there. In some ways, the lives of some Romantics also bear testimony to this fateful connexion. Nikolaus Lenau, Gérard de Nerval and the painter Caspar David Friedrich, are three whose lives ended in madness. Granted that in actual life there are many different causes of mental collapse, it is legitimate to surmise that an outlook on life which throws such a burden on man's free will may be held partly responsible.

Was nihilistic subjectivism doomed to lead into a cul-de-sac? If still in doubt, we must try to lay bare the souls of those Romantics who embody, in their lives or works, the Romantic sentiment of the malady of the soul. The task of psychological reconstruction, always problematical, is helped by the astonishing range of Romantic self-revelations.

One thing is immediately clear: the complexity of this sentiment. Two main variations can clearly be distinguished. There existed, first of all, the unredeemed *Weltschmerz* of poets and thinkers such as Leopardi in Italy and Schopenhauer in Germany. Together with Christian faith they had abandoned Christian hope, that strongest and most lasting source of ultimate bliss, and yet they felt equally repelled by the newfangled hope of secular progress.[5] This extreme kind of *Weltschmerz* was, I believe, a new phenomenon not to be compared to the earlier *Weltschmerz* as it had found expression for example in Edward Young's *Night Thoughts on Life, Death and Immortality* (1741–4).

There was also another, less radical, and therefore less despondent, group of Romantics whose *Weltschmerz* seems to have been derived from a half-conscious feeling of frustration. They sensed that the only salvation lay in a return to religion, but equally felt an inability or lack of determination to follow that road. Despite outward appearances, Lord Byron should, I think, be included in this second category.

Other Romantics, e.g. Alessandro Manzoni, no longer dazzled by Rousseau's modernized version of the Pelagian heresy, reverted to the traditional Christian 'pessimism' concerning human nature and the age-old Christian 'suspicion of the world', but this latter attitude, pessimistic though it may have appeared in the secularized Europe of 1800, was certainly not an expression of Romantic *Weltschmerz*.

To revert to the unredeemed type of *Weltschmerz*: the reason why some people today fail to comprehend its true nature is only too obvious. Since about 1800 all shades of nihilism have made great strides in Europe, so that by now, in the middle of the twentieth century, a considerable number of our contemporaries take nihilism for granted though they may still prefer to disguise it under such transparent cloaks as existentialism *à la* Camus or Jean-Paul Sartre. Such people no longer seem to be suffering as the result of their nihilist—or near-nihilist—outlook on life; or, to put it more cautiously, having become accustomed to the vast spiritual void around them, they have come to accept it almost as a matter of course, and if they suffer, as they often do, from a feeling of *malaise*, they do not consciously connect that *malaise* with their nihilist mentality, but rather attribute it to various kinds of imaginary or grossly exaggerated shortcomings and ills.[6] Obviously such people find it difficult to grasp that 150 years ago, when nihilism was still in the making, sensitive men who first contracted it in varying degrees,[7] suffered severely from the shock. But that is exactly what happened.

For example, Leopardi's initial reaction after the loss of his faith was a state of utter bewilderment.[8] To quote his own words: "I was terrified finding myself in the midst of nothingness, and myself nothing. I felt as if I were stifled believing and feeling that everything is nothing, solid nothingness."[9]

Of course, it is not suggested that the anguish of the void was the sole cause of the Romantic malady of the soul, least of all in the case of Count Giacomo Leopardi. Indeed, in this particular instance, the ills and afflictions that beset the unfortunate man were of so grave a nature as almost to obscure the deepest cause itself. There was, for example, the continuous financial anxiety in which Leopardi, the scion of an impoverished branch of the Italian *noblesse de province*, had to live. More depressing still was his perpetual ill-health and lack of physical vitality; even his eyesight, which he had overstrained in his precocious youth when he acquired his profound classical education, was seriously and, it seemed, irreparably impaired. If we add to this the narrow, uncongenial atmosphere of his native city, Recanati, in the Marches, "an ignoble city", as he dubbed it, where he was for a great many years virtually imprisoned by his tyrannical father, we may suppose that the chalice was full. But this was not all: Leopardi's bodily deformity—like Alexander Pope and Søren Kierkegaard, he was a hunchback—and perhaps also his shyness were repulsive or ridiculous to the opposite sex, to whom he felt very strongly attracted. Truly pathetic is his outcry in *Ultimo Canto di Saffo*:

Virtù non luce in disadorno amanto.[10]

Wrong though it would be to belittle these miseries, we must beware also of the opposite mistake. In our time, self-styled psychoanalysts, those modern sciolists, have suggested that Leopardi's malady of the soul was primarily due to his unsatisfied sexual desire, a theory which is as shallow as it is fashionable. Moreover, it is preposterous; hardly less so than if one were to interpret the sufferings of Goethe's Werther in the same crude manner. Nor is the analogy far-fetched, for Werther, that prototype of the man afflicted by *Weltschmerz*, also lacked any firm belief that could have upheld him in his tribulations.[11]

The so-called psychoanalytical explanation is as much an oversimplification as its materialist counterpart. The latter would, in this particular case, give undue weight to the sociological setting: the impoverished nobleman in an age of the triumphant bourgeoisie (or some formula to this effect). That other materialist idea, according to which man's spirit is completely dependent on his physique, was strongly repudiated by Leopardi when he warned his readers not to blame his opinions on his maladies.

Perhaps Leopardi's greatest misfortune was that in his childhood Christianity, or a warped version of it, had been crammed down his throat by a bigoted and unloving mother. When eight years old he was forced to put on priestly robes, four years later he received the tonsure, and before he reached the age of discretion he had already revolted against the faith which those hated robes were supposed to symbolize. His road to unbelief was neither straight nor easy; at the age of twenty-two, when he was planning to write a series of Christian hymns, he was still struggling to return to the faith.[12] However, soon afterwards he finally broke with Christianity. Thenceforward he increasingly projected his own unhappiness on to his picture of the world; his day-book, *Zibaldone*, shows us this process at work. It was then that he developed that bottomless *Weltschmerz* so characteristic of his mature *œuvre*, of the brilliant prose dialogues of the *Operetti Morali* no less than of his finest *Canti* by which he proved to be his country's greatest lyrical poet since Petrarch.

Inescapably miserable and utterly meaningless—this is his verdict upon life. Happiness never exists, though man, who feeds on illusions, always expects it of the future. Toil, fatigue, pain and sorrow, these are the realities of life:

> assai felice
> Se respirar ti lice
> D'alcun dolor.[13]

And the destination of this pitiful journey? An immense and horrid abyss that swallows up everything, even the memory of man's senseless martyrdom. For the hope of an hereafter is but a childish illusion:

> vana speranza onde consola
> So coi fanciulli il mondo.[14]

Here we can see quite clearly that once death has lost its meaning, life too cannot be meaningful any longer. This is why Eleander, the protagonist of the most famous of Leopardi's Dialogues, laments over the vanity of all human things; why, in another dialogue, between Plotinus and Porphyry, life is declared of so little importance that one should trouble neither to preserve nor to abandon it; why, finally, in Leopardi's greatest poem, the *Canto*

Notturno di un pastore dell' Asia, the unfortunate shepherd's persistent questions

> Dimmi, o luna: a che vale
> al pastor la sua vita,
> la vostra vita a voi?
> dimmi ove tende
> Questo vagar mio breve
> Il tuo corso immortale?[15]

remain without an answer. There is no point in turning to a living God, for there is no God. Some transcendent being does indeed exist; Leopardi calls it either Nature or Destiny. The darkest side of his nihilism is revealed by fragments of an ode in which he in-invokes the Zoroastrian Spiritual Enemy Ahriman, the blind and cruel power of nature that creates evil for evil's sake.[16] The Good Spirit, or Ahura Mazda, on the other hand, who in the Zoroastrian religion more than counterbalances Ahriman, is not invoked.

From his desolate point of view, Leopardi is at least consistent in the conclusion to his *Dialogue between Tristan and a Friend* where we are told that mankind knows nothing, is nothing and has nothing to hope for. When even the last 'inganni' ('illusions') are destroyed, there remains but the devastation of complete and utter despair as it is epitomized in his poem 'To Himself', from which these lines are taken:

> Amaro e noia
> la vita, altro mai nulla; e fango è il mondo.[17]

Another masterpiece of Romantic literature, Etienne Pivert de Senancour's *Oberman* (1804) must be referred to in this context. Purporting to contain a series of letters written by the hero to an intimate friend, the book in reality consists of a number of essays, some of which belong to the greatest of this *genre* since Montaigne. But apart from its literary value, *Oberman* represents a most important testimony, for it has been established that, apart from accidental trappings and the minimum amount of superficial disguise, the author has given us a very sincere picture of his own soul.[18] The book, which many critics had regarded as a *roman intime*, is to all intents and purposes a *journal intime*. In his introduction, the author remarked that 'if these long letters would make one man approximately known', they would be original as well as useful.

The impression conveyed in *Oberman* is that of a soul starved of ideals and values. Like Leopardi, Senancour bemoans the inexpressible void and nothingness that surrounds him on all sides.

As for his Italian counterpart, so for him too, life has become dull and meaningless. Cloudy weather makes him sad, but when it turns bright he finds that the sunshine is 'useless'. He feels less unhappy at dawn and dusk and also during the autumnal season. At one time it seems to him that he has no desires—and what is life without desires? Vegetating, instead of living, cannot satisfy him. At other moments he experiences a craving for everything, for nothing can ever satisfy him in his boundless disillusionment.[19]

Oberman rushes through life fleeing from the present, and yet the future holds no promise for him. The rare and fleeting moments in which he is free from *ennui*—'le mal d'Oberman', as it came to be called—he owes to the beauties of nature, for his soul still responds to grandiose romantic scenery, though here again he indulges in what he calls "cette volupté de la mélancholie", of which he bitterly remarks that it constitutes the most lasting enjoyment of the human heart. Senancour, himself born in Paris, had first experienced the delights of nature in the forest of Fontainebleau and later came to admire the rugged scenery of the high-lying mountain valleys of the Valais. Acoustic impressions gathered from nature meant more to him than visual ones.[20]

It is not that his life is particularly unhappy.[21] In this respect Senancour differs from Leopardi, although he too was plagued by physical disabilities, for, owing to paralytic symptoms in his shoulders, both his arms were withered. Nevertheless, he insists that it is the futility, and the futility alone, which renders Oberman, and therefore himself, miserable. His whole way of life, as he realizes only too well, has become too isolated; the introvert in the end is able to communicate only with himself. For all these reasons he does not know what to desire, and why all hope is extinguished in him. There are moments when the tomb appears an asylum where repose and calm may be found in the abyss of utter nothingness.[22]

Yet there are times when Oberman does not allow himself to be completely submerged by lethargy. Somewhere in the innermost recesses of his heart, it seems, he feels the urge to be entirely different from what he is, to be able to hope again, to discover a meaning in it all, in short to conquer the nihilism that has all but engulfed him. Although since his early days he had become estranged from the Christian faith, Senancour, according to his own 'déclaration essentielle' which was later published by his daughter Virginie, repudiated atheism. There was in him, as in his Oberman, the typically Romantic craving for infinity which is epitomized in the inscription on his tombstone:

Eternité, deviens mon asile.

CHAPTER SEVEN

The Lure of Nothingness.

THE futility of life is also the dominant theme of Schopenhauer's gloomy philosophy, but here such depth is reached that, in some ways, his nihilism has a strong diabolical tinge. Looking at his premises, we find that he not only denies the divine nature of Christ but dismisses Him as a demagogue.[1] Rejecting the divinity of Christ is only logical in a thinker who does not recognize any at all and regards theism as monstrous and totally absurd.[2] Like Ludwig Feuerbach, whose atheism, through the medium of Marx and Engels, has come to exert an even wider influence, Schopenhauer turns the biblical image upside down to assert that man creates demons and gods in his own image.[3] He fails to see any reason why a more perfect intelligence than that belonging to *homo sapiens* should exist anywhere in the Universe. The consolation proffered by Christianity or indeed any form of theism is not for him. Nor does his austere mind accept the blandishments offered by the apostles of infinite secular progress. His reply to them is to the effect that some stages in history are characterized by regress and even by a relapse into barbarism. Moreover, supposing a land of milk and honey could ever be realized, it would not last, since men would soon weary of its delights and attack each other in their boredom.

Since Schopenhauer no longer regards men as made in God's image, at least one essential distinction between human beings and animals is lost. This is why he contemptuously refers to the majority of mankind as 'bipeds'; and sometimes some quadrupeds —especially his poodle—seem nearer to his heart than any man: a trait Schopenhauer shares with other misanthropes. Again we find that life divested of its transcendental meaning must appear flat, empty and trite. There exists in Schopenhauer's philosophy, it is true, a metaphysical force, a blind inexorable Will, or Will-to-live, as he sometimes calls it; but its actions have no meaning whatsoever. For this grotesque demiurge does no more than stage the great tragedy of life, and watch it as a solitary spectator.

As with Leopardi and Senancour, so with Schopenhauer, the idea of man's utterly senseless existence produces gloom and despondency, only more so, for, as one critic put it, Schopenhauer's philosophy, "whatever its intrinsic value, will doubtless always be remembered as perhaps the most striking statement of the pessimistic *Weltanschauung* in the history of human thought".[4] From the very start the philosopher's mind is focused on man's torments and agonies, which, in an unparalleled jeremiad, he depicts in all their manifold shapes. Enjoyment and happiness, on the other hand, are sadly dismissed as a mirage, and thus the whole course of life seems to be oscillating between the two poles of suffering and *ennui*. All in all, the world appears as the worst of all possible worlds, whereas Leibniz had still held it to be the best of all possible worlds. Nor does the majority of mankind deserve a kinder fate, for on the philosopher's reckoning the average man is nothing better than a "dull scoundrel".[5]

Utterly lacking in that specifically Christian virtue of humility, Schopenhauer developed an ever growing contempt for mankind, whose meanness and malice he never ceased to castigate. Thus he arrives at his diabolical picture of "the world as a hell, which surpasses Dante's hell in that each man must be the Devil to his neighbour".[6] Truly diabolical, for in this extreme perversion two essential parts of the original Christian pattern, Purgatory and

Heaven, are omitted, and the Inferno alone holds sway. It is revealing that Schopenhauer quotes, in an approving sense, words which Goethe had put in the mouth of Mephisto:

> Alles was entsteht
> Ist wert, dass es zu Grunde geht.
> Drum besser wär's, dass nichts entstünde.[7]

This last idea leads us to Schopenhauer's peculiarly destructive concept of salvation which he finds in the renunciation of the Will-to-live. Suicide in itself, though not immoral according to his doctrine, would not suffice. Identity of consciousness would indeed be destroyed, but a kind of metempsychosis would take place and thus frustrate complete self-annihilation. The renunciation has to go deeper in order to extinguish the Will, that unique will-o'-the-wisp, which is almost—but not quite—immortal. Only in this way can the final goal be reached, 'das leere Nichts', empty nothingness.[8] It is hardly surprising that the Frenchman P. Challemel-Lacour thus summarized the impression which Schopenhauer's conversation made on him in 1859: "It was," he said, "as though I had felt the icy draught blowing in on me through the half-open door of nothingness."[9] Schopenhauer's photograph taken in the same year, and to a lesser extent the earlier daguerreotypes, tend to corroborate that impression.[10]

One final point must here be made. Although Schopenhauer at times posed as a Buddhist, and his insistence upon the renunciation of the Will-to-live was no doubt influenced by ancient Indian thought, it would be erroneous to regard it as the equivalent of the idea of extinction in Nirvana. The Buddhist conception that envisages the complete absorption in Brahma is a religious and mystical one, whereas Schopenhauer's idea is decidedly irreligious and characteristically non-committal.[11] Nor was there more than a superficial resemblance between Schopenhauer's thought and that of the medieval Christian mystics Eckhart and Tauler, whose spiritual companion (*Geistesgenosse*) Schopenhauer pretended to be.

On one of Francisco Goya's most harrowing plates from the series entitled 'Desastres de la Guerra', a corpse, half-buried in the earth and supporting itself on its elbow, has just traced on a sheet of paper 'Nada', the Spanish word for nothingness. At one time I used to think that this was meant to signify the senselessness of War. However, its message as I now understand it is far more ominous. What the artist means to convey is precisely that nothing exists beyond the grave. There is no hereafter, only a complete void.

Several times during the last thirty-five years of his long life, Goya went out of his way to deny the transcendental reality. The Christ he portrayed in the 'Betrayal of Judas' (1798, Cathedral of Toledo) and in the 'Garden of Olives' (1818, San Antonio, Madrid)—and also in the fresco in the cupola of La Florida, Madrid—is a pathetic, tortured figure, but decidedly not the Redeemer, and not the son of God, for the simple reason that there is no God. The fact that man, deprived of his belief in God, must be in danger of losing all sense of spiritual orientation was clearly realized by Goya. In the 'Desastres de la Guerra', the next plate in the series shows a number of human beings, roped to each other and obviously full of anguish, aimlessly wandering up and down the globe. This time the caption leaves no margin for doubt. It reads 'No saben el camino' (They don't know the way).

Yet even as late as 1819 Goya seems still to be wavering between faith and unbelief. This is borne out by his painting, 'The Last Communion of St. Joseph of Calasanz', which hangs in the Church of Escuelas Pias de San Antón Abad at Madrid, and which has rightly been hailed as marking one of the peaks of religious art. The saint's countenance is transfigured by the sacrament, as a supernatural radiance streams from heaven.

However, Goya's prevailing mood after 1793 was certainly not only violently anticlerical but also atheistic. Somewhat illogically, God, whose very existence was denied by Goya, was also denounced by him for acquiescing in all the horrors and misery on earth. As with Leopardi and Senancour, Goya's *Weltschmerz* and defiance of God have been ascribed to physical causes, in this case to a mysterious illness leading to intermittent deafness which had plagued him since 1792. That affliction, which the foremost painter of the age shared with the foremost composer, is believed to have caused a complete metamorphsis in Goya, so that the painter of fashionable portraits and man of the eighteenth-century Rococo turned into a misanthrope. Others have tried to explain the change in Goya's mentality exclusively in political terms. He had indeed started as a rationalist and had hailed the French Revolution as the dawn of the Age of Reason, but his enthusiasm, too, turned into disillusionment. French imperialism and atrocities in Spain after 1808 provided further motives for political disenchantment. Yet neither physical tribulations nor political vicissitudes suffice to explain the unprecedented degree of Goya's bitterness which is to be fathomed only by regarding its theological dimensions.

From now on Goya concentrated so much on the portrayal of the most painful aspects of life that almost the whole *œuvre* of those last thirty-five years might be interpreted as the pictorial illustration to Schopenhauer's jeremiad in *Die Welt als Willle und Vorstellung* published nine years before Goya's death. True, one outstanding feature of Schopenhauer's hell on earth is missing: boredom. Here, in Goya's whirlpool of cruelty and debauchery, there is no room for it. Human greed, drunkenness, hypocrisy, sexual lust and sadisms of all kinds, these are the constantly recurring themes elaborated with an astounding inventiveness. Nor does it take a warmonger to observe that even his portrayal of war, confined to military disasters and wretchedness, is one-sided. On the other hand, so sensitive an artist as Goya should perhaps be credited with the gift of prophetic insight. It may be that his mind somehow anticipated the accentuated horrors of the twentieth century. One of the plates of the 'Desastres de la Guerra' shows us an amorphous group of starving and emasculated victims, old and young alike, all clad in rags, and on the other side of the picture two well-fed gentlemen, elegantly dressed, without the slightest touch of compassion on their faces. The caption reads: '¿Si son de otro linage?' (Do they belong to another race?). Another sinister plate conveys something of the horrific atmosphere of Buchenwald.

Goya's later works are sometimes interpreted as standing for the democratic ideal.[12] There is some justification for that view as long as it is remembered that the artist was far from believing in the Romantic legend of the People. The plate entitled 'Popula-

The Lure of Nothingness

cho' (The Populace) in the 'Desastres de la Guerra' reveals common men and women as cruel torturers in their turn.

We have seen that for Schopenhauer mankind did not deserve a kinder fate. Similarly Goya never ceased to castigate human nature. The lesson is most forcefully driven home on plate 74 from the 'Desastres de la Guerra' entitled '¡Esto es lo peor!' (This is the worst!). Surrounded by a disconcerted but reverent group of human beings, the wolf sits writing on his roll: 'Misera humanidad, la culpa es tuya' (Miserable humanity, the fault is yours). Again, as in Schopenhauer's case, Goya's almost exclusive preoccupation with the dark side of life helps to produce a diabolical picture of the world. It has been observed that while Hieronymus Bosch, the fifteenth-century Flemish artist, introduced men into his infernal world, Goya introduced the infernal into the world of man.[13] In the end it is no longer human beings, however vile or insane, but gruesome monsters that haunt his 'Disparates' and, with a vengeance, his 'Pinturas Negras'. Their inexpressible horror, as Aldous Huxley has pointed out, is based on their 'mindlessness, animality and spiritual darkness'.[14] There may have been an inner logic in this development. Once God was denied and the Evil became only too conspicuous, the concept of man made in the image of God had to be replaced by that of ghouls with satanic grimaces.

Closer scrutiny reveals that Romantic nihilism did not in fact mean the complete absence of hope or belief of any kind. If the nihilists did not believe in anything else they firmly believed in nothingness itself. If they lacked any other hope, they still hoped for utter extinction. Faith and hope, no longer able to cling on to life in this world or the next, fastened on to death, or more precisely to death conceived as the negation of all manner of life.[15] If even transient sleep was extolled, as for example in Leopardi's *Dialogue between Earth and Moon*, death, it was confidently believed, would be but an eternal sleep, an everlasting general anaesthesia, an insensibility to all kinds of pain and suffering. To repeat, death thus pictured appeared as the only salvation to those suffering from unredeemed *Weltschmerz*. Leopardi, for one, fervently hoped for death, the healer of all pain and suffering; his poem, 'La Quiete dopo la Tempesta',[16] as well as his 'Dialogue between Tristan and a Friend', are conclusive evidence. In the 'Ode to Arimane' he implores the demon to grant him that he may not survive the seventh lustre, the age of thirty-five, which Dante, following the biblical tradition, had regarded but as half of man's allotted span of life.

Examples of Romantic longing for extinction are only too numerous. Friedrich Schlegel, in his youth for a long time without a centre of gravity, contemplated suicide on repeated occasions;[17] so did even Goethe just before he embarked on writing *Die Leiden des jungen Werthers*. Young Chateaubriand once attempted suicide; so did Lenau. Ugo Foscolo glorified suicide in *Le Ultime Lettere de Jacopo Ortis* (1802); Vigny dealt at great length with the same problem in the first version of his novel *Stello*, and, perhaps not surprisingly, two of Senancour's essay-letters in *Oberman* contain a subtle defence of man's right to take his own life, a course actually adopted by Goethe's Werther, Lenau's Faust, Lamartine's Raphael, Musset's Rolla, Mickiewicz's Konrad,[18] and in real life by Caroline von Günderode, Mariano José de Larra, Gérard de Nerval and T. L. Beddoes. In other cases again, though suicide was not committed, death was courted in various ways. Both Pushkin and Lermontov fell in duels. Of the latter duel an eye-witness describes how Lermontov aimed his pistol at the sky, with a peaceful, almost happy expression in his face.[19] Lord Byron's letters of 1823–4, as well as his poem "On this day I complete my thirty-sixth year", justify the surmise that, weary of life, he went to Greece to die. Finally, Shelley, in the face of grave warnings, embarked on his fateful voyage from which he was not to return. Shortly before, Jane Williams had said of him: "He is seeking what we all avoid, death." There exists, of course, also strong internal evidence for Shelley's *Weltschmerz* in the last years of his life, not only in the 'Stanzas written in Dejection' (1818) and the story 'Una Favola' (1820), where the poet is in love with Life and Death, two mistresses, of whom Death is a true lover, but still more conclusively in the symbolic dream-poem 'The Triumph of Life' which has remained a torso. In Rousseau's speech, the central part of the poem, Shelley's political disenchantment reaches its climax. Shelley had now come up against the problems of evil for which there was no room in the panaceas of his youth. But the evil had no counterweight; he did not perceive the existence of divine mercy. Nor did he share the belief in personal immortality.[20] His restless search was nearing its end, and in the concluding lines of his lyrical drama *Hellas* he epitomized the Romantic hope of repose:

> The World is weary of the Past:
> Oh might it die or rest at last!

Surely anyone who has pondered on the Romantic movement cannot avoid reflecting on the early death of many Romantics. True, the phenomenon was not universal: the octogenarians, Goya, Wordsworth and Manzoni, or Lamartine and Chateaubriand who almost reached the same age, are remarkable examples of longevity. Yet Keats, Shelley and Byron; Wackenroder, Novalis, Wilhelm Müller, Solger and Hauff; Pushkin and Lermontov; Leopardi, Petőfi, Słowacki, Wergeland, Stagnelius and Mácha; Larra and Espronceda; the painters Philipp Otto Runge, Franz Pforr, C.Ph. Fohr, Bonington, Girtin and Géricault; the composers Schubert, Weber, Arriaga, Chopin and Mendelssohn; the scientist Johann Wilhelm Ritter, and a host of *dii minores*, all met with death at a stage which, according to the standards then prevalent, must be regarded as untimely. Can we postulate some connexion between this phenomenon and the Romantic malady of the soul? Or diagnose *tædium vitæ terrestris* as one of the deeper causes of their early death? Perhaps; but still we must remember that this feeling was only in extreme cases the outcome of a nihilist outlook on life and death. With others, such as Novalis, the decisive motive, if we are to judge from his *Hymnen an die Nacht*, seems to have been the wildly impatient longing to be reunited with God and his beloved. Or again in Franz Schubert's case, his poem 'Mein Gebet', and, indeed, his A minor Sonata, testify to his longing for death in the sense of a new and completely transformed existence. More generally, however, we may conjecture, weariness of life was connected with that religious frustration so peculiar to the Romantics. To elucidate this last point will be the object of the following chapter.

CHAPTER EIGHT

Defiance of God and Religious Frustration

THE anguish of the void so intensely felt by so many Romantics could and indeed did evoke in their souls a great variety of responses. In some cases, as we have seen, their reaction was despondency or outright despair and, consequently, the more or less conscious longing for extinction. Others reacted in a more vigorous manner. They were driven to rebel against their Creator whom they believed to be cruelly indifferent to their own sufferings and those of their fellow human beings. But all the time they could not but continue the search for something, almost anything, that might fill the vast spiritual void and satisfy their craving for a metaphysical basis without which their life, as they had come to realize, lacked any meaning whatsoever. Nor were these various reactions at all clearly separated. Not infrequently it happened that the ceaseless search, carried on through all kinds of vicissitudes over a period of years, ended in failure and exhaustion which led in turn to irredeemable *Weltschmerz* and a rebellious intransigence towards God.

Alfred de Vigny is a case in point. In some respects his outlook on life was not dissimilar to that of Leopardi and even of Schopenhauer. He too regarded life as a malady which, he added consolingly, was transitory. In a more defiant frame of mind, however, he likened life to a prison from which only death would release us. He too was preoccupied with the idea of suicide, and, though he shrank from publishing his conclusions, seems to have contemplated a philosophical justification of suicide. True, unlike Leopardi, he did not altogether exclude the possibility of happiness. All the more he dwelt on its transience: "Si le bonheur n'était qu-une bonne heure?", he noted in his *Journal*. In the same year, 1834, he set himself the task of writing what he called 'melancholy satires' in the form of novels as well as for the stage.

Vigny's notebook, that rare masterpiece of introspection and intellectual integrity, posthumously published under the title *Journal d'un Poète*, was begun when he was twenty-six and continued at intervals throughout his life. Though considerably shorter than Leopardi's *Zibaldone*, it is the key to Vigny's thought.

The deeper reasons for Vigny's melancholy are not hard to trace. For one thing, he felt painfully conscious that he belonged to a social *élite* whose decline had long set in and whose complete downfall appeared inevitable. Army life, though he never idealized it, had initially appealed to his Stoic sense of duty; before long, however, it proved frustrating. After the Napoleonic interlude, the days of the aristocracy of courage seemed as numbered as those of the aristocracy of blood. Another facet of Vigny's unhappiness arose from his poignant feeling of isolation so often experienced by men of genius. To belong to the intellectual *élite* was to him as much a burden as a privilege. His novel *Stello* and the poem *Moïse* bear witness to this. In contradistinction to Senancour, Lamartine and many other Romantics, Nature held no solace for Vigny. Personal afflictions undoubtedly aggravated his melancholy. Sad childhood reminiscences, an uncongenial marriage from which for a time he sought relief in tempestuous and ultimately unsatisfying *liaisons*, the long-drawn-out mental disease of his mother to whom he felt deeply attached, his wife's perpetual ill-health and, towards the end, his own cruel suffering from cancer of the stomach—all these afflictions have to be weighed. Nevertheless, the root cause of Vigny's unhappiness lay almost certainly in his lack of sustaining faith and hope.

His road to unbelief was tortuous. It was as though his devout mother and his freethinking father had gone on fighting for Alfred's soul long after they were dead. In his youth he had gradually drifted away from the faith, but the yearning for it had persisted. Thus we find him confiding to his *Journal* in 1830:

> O God, all religions amount to the idea that man desires two things: that Thou exist and that his soul be immortal. . . . I have in me these two desires.

Seven years later, during the final stages of his mother's illness, the longing for a personal God and for religious certitude became almost overpowering. Under the immediate impact of her loss he addressed God in these words:

> Hast Thou received this virtuous soul in Thy bosom? Sustain me in this hope so that it should not be a transitory desire but may become a fervent belief!

For many years to come he continued to be intrigued by the phenomenon of faith. 'People talk of faith,' he noted in 1843. 'What after all is that thing that is so rare? A fervent hope. I have sounded all the priests who said that they possessed it, but that is all I have found. Never have I found certitude.' Time and again the sigh recurs. Georges Bonnefoy has rightly emphasized this constant undertone of Vigny's thought in his penetrating study *La Pensée Religieuse et Morale d'Alfred de Vigny* (1946). He has shown that even 'Le Mont des Oliviers', that poem which is so full of bitterness against God, was born of Vigny's ardent yearning for a faith. The unsatisfied religious craving was aggravated by the poet's burning sense of human compassion. For, unlike Schopenhauer, he had not closed his heart to the paramount Christian virtue of charity. On the contrary, the sufferings of man and indeed of all living creatures pressed heavily on his mind, and no doubt there is a sense in which he deserves the epithet "le poète de la pitié".[1] At times he voiced the noble sentiment of Stoicism to which his inborn *tenue*, that typical aristocratic bearing in face of the world, seemed to predispose him. We find this attitude epitomized in one of his finest poems, 'La Mort du Loup':

> A voir ce que l'on fut sur terre et ce qu'on laisse,
> Seul le silence est grand; tout le reste est faiblesse.[2]

One could perhaps trace in Vigny the beginnings of an existentialist outlook on life. If it be true that the existentialist tries to feel at home in anguish and nothingness, we might indeed describe Vigny as one of the forerunners of that recent group of thinkers. Nevertheless, the contrast outweighs the analogies. For although Vigny undoubtedly tried to come to terms with anguish and nothingness, he still could not take them for granted in the blasé and sophisticated manner of the twentieth-century existentialists. More often than not his stoic resignation therefore gave way to a violent and rebellious attitude to God. Since he could not accept the Christian doctrine of suffering, he rebelled against a Creator who, he believed, viewed all the misery in the world with the utmost indifference. It is noteworthy how close Vigny came to the teachings of Gnosticism on this point. But whatever affinity of ideas may have existed between Gnostics and Romantics, among his contemporaries Vigny was certainly not alone in his defiant stand. Lord Byron's *Cain* and Shelley's *Prometheus Unbound* had already sounded the same note—the former had made a deep impact on him—and Lenau, Musset and Mickiewicz were soon to follow. But Vigny, though not the first, proved to be the most daring champion of that Romantic revolt against God sometimes described as Romantic titanism.[3] As early as 1833 he had played with the fantasy of setting fire to a Church in order to revenge himself on God in case some anticipated misfortune should befall him.[4] Of far greater consequence, however, was the fact that in several of his poetical works, notably in *Eloa ou la Sœur des Anges*, he idealized him whom Christians—and Jews—regard as the supreme embodiment of evil. For Satan is here depicted as the champion of all unhappy creatures, to whom he is bound by a feeling of solidarity. Vigny uses Satan for his mouthpiece when that fallen angel tells Man that human grandeur transcends the grandeur of God since God can never equal the supreme human sacrifice of laying down His life in an act of love. Vigny even visualized a complete reversal of the Last Judgment when he wrote:

> That will be the day when God will come forward to justify Himself in front of all the souls and all that is alive. He will appear and He will speak and He will say in all clarity why there has been the creation and why there is suffering and the death of the innocent. . . . At that moment, mankind resuscitated will be the judge, and He that is eternal, the Creator, will be judged by all the generations who had life thrust upon them.[5]

Extremely radical though this antitheism may appear it was still not so intransigently nihilistic as Leopardi's or Schopenhauer's nightmares.

It has become customary to regard Nikolaus Lenau as a typical exponent of Romantic *Weltschmerz*. This view is only partly correct. At any rate, the almost exclusive preoccupation with the gloomy aspects of Lenau's mind, for example the nihilistic mood of his poem 'Der Indifferentist', has tended to obscure the brighter side, his deep yearning for a faith. Nikolaus Niembsch von Strehlenau [6] was the son of an officer of Silesian origin who was a debauched gambler; his death—Nikolaus was hardly five years of age—left the family in dire poverty and debt. But even more than the debts, his biological inheritance seems to have proved a heavy burden for his son, whether as hypersensitivity or irritability. Unlike Leopardi and Schopenhauer, however, Lenau had an affectionate mother. "My mother's love for me," he wrote after she died of cancer, "was of a most passionate kind." The grandparents on his father's side also supported him, but as they tried to alienate him from his mother their affection, he felt, was too dearly bought.

Lenau's studies covered a wide field; like Faust he could not rest satisfied with any one subject. The intellectual fare included philosophy at Vienna University, law at Poszony ("a dry and pedantic business"), agriculture and chemistry at Ungarisch-Altenburg, and medicine, a science that fascinated him, again at Vienna and, at the age of twenty-nine, at Heidelberg. Later was added the non-academic but no less ardent pursuit of the history of religious thought—and irreligious doubt. Nor could he ever settle in any region of the Old World or the New, for he knew both. Born in 1802 in a German 'language-island' in the Hungarian Banat, he moved as a youth from one seat of learning to the other, gravitating to the metropolis, but taking parts of his native Hungary in his stride. Next came the first of a long series of visits to Württemberg, interrupted by the fantastic endeavour to settle in Ohio in 1832–3. After his disillusioned return from America, which he had found utterly materialistic and spiritually hollow, [7] he alternated between ever more frequent travels and ever shortening sojourns in Württemberg and in Austria where he oscillated between Vienna and his beloved Salzkammergut. Of all the places he visited there Lake Traunsee, which had also captivated Schubert, was his favourite.

In Württemberg, the Swabian Romantic poets, Uhland, Kerner and others, received him most hospitably; in Austria too he could count on self-sacrificing friends. Nor could he complain about lack of appreciation on the part of the reading public. His lyrical poetry, which has an enchanting musical ring—he is one of the poets whose work has been most frequently set to music—and in addition is distinguished by the *piquanterie* of various Hungarian *sujets* (e.g. 'Schilflieder', 'Heidebilder' and 'Der Räuber in Bakony'), was already widely acclaimed both in Austria and Germany in the 1830s. It is true he had frequent tussles with the Austrian censorship authorities, but in this respect he was in excellent company. Moreover, since he managed to hold on to his Hungarian citizenship he was able to get away with a good deal more than a native Austrian.

In the realm of love, early folly and disappointment were followed in mature years by his passionate attachment to the congenial Sophie von Löwenthal, the wife of a friend. Though this love was denied its ultimate fulfilment, Sophie in happy moments helped to soothe his restless heart and inspired some of his noblest poetry. All in all, the impression of the outward setting and course of his life is one of light and shade—indeed strong light and strong shade—and unless we regard his mental collapse at the age of forty-two[8] as the outcome of inexorable biological fate, we are compelled to search for the key to Lenau's personality among the inner regions of his mind, those regions where, for a considerable part of his life, his decisions were free and undetermined.

All his life he was torn between such contrasting beliefs as Catholicism—the religion of his childhood—pantheism, and philosophical materialism, each of which he embraced in turn with the utmost fervour. But never for long; for at the back of his mind a corroding doubt was at work which cut at the roots of all his beliefs and eventually undermined the precarious balance of his personality. Until that tragic end was reached, however, the yearning for a faith had always fought against what he himself termed "melancholy scepticism". The great Italian historian of literature, Arturo Farinelli, described Lenau as "a melancholy rather than a pessimistic poet, a poet of transience and doubts rather than of futility and despair". Farinelli has also pointed out: "In spite of his sceptical opinions, he did experience, on repeated occasions, higher points in his life, whence he cast his glance upwards." [9] We may add that this was particularly true of that period in his middle thirties when, partly under the influence of the young Danish Protestant theologian H. L. Martensen, whom he met in Vienna in 1836, he found his way back to Christianity for a time. It was then that he wrote his dramatic poem *Savonarola*. During a visit to St Peter's churchyard in Salzburg, in September 1837, it seemed to him that "the dead are not lost to us for ever". On a previous occasion it had suddenly dawned on him that God's creatures needed a mediator so as not to despair and perish. By 1838, however, doubt had again got the better of faith. In April he wrote to his friend Martensen:

> The *Weltanschauung* which has found expression in my *Savonarola* has not uplifted me sufficiently, nor has it sufficiently fortified and reassured me against all the hostile assaults of a life that is spiritually and morally perplexed; I sometimes feel miserable, and during the periods of sombre moods it seemed to me that even God's cause was uncertain, indeed that it was almost *res derelicta, quae patet diabolo occupanti*.[10]

It was now that he embarked upon his epic drama *Die Albigenser*, in which, according to Lenau himself, doubt acts the role of the hero. A diffuse pantheistic belief is here combined with an apotheosis of the unfettered human mind.

But even at this late stage the yearning was still there; nor was it mute. It was in November of the same year, 1838, that Lenau in conversation with Max Löwenthal spoke of man's necessity to find his own helpless being penetrated and as it were supplemented by God.[11] In the same month he wrote the double sonnet 'Einsamkeit' (Loneliness) which begins with the pathetic outcry:

> Hast du schon je dich ganz allein gefunden,
> Lieblos und ohne Gott auf einer Heide . . .[12]

and ends in melancholy bordering on despair:

> Die ganze Welt ist zum Verzweifeln traurig.[13]

Significantly, one of Lenau's notebooks, published long after his death, contains an entry entitled 'Yearning for revelation'. Here

Leopardi (after the drawing by Luigi Lolli)

Goya (self-portrait)

again the poet is face to face with loneliness, and he gives vent to
the burning questions:

> Oh, why does loneliness exist for us? Where is God?

Twice more does the heart-rending question occur:

> Where is God? . . . Where is God?

Equally marked, though even more bewildered, was Alfred de
Musset's longing for a faith. Born in 1810, he spent the most impressionable period of his life in Paris under the restored Bourbon
monarchy. Before that régime came to an abrupt end, in July 1830,
he was already prominent among the *jeunesse dorée* of the capital.
His talent as a poet and his *esprit*, his distinguished connexions and
his attractive looks, dandy mannerisms, and a certain unmistakable
decadence all helped to launch him on a rapid career. Thus his
Contes d'Espagne et d'Italie (1830), a graceful if frivolous trans-
position of some of his own amorous adventures into a foreign
milieu, were widely acclaimed. It was then that he first accustomed
himself to devoting a good deal of his time and energy to an intoxicating and enervating round of dissipation, oscillating for ever,
as he afterwards put it, "between an ardent thirst and a profound
satiety". For a time, it is true, the evil spell seemed broken. This
was when he met the novelist Baroness Dudevant who, six years
older than Musset, had already acquired some fame under the
name George Sand. It is well known how Musset developed a
passionate attachment for her so different from the fleeting in-
fatuations of his many *caprices*. The journey with George Sand to
Italy in 1833-4 must be regarded as the high watermark of his
life. All too soon disharmony set in and brought estrangement in
its wake. After reconciliation, a second period of even more tempestuous happiness was followed by a final rupture. Inquisitive
researchers, mistaking the role of the detective for that of the
historian, have since busied themselves with vain attempts to
unravel the ups and downs of that spectacular *liaison*. What
matters here is that, however many complications may have arisen
owing to the character or circumstances of George Sand, an early

note of discord was undoubtedly due to the excessive instability of Musset's character,[14] and probably also to a strand of mental cruelty which was not sublimated, but exaggerated, by his love for George Sand. It is significant how time and again Musset in his letters to his mistress had to ask for forgiveness. As for his instability, this may have been caused partly by the strange habit of his mind to conjure up recollections of the past—often a lurid past —at moments when more balanced if less sensitive men might have lived only in the present. So strong and insistent was that echo of past sins that Musset sometimes called it his own *Doppelgänger*. Elsewhere he wrote:

> All these dull furies took me by the throat and cried out to me that they were there.[15]

After the rupture with George Sand, Musset felt for a time utterly prostrate, but it would be equally true to say that he never recovered from the repercussions. In the poem 'Nuit de Mai', the first of an exquisite quartet, he has vividly expressed his sorrow. In *La Confession d'un Enfant du Siècle* (1836), sorrow is mingled with remorse, and the picture he has drawn there of George Sand under the traits of Madame Pinson is idealized to such an extent that it can fairly be interpreted as an act of contrition on his part. But neither sublimation in lyrical poetry nor expiation in the form of veiled autobiography were able to offer more than momentary relief. In a period when his star as a poet and dramatist was still rising, he threw himself again into a whirlpool of debauchery, with the result that he was almost completely exhausted at the age of thirty-two, fifteen years before his death. What previously had perhaps partly been due to the exuberance of youth was now caused largely by his lack of self-control as well as by his decadent and morbid *curiosité du mal*, which seemed to make him drain the cup to its dregs. It was that strain in his mind which already at the age of eighteen made him translate Thomas de Quincey's *Confessions of an Opium Eater*. There is a sense in which it is true to say that Musset, too, committed suicide.

In the introductory chapter of the *Confession d'un Enfant du Siècle* where the youthful aberrations of Octave are recorded, Musset produces for his hero, and thereby for himself, an impressive array of extenuating circumstances. Indeed, to a large extent the example set by Octave's contemporaries, and, in the last analysis, the *Zeitgeist* itself are held responsible. Whatever we may feel about this plea, one thing is certain: that the chapter in question contains a searching diagnosis of the spiritual situation of that era. The generation of Frenchmen to which Musset belonged, growing up after Waterloo, is shown to be devoid of all positive values. Gone were the mysteries of transcendental religion, gone was Napoleon's glory. But the usurper, though himself vanquished by now, had only too visibly revealed the hollowness of the established régimes he had brushed aside with such consummate ease. The disenchantment was complete: respect for authority no longer existed, doubt had become the watchword of the day, scepticism tended to produce indifference, which, in its turn, often led to inertia or, worse, to callousness and debauchery. Thus the underlying *sentiment de malaise inexprimable* so subtly described by Musset in *La Confession* as well as in the dramatic poem *La Coupe et les Lèvres*, appeared as the corollary of nihilism.

Musset himself sincerely deplored this truly vicious circle. In spite of the scepticism which had eaten so deep into his heart he makes his hero Octave in *La Confession* predict:

> You will find that the human heart when it said: 'I believe in nothing, for I see nothing', has not said its last word.

The same Octave, and later Frank in *La Coupe et les Lèvres*, both lament that since their adolescence their minds have been poisoned by the writings of the eighteenth-century sophists whose destructive analysis tended to reduce creation to "a tidy cemetery" ('un cimetière en ordre'). With particular vehemence Jacques Rolla, Musset's truest self-characterization, reproaches Voltaire, who, throughout his long life, had done so much to undermine the imposing edifice of the old faith which at last had given way.

There were times when Musset's metaphysical craving seemed content with a vague brand of pantheism, "a belief in a God without form, without cult and without revelation".[16] How tenuous this belief was is incidentally revealed in the poem 'L'Espoir en Dieu' when Musset, immediately before imploring that impersonal deity, toys with the idea that perchance no such deity exists at all.

At other times, however, Musset was overwhelmed by the feeling of nostalgia for the faith in Christ whom, as he sadly remarked, he had never been taught to love. It is in a vein of deepest melancholy that Rolla, in whom Musset's personality was most truly reflected, exclaims:

> Je ne crois pas, ô Christ, à ta parole sainte:
> Je suis venu trop tard dans un monde trop vieux.[17]

And in a further passage of the same poem the religious frustration so peculiar to the Romantics is epitomized:

> Ta gloire est morte, ô Christ! et sur nos croix d'ebène
> Ton cadavre céleste en poussière est tombé.

> Eh bien! qu'il soit permis d'en baiser la poussière
> Au moins crédule enfant de ce siècle sans foi,
> Et de pleurer, ô Christ! sur cette froide terre
> Qui vivait de ta mort, et qui mourra sans toi![18]

Religious frustration: for Rolla, like Octave in the semi-autobiographical novel, yearns for the Saviour in the same breath as he rejects Him. Here, indeed, we have struck upon one of the *leitmotivs* of Romanticism: the simultaneous existence of, and dissonance between, the two keynotes: namely the quest for religion and the inability to embrace it.[19] Examples could be adduced from the whole range of Romantic Europe. One need only mention Jean Paul's novel *Hesperus* (1795), where the heart's unquenchable thirst for religion is contrasted with the intellect's intransigent repudiation of it.

It might be argued that both the search for God and the rejection of God are in some ways characteristic of human nature in general, and may be traced back to the fall of Man. Yet never before the Romantic era, it seems, were the two phenomena so inextricably interwoven, or at any rate never before was their paradoxical coexistence in man's soul exposed so mercilessly to the glaring light of consciousness. But there was more to it than that. For the first time since the advent of Christianity the eighteenth century had witnessed a considerable weakening of the Christian religion over men's minds. In the same measure as life and death were losing their meaning, men were beginning to yearn for a meaning. To those historical observers who regarded Christianity as a thing of the past, that Romantic yearning appeared to be the legacy of Christianity.[20]

PART THREE

Christian Revival:
Promise and Unfulfilment

CHAPTER NINE

The Assault on Unbelief

EVEN the vague religious yearning of a Musset or a Lenau included an echo, however faint, of the faith in Christ. It was of the very essence of the Romantic era that that echo grew stronger and more compelling until it helped to usher in a widespread revival of Christianity. At the same time, nothing could characterize the dual nature, and indeed the inner contradictions, of Romanticism better than the fact that the foremost Romantic herald of the Christian revival, the Abbé de Lamennais, was himself violently torn between faith and unbelief. Nor was this true only of certain periods in his life, as had been the case with some of the greatest religious figures of the past. In marked contrast to St. Augustine or Pascal, Lamennais it seems never experienced the blissful certitude of unshakeable faith.

Born seven years before the beginning of the French Revolution, in the picturesque town of St. Malo, Félicité Robert de la Mennais (for that was his original name) was descended from Breton and partly Irish stock. True, only one of his grandparents, namely his maternal grandmother, was of Irish descent, yet it may not be too fanciful to suggest that this enlivening admixture to Lamennais's blood perhaps accounts for some salient features of his character. Contemporaries already remarked upon the striking facial resemblance between young Félicité and his Irish ancestress, Madame Lorin de la Brousse. The Robert family belonged to the old bourgeoisie of St. Malo, the date of the ennoblement being the very last year of the *ancien régime*. Among the strongest and most lasting impressions of his childhood was the anti-religious terror of 1793–4, in the course of which an attic in his father's household had to be used, in the dark of night, for the purposes of the Christian cult. In his anonymous first publication, entitled *Réflexions sur l'état de l'Eglise en France au XVIIIᵉ siècle et sur sa situation actuelle*, written fifteen years after the event, Lamennais emphasized the strength of the Christian resistance of that time: "A large number of clerics, ready for martyrdom, braved every danger in France in order to administer to the faithful the succour of the sacraments and the comfort of hope. . . . Religion never appeared more beautiful."

It is significant that Lamennais first had to feel a strong repulsion for the excesses of atheist revolutionaries before he could experience the attraction of Christianity. For a time, however, this attraction remained largely theoretical; that is to say that Lamennais, say at sixteen, would outwardly put up a defence of Catholicism while inwardly remaining, to all intents and purposes, an agnostic.[1] Another six years elapsed before he received his first Holy Communion. The slowness of his conversion may have been in part due to the educational influence of the uncle on his father's side, Robert des Saudrais, whose mind, though not of an agnostic temper, was steeped in Rousseau's vague deism. Both uncle and father (Félicité lost his mother in early childhood), disillusioned by the Revolution, were gradually drifting towards Catholicism, but a far more more powerful pull in this direction came from Félicité's elder brother, the abbé Jean-Marie de la Mennais. The two brothers were very close to each other; the *Reflexions sur l'Etat de l'Eglise*, as well as the later work *Tradition sur l'Institution des Evêques* (1814), were joint efforts, but if we have reason to believe that here and there we can discern Félicité's brilliant phrasing, it is more than likely that the basic attitude no less than the initiative was Jean-Marie's. Before tracing other personal influences, it should be noted that Chateaubriand's *Génie du Christianisme* (1802) made a strong impact on young Lamennais. Through the medium of Chateaubriand he also came to appreciate Pascal's religious thought.

By the time Lamennais had reached his late twenties, he had, as we have seen, already offered his pen to the cause of the Church. Was he to go further and, like his favourite brother, also become a priest? Such was the ardent desire not only of his brother but also of some of his friends, the Breton abbé Bruté de Rémur, who introduced the brothers Lamennais to the famous theological seminary of Saint-Sulpice in Paris, and the young abbé Teysseyre, whose acquaintance he made there. Yet another character has to be mentioned, for it was he who clinched the issue—or so it appeared—when finally, as late as the winter of 1815–16, he persuaded Lamennais, who by then was in his thirty-fourth year, to become subdeacon and soon afterwards priest: the aged abbé Carron, whom Lamennais had befriended during his short exile in London earlier in 1815. It may not have been irrelevant to dwell upon these influences, for although Lamennais's ultimate decision to enter the priesthood was, after a prolonged period of hesitation, freely arrived at, it is well to bear in mind what that great connoisseur of the human soul, Sainte-Beuve, has remarked about Lamennais's need for spiritual guidance.[2] It is in this light that we have to interpret that ominous passage in the abbé Teysseyre's letter to Lamennais on the eve of his ordination: "You are going to the ordination in the same manner as a victim goes to the sacrifice." Earlier Lamennais had written to his brother in a vein of resignation: "I am opposed to nothing, I consent to everything; let them do what they like with my corpse."[3]

For years Lamennais had been suffering from *Weltschmerz* with a marked nihilistic tinge; his correspondence, especially during the years 1810–11, bears witness to this. As in the case of Leopardi, a variety of explanations have been put forward, each of which contains a certain amount of truth and yet misses the essential point. Thus Lamennais's physique has been held responsible, for he was prematurely born after seven months, he had a sunken chest, and his nerves were highly strung. Yet all this need not impress us much if, on the other hand, we consider that in his youth he enjoyed the pleasures of riding, hunting and fencing, and that he was as strong a swimmer as Lord Byron. Some writers have conjectured an early disappointment in love, to which, in their opinion, Lamennais was alluding many years later when he wrote: "Let those weep that have no Spring." However, the most penetrating and indeed the only convincing analysis of Lamennais's despondency has been given by the French historian Henri Bremond, who rightly points out that Lamennais's unhappiness was due to the fact that his hope of mystical consolation was never fulfilled. Already in 1810 he had uttered the sigh: "My greatest torment is to be deprived of all spiritual help."[4] After his ordination, his mind was still that of the darkest melancholy: "I am and henceforward cannot help being extraordinarily unhappy." [5] The mystical consolation, the hoped for and half expected sign from heaven, had failed to appear, a situation epitomized in Bremond's phrase, 'silence de Dieu'. What right had Lamennais to expect such a sign? One cannot forbear from asking this question.

While still hesitating about his vocation, Lamennais, for his all misgivings, seems to have envisaged the priesthood as a kind of haven for his restless soul, as when he wrote to his brother in 1811: "What pleases me about the course that I have decided upon, is that it would bring everything to an end." [6] When this hope too was dashed to the ground, the abbé Teysseyre had the ingenious idea of diverting Lamennais's excessive nervous energy into the channel of intellectual work. [7] Already in his youth Lamennais had proved that he was capable of sustained and extensive mental effort: witness his knowledge of Greek and Latin, no less than of four modern languages, his commentaries on Malebranche and Pascal, and his study of mathematics, which he taught for a time at the Collège de St. Malo, a religious seminary his brother had helped to found. Now, in 1816, it was clear to the abbé Teysseyre that if his plan was to succeed, Lamennais would have to be induced to tackle a difficult and momentous subject which his friend had planned before his departure to England and since discarded; this was to be an apologetic work entitled *Esprit du Christianisme*. Lamennais, reminded of the earlier plan, refused to resume it. Teysseyre then produced some notes which he himself had made with a view to a large-scale refutation of Rousseau's theories. At first Lamennais found his task irksome, but gradually the writer's vocation—his true vocation—grew on him, and he contrived to work himself into a creative trance, the outcome of which was the first volume of the *Essai sur l'indifférence en matière de religion* (1817), in many ways the most important work of Catholic apologetics in the nineteenth century. The abbé Teysseyre was hardly exaggerating when he praised Lamennais's *chef d'œuvre*, which he had done so much to stimulate, for combining the style of Jean-Jacques Rousseau with the reasoning of Pascal and the eloquence of Bossuet. [8] We may endorse this encomium and yet feel inclined to qualify it. For, as Adolfo Omodeo in *La cultura francese nella restaurazione* (1946) has pointed out, Lamennais's *Essai*, for all its brilliance, lacks the originality of Pascal's immortal *Pensées* or of the deepest thought of Bossuet. In a sense, the Italian historian's strictures when he speaks of the *Essai*'s 'grandezza imitata' are not unjustified. All the more original, it must be owned, was the manner in which Lamennais's work came into being. Not only had he almost to be forced to write his masterpiece, but from his manner of writing and other evidence it is clear that, once he embarked on his task, his impelling motive was as much to convince himself as to persuade his readers.[9] Besides, it has been remarked that he may have derived a kind of vicarious joy from the process of so vividly describing those mystical experiences which presumably had been denied to him.[10]

The title of the *Essai* would suggest that the author's violent attack was aimed mainly at indifference in religious matters. However, the first glance at the book itself reveals that the assault is directed against unbelief in all its various shades. Perhaps for the very reason that Lamennais suffered so much from the enemy within himself, he pursues that enemy wherever he appears, in the most merciless manner. Indeed, the marked polemical note of the *Essai* as well as some of his other writings almost suggests that his hatred of unbelief exceeded his love for the faith. Altogether it would appear that it was given to Lamennais to probe more searchingly into the psychological depth of unbelief than anybody had done up to his lifetime. In fact, part of his startling analysis reads like an anticipation of Dostoevsky[11] and Nietzsche.[12] There exists, for example, a less well-known treatise published by Lamennais in 1841 under the title *Discussions, critiques et pensées diverses sur la religion et la philosophie*. It contains this luminous passage:

When the faith which once united a man with God and raised him to God's level begins to fail, something terrible happens. The soul, impelled by its own gravity, falls incessantly and without end, carrying with it a certain intelligence detached from its principle, and which clutches at all that crosses its path as it falls, now with a sad restlessness, now with a joy resembling the laughter of a madman. Tormented by the necessity to keep alive, it is either coupled with the very matter that it is trying in vain to make fertile, or else it pursues fantastic abstractions, runaway shadows, shapes without substance, as it crosses the void . . . All that remains of love comes closer to that which mysteriously gives life to the brute forces of nature. One understands society no more as a manifestation of the spirit and its laws, but as a mechanical task of arrangement, or, if one suspects anything beyond it, of a crystallization more or less regular. . . . All the nobler instincts fall into a deep sleep. All the secret powers which preside at the formation of the moral world and at the development of being in its invisible essence, are partly extinguished and partly create a kind of internal torture of which the unknown cause casts him into inexpressible anguish and despair. His soul is hungry, what shall he do? He will kill his soul, since he cannot find any nourishment for it, where he is. If he suffers, this is so because he is still too high. Descend then, descend to the level of an animal, to the level of a plant, make yourself a beast or a stone! He cannot; in the shadowy abyss whither he plunges he carries with him his inexorable nature, and from world to world the echoes of the universe repeat the heart-rending plaints of this creature who, having departed from the place that the Almighty organizer in His vast plan has allotted to him, and henceforward incapable of anchoring himself, drifts without rest amidst the whole of creation like a battered vessel tossed hither and thither by the waves on a deserted ocean.

To return to the *Essai sur l'indifférence en matière de religion*: Lamennais's chief argument in favour of a return to Christianity, in this work as well as in the subsequent *De la Religion considérée dans ses Rapports avec l'Ordre politique et civil* (1825-6), is the indispensability of a Christian foundation for the task of social reconstruction. Thus the Christian religion is commended not for theological reasons but rather for reasons of sociology, as a panacea for all the evils which afflict the social life of man. Lamennais is at his best when he demonstrates how a society based on profane philosophy and religious indifference must, perforce, disintegrate from within and eventually degenerate into anarchism or despotism.[13] Memories of the French Revolution, and more recently of Napoleon's tyranny, added poignancy to his argument. We have since become only too familiar with this kind of argument, which Basil Willey has neatly dubbed "negative apologetic", and which has also been referred to as the so-called theology of crisis. But it is well to remember that when the Romantics, and Lamennais in particular, wielded this weapon, it was new and not yet blunted, and however problematical it may seem to us in retrospect, there is no doubt that it was used at the time with signal success. The verve with which if not the full case for Christianity at any rate an overwhelming case against unbelief was presented in the *Essai* was such that a contemporary remarked: "This work would awaken the dead." It certainly shook many people who had been hovering on the borders of faith, and was instrumental in bringing about a number of conversions.

Nor indeed was Lamennais's influence confined to his writings. In the rural surroundings of La Chênaie near Dijon, an estate that had come down to him from his mother's family, he founded, and was for a long time in charge of, a famous 'Ecole apologétique et de science religieuse'. To this we must add his contact with a galaxy of young writers (he was Victor Hugo's confessor).

Several contemporaries have described various facets of his magnetic personality. To give but one example, it might be fitting to quote Cardinal Wiseman's impression:[14]

How he did so mightily prevail on others it is hard to say. He was truly in look and presence almost contemptible; small, weakly, without pride of countenance or mastery of eye, without any external grace; his tongue seemed to be the organ by which, unaided, he gave marvellous utterance to thoughts clear, deep and strong. Several times have I held long conversations with him, at various intervals, and he was always the same. With his head hung down, his hands clasped before him, or gently moving in one another, in answer to a question he poured out a stream of thought, flowing spontaneous and unrippled as a stream through a summer meadow. . . . All this went on in a monotonous but soft tone, and was so unbroken, so unhesitating, and yet so polished and elegant, that if you had closed your eyes, you might have easily fancied that you were listening to the reading of a finished and elaborately corrected volume. Then, everything was illustrated by such happy imagery, so apt, so graphic, and so complete.

CHAPTER TEN

Reaffirmation of the Supernatural

THE Romantic attempt to revive Christianity assumed many different shapes. Often irreligion was attacked on the grounds that it must inevitably lead to the breakdown of civilized life on earth. Others again re-emphasized the other-worldly side of the Christian religion. Outstanding among them was the German Friedrich von Hardenberg, better known under his *nom de plume* Novalis. To a higher degree than any other Romantic this daring thinker and ethereal poet can be regarded as the re-awakener of a genuine Christian mysticism.

At the outset it should be noted that his concern for the hereafter was anything but a form of 'escapism' as the glib modern formula has it. For even from the narrowly practical point of view Novalis was certainly not maladjusted, let alone a failure. After completing his legal studies, which he had pursued at Jena, Leipzig and Wittenberg, he acquired a thorough knowledge of the coalmining industry, first at the celebrated mining academy at Freiberg in Saxony, and later more practically at Weissenfels. It was not without significance that whereas his meditations soared to lofty metaphysical regions, his duties often took him deep into the bowels of the earth. As a recognition of his good services to the Saxon mining industry he was appointed, at the age of twenty-eight, to the cherished post of *Amtshauptmann*. He died of tuberculosis a few months later, in March 1801, before the completion of his twenty-ninth year. Within the space of this short life his ceaselessly active mind also contrived to encompass the most diverse branches of knowledge, such as history, chemistry and the philosophy of mathematics, to name but three of his vital interests. In the world of letters he had already established a name for himself as an author of aphorisms, some of which rank as high as those of Friedrich Schlegel or Nietzsche.[1] However, he never regarded writing as a profession, but rather as a *Bildungsmittel* to help him develop and enrich his own mind. Altogether his social ambitions did not run very high. For a time during adolescence, it is true, he was dazzled by the prospects held out to him by his uncle Friedrich Wilhelm von Hardenberg, a very worldly dignitary of the *Deutsche Orden*, but soon he lost interest in the outward glitter that would have been his had he embarked upon a political or diplomatic career. More and more he came to agree with his father, who, unlike the uncle, entertained a strong Christian suspicion of the world and cherished above everything else the idyllic tranquillity of family life.

The transience of human joy and happiness was most forcibly brought home to Novalis at Eastertide 1797 when, within the brief space of twenty-six days, he lost both his fiancée Sophie von Kühn and his favourite brother Erasmus. It was this overwhelming double shock that at first seemed to deaden his soul (for a time he even contemplated suicide) but eventually helped to heighten his religious susceptibilities. The longing to be reunited with his beloved produced in him an irresistible yearning for personal immortality. Shortly after Sophie's death he spoke about his "vocation for the invisible world", and as his mind unfolded during the last four years of his life it came to divine ever-widening vistas of those higher regions. Other influences pointed in the same direction. He became acquainted with young Schelling, who introduced him into the realm of the new transcendental philosophy. From Fichte, at whose feet he had sat as a student, he received further encouragement. The philosophical works of Hemsterhuis, which he re-read most thoroughly in 1797, enhanced his awe before nature's mysteries. Finally, his contacts with Romantic circles in Dresden in 1798 and in Jena in the two following years confirmed him in his chosen path.

It was characteristic of the marked pantheistic mood of the time that of the divine persons of the Trinity it was the third, the Holy Ghost, that might be said to have engaged almost the whole of his religious attention at first. The ideas of Plotinus and of the sixteenth-century thinker Jacob Boehme clearly left a deep imprint on his receptive mind. Only gradually did God the Father come into the picture, and still later the Son. Of all the divine attributes, infinitude at this stage made by far the strongest appeal to Novalis, as to many other Romantics.[2] Next came the awe-inspiring realization of the all-creating power of God. Closely linked with it was the well-known 'renaissance of wonder' which has sometimes been regarded as the very essence of the Romantic movement.[3] No longer were the marvels of the universe taken for granted in a blasé and matter-of-fact frame of mind. Echoes of the Book of Genesis no longer fell on deaf ears, and thus the all-powerful nature of God stood revealed once more in its full and yet ever mysterious glory. Novalis, in his diary, described this change of mentality in these words:

> He to whom it has become evident that the world is God's realm, and whom the great conviction has penetrated in its immense fullness, will proceed undaunted on the sombre path of life looking into its tempests and perils with a deep and divine tranquillity.[4]

Thence there was but one step to the desire to approach that supernatural being by way of contemplation in the hope of attaining the highest ideal of a mystical union. The anti-rationalist facet of Romanticism, which has been discussed in a previous chapter, provided yet further stimulus. For just as medieval mysticism of the fourteenth century was, at any rate in some of its aspects, a reaction from the excessive rationalism of the Scholastics, Romantic mysticism, as it found expression in Novalis and kindred minds, was of course in part a reaction from the arid rationalism of the Enlightenment. Moreover, just as the great fourteenth-century contemplatives, for example Eckhart and Tauler, emphasized the need for a culture of the feelings, again Novalis as well as some of his fellow Romantics laid the deepest stress on the emotional side of religion.

To Novalis the emotional approach to religion was familiar from his early youth, for he had grown up in the Pietist atmosphere of his parental home where Count Zinzendorf's religious teachings and inspired example were held in the highest esteem. Thus the first seeds of Novalis's love of Christ had been sown early in his life, yet it was not until he fully grasped the meaning of Redemption that those seeds blossomed forth to bear marvellous fruit. The great turning point in his life is recorded in one of his posthumously published *Geistliche Lieder*:[5]

> Unter tausend frohen Stunden
> So im Leben ich gefunden,
> Blieb nur eine mir getreu;
> Eine, wo in tausend Schmerzen
> Ich erfuhr in meinem Herzen
> Wer für uns gestorben sei.'[6]

Until that event his soul had as it were been entombed, but now suddenly it partook of a spiritual resurrection:

> Ward mir plötzlich wie von oben
> Weg des Grabes Stein gehoben
> Und mein Innres aufgetan.[7]

In the first of the *Geistliche Lieder* Novalis says that it was only through Christ that he became a human being:

> Mit ihm bin ich erst Mensch geworden.

It has rightly been remarked that the *Geistliche Lieder* could only have been written by one whose soul had experienced both unredeemed gloom as well as the shining light of Redemption.[8]

After his full conversion to the faith in Christ, Novalis began to assume that remarkable ambivalent attitude to life in this world and the next which made him embrace both with almost equal fervour. In this respect the affinity between him and the Swedish theosopher Swedenborg is particularly striking. While Novalis was at times secretly hoping for an early death that would reunite him in a transfigured form with his beloved Sophie, he concluded a second bethrothal with the gentle Julie von Charpentier. At a time when his mind was revelling in images of "the lighter existence after death" and of "sunny glimpses of the other world", human science and scholarship also held him enthralled. But perhaps it would be more to the point to say that the borderline between earthly and supernatural life became increasingly blurred for him—as it did for Blake and Schubert. The latter is credited with having said: "It sometimes seems to me as if I did not belong to this world at all." Of Novalis, his colleague and friend Kreisamt-mann Just, who has left us a short biographical sketch of him, re-marked: "He created for himself in the visible world an invisible one." And Ludwig Tieck, who knew him no less well, reports: "It had become most natural to him to regard the nearest and most common thing as a miracle, and the strange and supernatural as something common; thus everyday life surrounded him like a wonderful fairy-tale, and in that region which most men would divine, or else cast in doubt, as something far away and incompre-hensible, he was fully at home." [9]

Heaven as man's fatherland which must for that reason also be his ultimate goal: this is the dominant theme of the first of the *Geistliche Lieder*; it is also the theme of Novalis's most celebrated creative achievement, his *Hymnen an die Nacht*. In that great cycle, composed of harmonious poetic prose and lofty religious poetry, the Romantic reaffirmation of the supernatural found sublime expression. Again, significantly, the *Hymnen an die Nacht* open with an apotheosis of light, the medium of life. Gradually, however, the scene shifts from the splendour of light to the awe-inspiring darkness of night. But his is not the night of the nihilists, not the negation of life. On the contrary, the night that Novalis beholds in his mystical vision is that medium in which alone the true and lasting life is revealed:

> Getrost, das Leben schreitet
> Zum ewgen Leben hin. [10]

In contradistinction to men like Chateaubriand and Lamennais who wrote eloquently about mysticism, Novalis, we may con-jecture, lived it. To what extent divine grace helped him to do so, is by the nature of things inscrutable. What can, however, be es-tablished is that he was utterly single-minded in his search for God.

CHAPTER ELEVEN

The Return to Catholicism

YET another unmistakable feature of the Romantic revival was the trend towards Catholicism. True, other branches of Christianity, too, experienced that revitalization to which the Romantic Movement contributed so much: for example, sections of the Lutheran Church rallied round a new orthodoxy. But Catholicism certainly made the most spectacular gains. The roads converging on Rome were manifold. Some Romantics who were to become ardent Catholics had been Catholics in their youth, had then drifted away from religion, only to return to the Church, their faith invigorated. Chateaubriand and Lacordaire in France; Görres, Clemens Brentano and Annette von Droste-Hülshoff in Germany, Manzoni in Italy, Garrett in Portugal, are illustrious examples. Others, however, were converts from Protestantism or Anglicanism whose conversion might be regarded as a return to the religion of their forefathers. Here the outstanding names are Friedrich Schlegel and Cardinal Newman,[1] but many others, as for example, Frederick William Faber,[2] Adam Müller, or the German 'Nazarene' painters in Rome, with their leader Friedrich Overbeck, were hardly less noteworthy. One or two of the so-called Nazarene school of painters had found their way to Catholicism from Judaism. The most remarkable of the ex-Jewish converts was Dorothea, the wife of Friedrich Schlegel, who was a daughter of the enlightened Jewish philosopher Moses Mendelssohn.

The Silesian Catholic Joseph von Eichendorff went so far as to interpret the whole Romantic movement in Germany from the predominant motive of Protestant nostalgia for Catholicism. This was no doubt an exaggeration, yet reduced to its proper dimensions Eichendorff's diagnosis contains more than a grain of truth. Of special value in this context is the testimony of Goethe, himself a non-Catholic, who in explanation of the new religious tendencies in Germany remarked to a friend in 1815: "The Protestants feel a void," and added: "They want to create a new mysticism." What was it that gave some Protestants that feeling of a void? And why did others who drifted from Protestantism to agnosticism and later found their way back to religion so often become Catholics rather than go back to the Protestantism in which they had grown up? These are delicate points which even in historical retrospect are not easy to discuss across denominational frontiers. But no one dealing with the problem of the relationship between Romanticism and Christianity can afford to sidetrack them. Again our chief witness is none other than Goethe who, though never converted to Catholicism, had a great deal to say about the reasons for the comparative decline of Protestantism. Out of several utterances we may pick that of 1805 made in conversation with Heinrich Voss: "Protestantism," Goethe remarked, "has given the individual too much to carry." And he added: "Nowadays a burdened conscience must carry that burden all by itself, and thereby loses the strength to come into harmony with itself again. People ought never to have been deprived of oral confession." In his autobiography *Dichtung und Wahrheit*, Goethe relates how at one stage he had been vexed by religious doubts which he would have liked to put straight in the confessional. Similarly, Ricarda Huch, in her study of German Romanticism, strongly underlines the fact that several of the converts felt attracted by the confessional.[3] In Goethe's opinion, the Protestants had altogether too few sacraments.[4] In the same vein, Alfred de Vigny, himself a lapsed Catholic, criticized the Reformation for having deprived religion of the daily miracle of Mass.[5]

Goethe also censured the excess to which Protestant individualism had led at a time when, as he said, people in every important city were beginning to establish new principles of biblical interpretation. Repelled by this phenomenon, some Protestants and some lapsed Catholics alike began to feel attracted to the authoritative element in the Catholic Church. Characteristically, it was Friedrich Schlegel, in his youth the daredevil Romantic individualist *par excellence*, who after his conversion to Catholicism was among the first to denounce Protestant individualism and to extol the tradition of authority in the Catholic Church which he had come to recognize as the rightful authority.

Another fact of Protestantism that found disfavour with the Romantics was its austerity in the matter of symbols and ornaments. The Protestant religion, Novalis noted critically in 1798, is less visible. Atterbom, the Swedish Romantic writer, who visited Berlin in 1817, was appalled by the unprepossessing interior of the Protestant churches in that city. The contrast was even more glaring in formerly Catholic churches which later had been taken over by the Protestants. This is how it struck Chateaubriand, in 1833, on the occasion of a visit to Ulm Cathedral:

> The Reformation makes a mistake when it shows itself in the Catholic monument upon which it has encroached; it cuts a mean and shameful figure there. Those tall porches call for a numerous clergy, the pomp of the celebrations, the chants, pictures, ornaments, silk veils, draperies, laces, gold, silver, lamps, flower and incense of the altars. Protestantism may say as much as it pleases that it has returned to Primitive Christianity; the Gothic churches reply that it has denied its fathers; the Christians who were the architects of its wonders were other than the children of Luther and Calvin.[6]

Similar feelings were expressed in the striking *Letters from England* (1807), which as has been mentioned above, purported to be translated from the original Spanish but were in reality the work of Robert Southey. It is of course impossible fully to disentangle Southey's own views from those of the pseudo-Spaniard, behind whose back he was hiding. Yet "the keen lashing given to Protestant absurdities" (this is how it struck a contemporary) is done with so much verve that it is hard to believe that Southey was not to some extent voicing his own feelings. However much he may openly have criticized aspects of Catholic Portugal and later gone so far as to oppose Catholic Emancipation in England, his *Letters from England* allowed the surmise that there had been a stage in his life when at any rate some features of Anglicanism seemed disquieting to Southey.

It is no wonder that the Romantics, with their colourful aesthetic sensibility, felt more in sympathy with the Catholic attitude to religious cult and ceremony. At times the Romantic–Catholic alliance, if such it may be called, seemed indeed precariously based on aesthetic values. In Germany, Romantics such as Tieck or August Wilhelm Schlegel, neither of whom became converts, were fascinated by the outward splendour of the Church. Time and again they used the imposing edifice of the medieval Church as a kind of backcloth. Catholic church architecture, religious paintings, chants, processions and the like, provided suitable ingredients for the making of a Romantic novel or the composition of a Romantic essay on the Middle Ages. When August Wilhelm Schlegel told Benjamin Constant that one could write about religion without having a religion oneself, Constant felt baffled, and noted in his diary:

> A. W. Schlegel laments the passing of a religion in which he does not believe.

But the paradox resolves itself when it is realized that what Schlegel and others with him were lamenting was chiefly the passing of an age of outstanding artistic achievement which had been the visible result of medieval religious fervour. Alfred de Vigny, on the other hand, obviously went too far when he implied that the concern for Christian art was the only obstacle left in the path of atheism:

> Et l'église sans foi, ce triste corps de pierre
> Qui dans l'autre âge avait pour âme la prière,
> L'église est bien heureuse encore qu'aujourd'hui
> Les lévites de l'art viennent prier pour lui.[7]

Such an ambiguous attitude to religion was, it is true, not uncharacteristic of certain trends in Romanticism. At the same time nothing is more misleading than the widespread notion according to which Romantics who became devout Catholics somehow ceased to be Romantics. Catholic devotion, it must be insisted, was one of the potentialities latent in Romanticism, just as was the other extreme, nihilism, or a variety of half-way houses. The rest of this chapter should serve to illustrate this point.

Alessandro Manzoni was born in Milan in 1785. He owed much to that great centre of culture which by the turn of the century was in many respects leading among Italian cities. An even stronger impact, however, was caused by his prolonged stay in Paris during the impressionable years between twenty and twenty-five. It was in the metropolis of the *Empire* that he drifted further and further away from the Catholicism of his childhood; it was here too that he recovered his belief. An anti-clerical note was sounded already in some of his earliest poems, e.g. in 'Del Trionfo della Libertà' written before he moved to Paris. In fact an Italian schoolfriend, by the ominous name of Pagani, is believed to have first drawn him away from the Church. Anti-clerical and anti-Catholic influences were bound to be more marked in the circle in which he was at first moving in Paris. His mother, the redoubtable Donna Giulia, daughter of the enlightened reformer Cesare Beccaria, had made the acquaintance of some of the *Idéologue* sect of philosophers, among them Madame de Condorcet, widow of the famous herald of secular progress. The friendship that united Manzoni with Claude Fauriel, who had already established a considerable reputation as philososopher and man of letters, was of special significance. Heirs of the *Encyclopédistes*, the *Idéologues* obviously further alienated him from the Church, and, indeed, for a brief spell he seems to have gone so far away from it as to turn atheist. However that may be, by 1807, after his first two years in Paris, when he decided to marry the Calvinist Henriette Blondel, the fact that she was not a Catholic seemed to him an advantage.

Yet only a few years later Manzoni, since 1810 already reconciled to Catholicism, helped to convert his wife, who, in her turn, had come to deprecate what she called the gloomy impact of Calvinism. Manzoni's return to the faith in which he had been nurtured has been the subject of much critical scholarship. It has been pointed out that the most tragic aspect of the Wars that had been unleashed by Napoleon, i.e. the countless hecatombs of human casualties, may have been a contributory factor.[8] Perhaps for Manzoni too, to use Jean Paul's poignant phrase, "the churchyard assumed the role of the preacher". Others have stressed the part played by Jansenists,[9] notably among them the Abbé Degola who was in charge of the instruction in the Catholic faith. Indeed, it has been surmised that Manzoni himself learned a certain amount from these instructions. That he fell under Pascal's spell is certain, and in this sense A. P. d'Entrèves's remark that "Pascal is the real key to Manzoni's religious experiences"[10] is correct, but the same critic also emphasizes the impression made on Manzoni by the other great moralists of the seventeenth century. Yet all these pointers, important though they are, still do not fully solve the deeper problem. What was it, we are tempted to ask, that made Manzoni embrace his recovered belief with such signal fervour? The answer he himself gave many years later was: "It was the Grace of God." And on another occasion: "Thank the Lord who appeared to St. Paul on the road to Damascus." This, it would seem, is as far as we can take it, for it is well to remember what Gaetano Negri, who knew Manzoni well in later years, has said: "No one will ever know the phases of the psychological drama by which Manzoni passed from scepticism to ardent faith, as he was a completely reserved person. He never allowed anyone to delve deeper into his conscience than he wanted."

Manzoni's return to a strengthened Christian faith certainly did not mean that he was no longer one of the Romantics. Quite the reverse: he was the acknowledged leader of Romanticism in Italy; and as for the alleged incompatibility of Christianity and Romanticism, this can be refuted by invoking Manzoni's own testimony. When Massimo d'Azeglio expressed his regret that such a great poet should adhere to the Romantic school, Manzoni retorted by pointing out that Romanticism appealed to him for the very reason that he considered it contained a Christian tendency. Romantic literature, he held, can and should be based on Christian inspiration, historical truth, and a simple form of presentation; it should be drawn from the bottom of the heart. The same letter to d'Azeglio is important also in another respect, in that it contains an exposition of Manzoni's ideas on Christian liberalism which plays a large part in the shaping of his *chef-d'œuvre*, *I Promessi Sposi*. As a paragon of a Romantic historical novel that work has been discussed in a previous chapter of this study. What matters here is the fact that that "Christian romance", as Leopardi so aptly called it, is so obviously imbued with a deeply felt Catholicism. To illustrate this point, the following passage shall be quoted (though many others might have been chosen):

It is one of the singular and incommunicable qualities of the Christian religion that it is able to guide and console anyone who in whatever circumstances seeks refuge in it. If there exists a remedy for that which has passed, it will prescribe and administer it, moreover it will lend insight and strength to put it into operation at any price. If no such remedy exists, it provides the means of carrying out in reality the proverb about making a virtue of necessity. It teaches us to pursue in a spirit of wisdom that which has been undertaken from lightheartedness; it makes the soul embrace with affection what has been imposed upon it by force, and invests a choice that was rash but irrevocable with all the sanctity, all the wisdom, and, let us put it frankly, all the joys of a vocation. It is a highway so made that, by whatever labyrinth or precipice man may reach it, he will after a few steps walk along it safely and willingly, and will happily arrive at a joyful destination.

The comfort to be derived from a strong Christian faith pervades the whole of this work. Clearly, Manzoni's chief object in writing *I Promessi Sposi* was to edify, not merely to provide aesthetic pleasure or intellectual enjoyment. Many a reader must have concurred with the opinion of Lamartine who told the author: "Never have I read pages on religion which moved me so much as yours." It was because Manzoni's religious sentiments were so unquestionably genuine that he was justified in criticizing the cynicism of Balzac, who, when visiting Manzoni, brazenly admitted that he had embarked on writing his one religious novel *Le Médecin de Campagne* as a kind of literary speculation. Manzoni's comment was to the effect that to treat *le genre religieux* successfully it must be done with deep conviction. However, he was too tactful, or maybe too shy, to express this opinion in the presence of his visitor.

The moral—or, as the author himself put it, the juice—of the whole tale is drawn right at the end of *I Promessi Sposi* when Manzoni turns once more to the crucial problem of suffering on which the reader's attention had been focused so often throughout the novel, and we are told: "When troubles come, whether by our own fault or not, confidence in God can lighten them and turn them to our own improvement." No one, and least of all Manzoni himself, would have claimed that this reflection was original.

Indeed, its essence had been anticipated by the ancient Greeks, who hailed the discipline of suffering as δαιμόνων χάρις, the mercy of the gods. Christian thinkers, not uninfluenced by ancient Jewish thought, had elaborated the theme throughout the ages. However, seen against the background of the secularization of our culture in the Modern Age, it would appear that the renewed emphasis on suffering was a characteristically Romantic trait. In marked opposition to the optimism of the Enlightenment, the Romantics can be said to have rediscovered the inevitability of human suffering. Thus, among Romantic painters, Géricault was called by Michelet "the Correggio of Suffering" because he had painted shipwrecks, mad scenes and executions.[11] What Leopardi and Schopenhauer have to say on this score, has been shown above. Alfred de Musset, too, in spite of his excessive craving for pleasure, was not unaware of this problem. In his poem 'Nuit de Mai', the Muse comforts the poet with the thought:

> Rien ne nous rend si grand qu'une grande douleur.

But the greatness Musset visualized when he wrote these lines was the greatness of the artist. He did not perceive the phenomenon of suffering in its religious context. Yet the very fact that Romanticism, unlike its more secular predecessor, occupied itself so intensely with the problem of suffering, helps to prove Manzoni's contention that Romanticism contains a Christian tendency. This reflection should not allow us to forget that few Romantics faced this problem in so peculiarly Christian a manner as did Manzoni, nor that few Romantics contrived to harmonize as successfully as did Manzoni the Christian and the Romantic worlds. For as a Romantic Manzoni took it for granted that it was the human heart that must be the central object of literature, while as a Christian he believed no less firmly that it was the Christian religion "which had revealed man to man", and which alone offered the key to the tangle of the human heart. The latter view found expression in Manzoni's apologetic writings entitled *Osservazioni sulla morale cattolica*, which appeared in 1819, two years after the publication of the first volume of Lamennais's great work of apologetics. When the first volume of the *Essai sur l'indifférence en matière de religion* appeared in an Italian translation

Manzoni wrote a short introduction for it. His own *Osservazioni* were reflections that occurred to him on reading Sismondi's *Histoire des républiques italiennes du moyen âge* which contained a fierce attack on Catholicism. The Genevan Calvinist advanced the argument that Catholic morality had been a reason for the corruption of Italy. Manzoni refuted this allegation in a quiet and scholarly manner, avoiding as far as possible the polemical tone that characterized Lamennais's impetuous style. Italy's moral decline was not denied or even minimized in the *Osservazioni*, but it was attributed to flagrant transgressions of the canons of Catholic morality. In passing, it may be noted that Manzoni never indulged in that overweening national pride to which some Romantics, and many who have followed in their footsteps, proved so susceptible. A second part of *Osservazioni* was planned by Manzoni, but of this only fragments are extant.

During the time Manzoni was working on the *Osservazioni*, and thereby laying the theological foundations on which his masterpiece was to rest, his lyrical vein found an outlet in *La Pentecoste*, the most inspired of his religious poems *Inni Sacri*. The overpowering might of the spirit of Christian love is celebrated in this poem in a manner at once solemn and full of enthusiasm. Here if anywhere a Romantic has succeeded in capturing the spirit of unalloyed Christian harmony. Among Romantic poets perhaps only Joseph von Eichendorff can be said to have equalled this achievement. If it be possible at all to gauge the sincerity and depth of another man's faith, Manzoni's *La Pentecoste* and some of Eichendorff's religious poems, notably *Der Einsiedler*, may be regarded as conclusive testimony of their authors' religious convictions. Goethe, who declared that he could read Manzoni's soul in his *Inni Sacri*, thus recorded his impression: "He shows himself Christian without fanaticism, Roman Catholic without hypocrisy, devout without bigotry." This was high praise, coming as it did from one who saw so clearly through the artificiality of much that passed under the name of Catholic revival.

Manzoni was forty-two years of age when he published the first version of *I Promessi Sposi*. In spite of its resounding success, he continually remodelled the novel until the definitive version appeared some fifteen years later in 1842. During this period of his life the close friendship that united him with the liberal Catholic thinker Antonio Rosmini Serbati, founder of the religious order of Rosminiani, proved a greatly enriching experience. Though he had not met Rosmini until 1826, this bond, which lasted for nearly thirty years until Rosmini's death, meant as much to him as that which had united him with Fauriel in earlier years. Blessed by good fortune in so many ways, Manzoni was by no means spared the adversities of life. In 1833 he lost Henriette, and a series of family disasters culminated in the death of his eldest son Pietro forty years later, a month before his own death in the spring of 1873. He was intensely grieved by these bereavements, but there is reason to believe that his faith helped him to come to terms with them. "A gentle wisdom reflects all round him": this is how Tommaseo, who knew him well in later years, summed up a description of Manzoni's countenance. Gentle and quiet he must indeed appear, especially if compared to his tempestuous Romantic contemporaries. Nor, as has already been observed, can his long life-span of eighty-eight years be regarded as at all typical for the Romantic era. And yet he was essentially one of the Romantics, and, moreover, one of the greatest of them all. It was therefore a fitting tribute when Giuseppe Verdi, Italy's foremost Romantic composer, dedicated his *Requiem Mass* to the memory of Alessandro Manzoni, on the first anniversary of whose death it was first performed.

CHAPTER TWELVE

Oecumenical Trends

IT was symptomatic of the revival of Christianity that the barriers between various Christian denominations no longer appeared to be serious obstacles on the road towards an oecumenical Christian outlook. Nor was this due to weariness or indifference, as had been the case during the age of enlightened toleration. Rather the reverse, for what now helped to produce that phenomenon was the

upsurge of a genuine Christian enthusiasm. There was no mistaking the trend. Whereas the Protestant Pietist Novalis, in his
Christenheit oder Europa, painted the Catholic Middle Ages in the
brightest hues, the Catholics Goerres and Clemens Maria Hof-
bauer declared that the Reformation had served a wholesome
purpose, and another prominent Catholic thinker, the Bavarian
Franz von Baader, helped to rediscover the great Protestant
mystics of the past—above all Jacob Boehme. According to his
own testimony, Baader derived the greatest pride from the epithet
"Boehmius redivivus" bestowed upon him by A. W. Schlegel. In
our context, however, Baader's significance lies not so much in his
re-interpretation of the Protestant and Catholic mystics—for
Eckhart and Saint-Martin too attracted him greatly—but in his
endeavour to utilize the wisdom of the mystics for the ambitious
aim of a reunion of Christendom.

As in the case of Novalis, Baader's range of interests was by no
means exclusively theological. Born in Munich in 1765 the son of
a distinguished physician, he studied medical and other scientific
subjects in Vienna and Southern Germany, qualified as a medical
doctor, but afterwards entered the mining industry. Ten years
before Novalis, he studied its theoretical side at Freiberg, and followed this up by a four-year visit to England and Scotland (1792–
6) where he learned a great deal about the practical side of mining.
The social problems created by the Industrial Revolution also
then first engaged his attention. Enriched by his experiences, he
returned to Bavaria and entered upon a notable career as a civil
servant in the mining department. The scientific bent of mind also
came to the fore in his elder son Joseph, who became one of the
earliest champions of railway development in Germany. Franz
von Baader himself made some inventions in the glass industry,
but the financial hopes he based on them proved illusory and were
to involve him in ill-considered speculations.

Apart from these preoccupations, philosophical questions had
concerned him for some time past, but it was not until the last
stages of the Napoleonic Wars that the centre of his interests shifted
towards religious issues. It was then that he began to evolve far-
reaching oecumenical designs for reconciling all branches of Christianity. One of the earlier schemes has come down to history, for it

is believed to have helped stimulate the idea of the Holy Alliance[1] in the mind of Tsar Alexander I. The pamphlet in question is entitled *Ueber das durch die Französische Revolution herbeige-führte Bedürfnis einer neueren und innigeren Verbindung der Religion mit der Politik* (1815). Memoranda from Baader, almost identical with the pamphlet, reached the three most powerful monarchs on the Continent—i.e. the Orthodox Tsar, the Catholic Emperor Francis of Austria and the Protestant King Frederick William III of Prussia—at the turn of 1814–15. The greatest emphasis was placed upon the idea that no league of States could last without a league of souls. Religious unity was declared to be one of the main prerequisites of a genuine peace in Europe. Thus the crucial question had to be faced of how that essential unity was to be brought about. There existed on this score a wide divergence of opinion in Romantic circles. Some Romantic thinkers, as we have seen, held that salvation could only be found in a return to the bosom of the Roman Catholic Church. Baader and others with him, however, envisaged a re-integration of Christendom on a different, namely supra-denominational basis. In order to achieve it, the three main branches of Christendom would have to be prepared to learn from each other's merits and faults. This latitudin-arian approach, it may be noted, was characteristic also of certain sections of the German Pietist movement with which Baader kept in close touch. From E. Susini's publication of Baader's *Lettres inédites* (1942) it emerges that he even helped to organize the large-scale migration of German Pietists to Russia that took place soon after 1815. On the Russian side the official in charge was Baron von Berkheim, son-in-law of Madame de Krüdener, who was then held in the highest esteem by the Tsar.

To one eagerly watching the portents in the Eastern sky, the moment must have seemed highly auspicious for a move in the direction of religious reconciliation. The six or seven years after 1812 were undoubtedly the hey-day of religious toleration in Russia, of which the admission of the British and Foreign Bible Society in 1812 and the establishment of the supra-denomina-tional Russian Society two years later were most conspicuous proof.[2] The Moldavian nobleman Alexander Stourdza, one of the Tsar's collaborators, expressed not only his personal view when

Lenau

Lamennais (after a lithograph by von Belliard)

he wrote in his *Considérations sur la doctrine et l'esprit de l'église orthodoxe* (1816) that, "we live at a time when all Christians without distinction ought to unite their efforts in order to struggle against perdition and unbelief." Indeed, no less august a person than Tsar Alexander I, perhaps influenced, and certainly impressed, by Baader's ideas, had come to share the latitudinarian outlook that found so startling an expression in his draft of the Holy Alliance treaty, that last attempt at basing international relations in Europe upon Christian foundations. In the same direction lay the sympathies of Prince A. N. Golitsyn, Procurator General of the Holy Synod and since 1817 Minister of Cults and Education, who in a letter to Baader asked the latter to send him from Germany priests and clergymen of various denominations. Moreover, Baader received further encouragement from his nomination to the official post of literary correspondent of the Russian Ministry of Cults, which implied that at regular intervals he had to dispatch to Golitsyn lengthy reports mainly about the religious situation in Germany. Though this may be hard to believe, Baader even seems to have been commissioned to write a textbook for the Russian Orthodox clergy.[3] However that may be, he seriously contemplated the foundation of a Christian Academy in St. Petersburg. In an elaborate scheme, which, alas, never came to fruition, he assigned to the Academy the double task of reuniting modern science and religion, as well as promoting a *rapprochement* between Christians of various creeds. Anticipating the Slavophil argument of which so much was to be made at a later date, he declared Russia to be the most suitable site for this purpose, since that country, unlike the West, had not yet been affected by the pernicious process of atheist dissolution. Furthermore, the Orthodox Church was in Baader's opinion predestined for the task of mediating between the two main branches of Western Christendom, for he believed it allowed a wider margin of intellectual freedom than did Catholicism, and yet avoided the abuse of freedom so characteristic of some Protestant circles. Criticizing those who could think only in terms of the Catholic–Protestant issue he never tired of demanding *Audiatur et tertia pars*.

In 1821, a dramatic international event, the outbreak of the Greek War of Independence, focused European attention on the

Orthodox Church, especially after the murder of the Patriarch Gregorius in Constantinople. Russia was expected to assume the role of champion of the Orthodox Christians in their struggle against the infidel Turks. To Baader the moment seemed opportune for a renewed initiative. Hitherto his contact with Russian statesmen and thinkers had been confined to correspondence. His knowledge of the Russian Orthodox Church derived only from his reading—e.g. Stourdza's above-mentioned *Considérations*, that made a great impact on his susceptible mind. Now the stage seemed set for a direct approach, and Baader, full of high hopes, decided to travel to Russia with the object of going straight to St. Petersburg, where he would meet his friend Prince Golitsyn face to face and pursue his far-reaching schemes unimpeded by distance or any other obstruction. For it had not escaped his notice that, owing to intrigues of a semi-political nature, the Russian Embassy in Munich had been very tardy and repeatedly even failed to forward his dispatches to Golitsyn. Perhaps this fact might have been a pointer to potential trouble. But Baader was by now fully determined to seize the bull by the horns. We may note in passing that he had not received any sort of invitation from the Russian government and that his journey was not even officially announced. Accompanied only by his young disciple, the Baltic baron von Yxküll, he left Munich in the summer of 1822. He was glad to turn his back on his native city, where he had incurred the hostility of some Bavarian Catholics who resented his contacts with the Pietists and the Orthodox Church. Besides, two years earlier his post in the civil service had been abolished though he continued to draw his usual salary.

To cut a painful story short: Baader never reached his destination, though he was away from Munich for more than twelve months. This is not the place to give a detailed account of the political and bureaucratic chicanery to which he was exposed both in the Russian Baltic and in Prussia. One incident, however, stands out in almost symbolic relief. Indeed, the scene might have sprung from Franz Kafka's grotesque imagination. When Baader got as far as Riga, he was received by the Governor of the Baltic provinces, Count Paulucci, a native of Piedmont, who had entered the Russian service just before 1812. Paulucci, a friend of Joseph de Maistre and adherent of an ultra-conservative outlook on religion, detested anything that was connected with the Pietist revival, which he regarded as politically subversive. In the course of a brief interview the Governor intimated to the unusual traveller, in no uncertain terms, that he regarded him as an *exagéré*. Baader, greatly shocked, had yet the presence of mind to retort that a religious man must of necessity be an *exagéré*. Worse things were in store for him. On order from St. Petersburg he had to turn back to the frontier town of Memel, where for seven interminable months he clung to the hope that the misunderstanding, as he interpreted it, would be cleared up, after which he would be granted permission to proceed to the Russian capital. His dreams were rudely shattered when a letter from Prince Golitsyn reached him in which he was explicitly forbidden to come to St. Petersburg. Moreover, his post as a correspondent of the Russian Ministry of Cults was abolished. Golitsyn, in his turn, had acted upon an ukase of the Tsar signed at the Congress of Verona. Baader's painful return journey was aggravated by the behaviour of the Prussian police, who, during his stay in Berlin, shadowed him as if he were an undesirable and dangerous person.

How are we to account for the débâcle of Baader's mission? The answer, it would seem, lies chiefly in the extraordinary change of attitude on the part of Tsar Alexander I and some of his advisers that had taken place from about 1819 onwards. With increasing momentum the Tsar had come to view the Pietist movement and all that was connected with it through the gloomy spectacles of Metternich, who, in his Political Confession of Faith, a document composed for the Tsar at the Congress of Troppau, decried the Pietist brotherhoods as revolutionary gangs in a Christian mask. It lies outside the scope of this study to investigate the Tsar's reasons for accepting so highly prejudiced an opinion after having patronized the movement for some years past. Suffice it to mention that the Russian Orthodox Church, on whose magnanimity Baader had counted so much, had a great deal to do with the change of policy. Significantly, the narrow-minded and sinister monk Photius, who played so large a part in the overthrow of the tolerant Prince Golitsyn, went so far as to stigmatize the liberal policy of the statesman he wished to supersede as the work of Satan. In the same vein the reactionary Admiral Shishkov now dared to denounce the Bible Society, which previously had enjoyed the Tsar's special care, as a terrible conspiracy against the government and religion. But even at the time when religious toleration had been officially sanctioned, large sections of the Russian Orthodox Church had been opposed to, or at any rate not interested in, the new policy, which never represented the views of more than a very thin layer of society. It was Baader's wishful thinking that more or less identified that vanguard, if thus it may be called, with the Russian Orthodox Church as a whole. Nor, it seems, did he fully appreciate the extent to which the Church in Russia had since Peter the Great been dependent upon the State. These were errors of judgment which might have been avoided. However, one can hardly blame Baader for not realizing, in 1822, that the period of religious toleration and reawakening that had been inaugurated in Russia ten years earlier had already become a thing of the past. Embittered and yet undaunted by his setback he continued to work in his own way for *Una Sancta Ecclesia*. From the Russian Orthodox side promising signs were not missing even now. There was, for example, the rather encouraging treatise on the present state of the Russian Orthodox Church written at Baader's behest, in 1840, by the Orthodox scholar E. Shevyrev.[4] Furthermore, there was his new friendship with the new and enthusiastic Prince E. P. Meshchersky. But above all there was, as Susini has discovered, the new and cherished contact with Uvarov,[5] Minister of Cults under Tsar Nicholas I.

Contemporaries, among them Goethe, Lenau and Montalembert, have testified to the depth of Baader's intellect as well as to his dazzling oratorical gifts. Here if anywhere was what the Germans call a *Feuergeist*. With almost volcanic forcefulness he threw out ideas, religious, philosophical or scientific. For many years immersed in the theology of Thomas Aquinas and in the theosophical literature of the medieval and more recent past, he nevertheless concerned himself also with problems of the present and the future which he perceived more clearly than many of his great contemporaries. To name but two of these problems: the situation of the working class in industrialized States, and, more important still, the danger of spiritual nihilism. Yet the unbiased student of Baader can for all his admiration hardly suppress a few qualifying reflections which should serve not so much to dethrone Baader from an imaginary pedestal but to show him in the proper perspective, in the first place as a typical Romantic personality, and secondly as a fallible if outstanding human being.

We have seen that Baader cherished the ideals of toleration and reconciliation. Yet he himself, like some other heralds of the same ideals, was anything but tolerant in his attitude to persons, nor could he be reconciled to those of his contemporaries, such as Schelling and Goerres, who had at first accompanied him on his intellectual journey but had then gone their own way. Another discrepancy is even more glaring. Baader may be said to have conceived some of the most profound and edifying ideas on Christian marriage, yet is reported to have neglected his first wife Franziska, *née* von Reisky, whom he had married in Prague in 1800, and who died six years before him in 1835. The substance of our third proviso must rest on the authority of that much-travelled Frenchman Charles de Sainte-Foi who, at one time Lamennais's disciple at La Chesnaie, lived in Munich for several months in 1831 and fell under Baader's spell. Yet he remarked in his *Souvenirs*:

> This Catholic philosopher knew but the theory of Catholicism. He held forth admirably about the efficacy of the sacraments and of prayer, but does not seem to have used those means much for himself which he so warmly recommended to others.[6]

Although we cannot be sure about the extent to which this observation may be correct, the note of discord in Baader's soul is clearly audible. That inner disharmony may well have been the deeper reason why this intuitive thinker and master of the spoken word found it impossible to present his thought on paper in the form of a coherent philosophical system. His published work is dispersed in innumerable shorter contributions, for the most part written in an involved and almost cryptic style. The most remarkable among them bears the characteristic title *Fermenta Cognitionis*: the Leaven of Thought.

CHAPTER THIRTEEN

Emotional Christianity

IN discussing Novalis in a previous chapter, mention has been made of the Romantic stress on the emotional side of religion. This aspect, however, is of such great importance that it warrants closer examination. For this purpose one more figure will be introduced: Friedrich Ernest Daniel Schleiermacher.

As was the case with Novalis, Schleiermacher owed his earliest religious experiences to Count Zinzendorf's *Brüdergemeine*, that Pietist sequel to the Bohemian (or Moravian) Brethren. On leaving his native Silesia, it is true, he too passed through the stage of revolting against the religion of his childhood, and at the age of eighteen he confessed in a letter to his father, who was a Protestant army chaplain, that he no longer shared the belief in the divinity of Christ or in mankind's redemption through Christ. Later on in his life he was to become the great reawakener of Protestantism in Germany. Indeed he has been hailed as "the Second Reformer". A further example of a return to Christianity—though in this particular case the road most decidedly did not lead to Rome.

It would go far beyond the scope of this chapter to trace the various facets of Schleiermacher's powerful personality. It is enough to mention that he became the foremost Protestant preacher of his time and that his sermons at the Dreifaltigkeitskirche in Berlin during the trying time between Prussia's humiliation of 1806 and her triumph in 1813 are regarded as some of the finest specimens of political oratory in Germany since the time of Luther. Nor should it be forgotten that Schleiermacher, who was in close contact with Wilhelm von Humboldt, helped to found Berlin University, and in his double capacity as Professor of Protestant theology and Secretary of the Prussian Academy did much to stimulate higher learning and scholarship far beyond the realm of theology. Himself an accomplished classical scholar, he translated Plato's *Dialogues*, a task he had embarked upon with the assistance of Friedrich Schlegel, whom he befriended in Berlin before the turn of the century. Nor did the social question escape his attention. Especially during the last years of his life, after the July Revolution of 1830, he enjoined upon the higher classes the duty of developing a keener sense of responsibility towards the materially handicapped classes. For this purpose he advocated the idea of social insurance and other reforms typical of the Modern Welfare State. Here then was yet another case of a Romantic who kept his eyes wide open and did not inhabit the proverbial ivory tower.

Schleiermacher was a prolific writer, but of all his works the *Reden über die Religion an die Gebildeten unter ihren Verächtern*,[1] published anonymously in 1798, had the profoundest impact on his contemporaries. It is therefore legitimate to focus attention on this work of apologetics, especially since it contains so much that is typical of the Romantic mentality though it was conceived only on the very threshold of the Romantic era. Conversely, Schleiermacher's own return to religion was certainly stimulated by his contacts with Romantic contemporaries. Right at the outset it should be noted that the *Reden* appeared in the Prussian capital in 1798. Berlin might well have seemed a singularly inauspicious place for a religious revival. On the other hand it might have been argued that here if anywhere the cause of religion was in dire need of an able apologist. Indeed, religion was at a rather low ebb in that upstart European capital. Anti-religious views, which had been fostered by the royal free-thinker Frederick the Great and his entourage, had spread alarmingly so that Gotthold Ephraim Lessing had already coined the phrase that the much vaunted "intellectual freedom of Berlin" reduced itself to everybody's freedom to utter as much insulting nonsense about religion as he pleased. Friedrich Schlegel's testimony points in the same direction. At about the time when Schleiermacher was writing his *Reden über die Religion*, Schlegel wrote to his brother that people in Berlin were fanatical in their anti-religion.[2] Such then was the setting in which Schleiermacher's work of apologetics originated. Perhaps this helps to explain the fact that the *Reden*, far from being a piece of sound Christian apologetics, are in reality an impassioned argument for religion in general. Perhaps the detour via 'religion', or as it would previously have been styled 'natural religion', was one of the directions taken by the Romantic return to Christianity.[3] "People are already talking about religion," Friedrich Schlegel noted in his *Ideen* in Berlin in 1800. It may be significant that he did not yet report them as talking about the Christian religion.

The vagueness of Schleiermacher's religion was accentuated by, and to some extent the outcome of, his extreme emotionalism. With him, as with his friend Novalis, that tendency became so marked because it had arisen from the combination of two trends, namely his early allegiance to the *Brüdergemeine* as well as the prevalent Romantic mood. For there is no doubt that that Protestant sect which had inspired Wesleyanism in this country, was characterized by a highly undogmatic and emotional approach to Christianity. However much religious sentiment, Christian ethics and Protestant dogma may have been integrated in the original Protestant movement of the sixteenth century, later events, and in particular the Thirty Years War and its aftermath, witnessed in Germany a disintegration of those three component parts.[4] It was then that the dogmatism of the Lutheran Church came to be opposed by the ethical rigour of late seventeenth-century Pietism as well as by the deep emotionalism that marked Count Zinzendorf's *Herrnhuter Brüdergemeine* at the beginning of the eighteenth century.

For Schleiermacher religious sentiment is the master-key and indeed the only key to religion. Theology for him is nothing but religious feeling that has become articulate. The preacher, therefore, should aim at *Selbstmitteilung*, that is to say he should unbosom himself to his congregation. Romantic self-revelation, inaugurated by Rousseau in his *Confessions*, and so lavishly indulged in by Romantic poets and men of letters, thus found its way into the pulpit of the Protestant Church, for it should be noted that emotionalism and insistence on *Selbstmitteilung* remained prominent features of Schleiermacher's approach to religion even at a time when the hazy religiosity of the first edition of the *Reden* had given way to a more dogmatic type of Protestant Christianity.

How nebulous and non-committal was the 'religion' of 1798 can be gauged from the fact that not even the belief in a personal God and the immortality of the individual human soul were regarded as integral parts of it. Indeed, dogma of any kind was declared to be an abstraction from, and a studied contemplation of, religion, but not part of religion itself. Nevertheless, in spite of the fact that all dogma was rejected in the *Reden* of 1798, we find in them an appeal for the foundation of a Church: one free of dogma but still a Church. Another Romantic paradox, we note, and this time in more senses than one. Schleiermacher was not alone in this respect, for Novalis, too, toyed with the same idea in *Die Christenheit oder Europa*, and so did a lesser man, Zacharias Werner, before he came to espouse Catholicism in rather too hectic a fashion.

A corollary of Schleiermacher's antidogmatic attitude was what one might call his relativism in religious matters. Thus he remarks in the *Reden*: "Everyone must be aware that his own outlook is only part of the whole, and that on the same objects that affect him in a religious way there exist views which are equally devout and yet totally different from his own." So far-reaching a relativism was probably due to several factors. To some extent it may have been an echo of Zinzendorf's teaching, for Schleiermacher, in his own words, always remained "a *Herrnhuter* of a higher order". Above all, however, we have to remember the characteristically Romantic concept of personality which has been touched on in our introductory chapter. Each individual Christian church or sect, or in the last analysis each individual human being, was considered to have a right to its own personality. In the same vein Schleiermacher could later write in a work entitled *Christliche Sitte* that "there exist distinctions between Catholicism and Protestantism which are and always will remain within their rights". The manifold interpretations of Christianity—this was the underlying assumption—all served to supplement each other, and to bring out some essential feature of Christianity that might otherwise be lost. If even the relative rightfulness of Catholicism was recognized from the Protestant side, it was understandable that differences inside Protestantism appeared to be negligible. Schleiermacher was therefore consistent in his attempt to bring

about a union within German Protestantism. This was a twofold
task. In the first place, the Lutheran and the Reformed Churches
were to be brought into closer alliance: an endeavour that was
sponsored by the Prussian King Frederick William III and met
with a certain measure of success. It should be mentioned in this
context that the King's Erastian method of attempting Union was
opposed fiercely by Schleiermacher. Secondly, the ever-widening
rift between Protestant pietist and Protestant rationalist trends
was to be bridged; but this enterprise proved far more arduous,
and indeed was never achieved.

Schleiermacher's Romantic relativism in matters religious was
by no means confined to the world of Christendom. Christ, whose
divinity he did not accept in 1798, was, it is true, acknowledged
as the foremost but not as the sole mediator between God and
man.[5] No real incarnation had ever taken place, but several emissaries of God had arisen, of whom Christ was the loftiest. Moreover, new emissaries were needed now and in all future times.
Similarly, the community of saints, one and indivisible, comprised
all religions.[6] Far-fetched though the analogy may seem, the syn-
cretist prayer to the several founders of world religions and other
great religious figures that forms that startling final page of Arnold
J. Toynbee's *Study of History* (1954)[7] would seem to be composed
much in the same spirit as Schleiermacher's first edition of the
Reden über die Religion.

Karl Barth, in his study of Protestant theology in the nineteenth
century, rightly points out that, in spite of his contrary intentions,
Schleiermacher called in question the decisive presuppositions of
Christian theology, and this owing to his failure to elaborate
sufficiently the contrast between God and man, and correspond-
ingly between Christ and man.[8] Seen from this angle, we would
seem to be faced by an anthropocentric theology which had obviously travelled a long distance from the theology of the Reformation. Yet anthropocentricity is only one aspect of it. Whereas the
human side of Jesus is stressed at the expense of Christ's godhead,
the Third Person of the Holy Trinity, the Holy Ghost, receives
almost exclusive veneration. Here there is, as Karl Barth has convincingly shown, the second centre of Schleiermacher's theology
and here, we may remember, we find ourselves again in the full

stream of Romantic ideas. Adoration of the Holy Ghost, at the expense of the other Persons of the Trinity, emotionalism and finally, pantheism are, as it were, natural allies.

Of the marked pantheistic note in Schleiermacher's doctrine there cannot be the slightest doubt. "The object of our religion," we are told in the *Reden*, "is to love the spirit of the world and to look upon his works joyfully." Even more revealing is the remark: "God is not everything in religion, but only one element, and the Universe is more." The idea of immortality, too, appears in a pantheistic garb: "In the midst of the finite to become one with the infinite and to be eternal in one moment, this is the immortality of religion." [9] In the third edition of the *Reden* (1821), the pantheistic note is much less visible. Now God is more or less clearly distinguished from the world. Yet even Schleiermacher's late *chef d'œuvre*, *Der christliche Glaube* (1821) betrays, as Franz Schnabel has remarked,[10] a strange uncertainty on ultimate questions.

CHAPTER FOURTEEN

Unfulfilment

BOTH the promise and the unfulfilment of the Romantic revival of Christianity are epitomized in the great and tragic figure of Lamennais. It lies obviously outside the scope of this chapter to follow that restless man through all the vicissitudes of a career that has been the subject of so many searching investigations, among which the three volumes by the Abbé Boutard, the biography by Duine and the more recent study by Alec R. Vidler are outstanding.[1] All I am attempting to do here is to outline and comment upon the principal issues.

It has rightly been remarked that Lamennais rendered immense services to religion.[2] We have seen that by his *Essai sur l'Indifférence en Matière de Religion* he revivified Catholic theology, especially on its apologetic side. However far more ambitious were his attempts to awaken the Church to the two great modern issues of liberalism and the social movement of the working class. Nor is the analogy of the awakening far-fetched, for in many European countries the prelates of the Catholic Church—as well as other religious leaders—were then enjoying a somewhat complacent slumber. True, their inertia may in part have been caused by exhaustion after the prolonged period of crises that culminated in the Civil Constitution of the Clergy and Napoleon's attack on the Church. When the régimes of the Restoration in 1814–15 extended their protection to the Church and restored some of the clergy's ancient privileges, it was understandable that the offer was accepted. At the same time there can be little doubt that the Church placed too much trust in the forces of the Restoration, and too little confidence in their social and political adversaries. It could not escape the notice of clear sighted observers, such as Lamennais, that the rulers of the Restoration were using religion, as often as not, as an *instrumentum regni* in much the same manner as the 'wise man' who according to the sophist Critias had discovered that a belief in gods might act as a useful deterrent. There existed, as Lamennais saw it in 1830, a real danger that religion would be smothered by the heavy-handed protection of the governments.[3] Furthermore, the political alliance between the Church and the powers that be could well prove a mixed blessing for the Church at a time when the unconstitutional measures of Charles X in France, that had received the approval of the Archbishop of Paris,[4] led not to the strengthening but to the downfall of the Bourbon régime. Lamennais, it should be noted, had foreseen the latter event for some time past.

It would thus appear as if Lamennais's reasons for advising the Church to discard her alliance with the régimes of the Restoration in Europe had been twofold. In the first place, he discerned the ulterior motives of the Church's ally; secondly, he had towards the late 1820s arrived at the conclusion that the Church was supporting the wrong cause. When, after the July Revolution of 1830, the Church accommodated herself to Louis Philippe's Bourgeois Monarchy, Lamennais still believed that she had espoused a lost cause. There existed, however, a third and decisive reason for Lamennais's attitude at that juncture. What he was most afraid of was lest the Church's spiritual power be compromised by her temporal power. It is well to remember that some of his prominent Catholic contemporaries—for example the Italian Romantics Alessandro Manzoni and Antonio Rosmini Serbati—thought on much the same lines. Rosmini, however, for a long time refrained from publishing his treatise *Of the Five Wounds of the Holy Church* which he had completed by 1833.[5] Lamennais, on the other hand, impetuous as ever, fully displayed the courage of his conviction when in conjunction with a set of enthusiastic collaborators he began to publish *L'Avenir*, the first daily paper to sponsor the cause of Catholicism. Among the political causes championed by the paper was that of the oppressed Catholics of Belgium, Poland and Ireland. The first two of these countries were then in the throes of revolutions against their Dutch and Russian overlords. As for Ireland, young Montalembert, Lamennais's most brilliant disciple, showed in his article 'Du catholicisme en Irlande' that Catholic Emancipation had made no difference to the shocking way in which the Catholics were impoverished by the Established Church of Ireland. Yet the Irish Catholics, though poor, were free, and Montalembert emphasized how much the cause of Catholicism had benefited from the complete separation from the State. That this separation was so complete was due in no small measure to the bold stand made by Daniel O'Connell in the famous Veto question: i.e. the 'right' of the Crown to hand-pick Ireland's Catholic bishops.[6] The breadth of the concern of *L'Avenir* was further exemplified by a proposal to found a kind of Liberal Catholic International with a programme that would have resembled that of the Christian Democratic parties of our own time.

Rightly, or wrongly—or, since the historian might as well take sides, on the whole rightly—it seemed to Lamennais and the group around him that from about 1830 onwards the best chance for a thorough-going Catholic revival lay in a *rapprochement* between the Church and the forces of liberalism, and—more debatably—in a *renversement des alliances* by which the Church would come forward as the ally of the liberal forces that were as yet scattered all over Europe but to whom the future belonged. But the same number of *L'Avenir* (15 November 1831) that advocated the formation of a kind of Liberal Catholic International contained an even more far-sighted idea when it drew attention to the duty of raising the material conditions of the lower classes. A few days earlier the paper had carried an article, written by Charles de Coux, in which it was pointed out that the problem of the industrial proletariat overshadowed everything else.[7] Lamennais himself returned to this theme time and again. "That immense question of pauperism," as he called it, weighed heavily on his mind.

If the Church had heeded Lamennais's and Charles de Coux's warning, perhaps "the great scandal of the nineteenth century", as Pope Pius XI was to call it—namely that the Church lost the working class—could have been avoided. One cannot but regret that the spirit that informed Leo XIII's encyclical *Rerum Novarum* (1891) was not adopted by the Church during the 1830s or 1840s when the social problems created by the Industrial Revolution were most pressing. At that very time the Church had at long last abandoned her misguided stand against the Scientific Revolution. In 1835, almost three centuries after their publication, Copernicus's truly epoch-making writings were removed from the *Index librorum prohibitorum*. But the world still had to wait the best part of three score years for *Rerum Novarum*, by which time the Church had lost her temporal power while, as Lamennais had predicted, her prestige in spiritual matters had been greatly enhanced.[8]

To return to the 1830s: not only were Lamennais's warnings not heeded, but the Papal encyclical *Mirari vos* condemned some of the main ideas expounded by *L'Avenir*. The idea of the need for a regeneration of the Church was repudiated, liberty of publication rejected, and the separation of Church and State disapproved. As to the key passage which ran; "Our dearest sons in Jesus Christ, the Princes", it was, to say the least, arguable that it could not easily be brought into harmony with the sentiment expressed in the Sermon on the Mount.[9] However that may be, it is hard not to sympathize with Lamennais, who claimed for himself, as indeed for any Catholic, the right to question the authority of the Pope in matters of politics. "Is there not a real distinction between politics and religion, and am I bound to believe the Pope in the former?" he asked in *Affaires de Rome* (1837). When, sixteen years after Lamennais's death, the Vatican Council promulgated and clarified

Papal infallibility, questions of Christian morals and dogma only were included.

Lamennais's disappointment about the Papacy's negative attitude was greatly enhanced by his suspicion that Pope Gregory XVI had yielded to strong pressure exerted on him by the secular powers. That this suspicion was only too justified cannot be doubted, since the publication of the documents in Adrien Boudou's study *Le Saint Siège et La Russie, 1814–1847* (1922), in Liselotte Ahrens's book *Lamennais und Deutschland* (1930), and, more recently and exhaustively, in Andreas Posch's important contribution 'Lamennais und Metternich' (1954).[10] Both Tsar Nicholas I and Prince Metternich brought strong diplomatic pressure to bear upon the Holy See whom they urged to issue a severe condemnation of *L'Avenir* and all it stood for. There exists a revealing dispatch addressed to Metternich on 18 May 1834, by Count Lützow, the Austrian Ambassador in Rome: "His Holiness . . . directed me to say that he is always happy to know your opinion, which he likes best of all to know and to follow". A few weeks later, the Papal encyclical *Singulari nos*, the strongest condemnation of, and counterblast to, *Paroles d'un Croyant*, published by Lamennais earlier in the year, was perhaps in its very wording influenced by Metternich, who, with good reason, declared himself to be highly satisfied with the encyclical.[11] Lamennais's efforts were thus frustrated by the very alliance of Papacy and political reaction which, not without justification, he regarded as detrimental to the cause of Catholicism.

Subsequent events during the century between Lamennais's death and our own time vindicated some of the noblest aims of this daring thinker. Of him it can truly be said that he was far ahead of his time. This much has to be stated frankly and unequivocally. But I cannot agree with those who are attempting to prove a fundamental consistency in Lamennais's attitude. It was Sainte-Beuve who initiated this astonishing *tour de force* which is based upon the argument that Lamennais's governing aim throughout was the regeneration of society. This argument itself is strong as far as it goes (and I have used it myself in a preceding chapter), but it should be realized that it does not go all the way. However consistent Lamennais may have been in this one important point, he was most inconsistent as far as the still more fundamental issue of faith was concerned. There was a long stretch of years in his life during which faith had as it were the upper hand; it was then that he tended to believe that a true regeneration of society could only be built on the basis of Catholicism. But even during that period itself he seems to have been continuously torn between faith and unbelief. "I always saw an open abyss at my side; I turned my eyes away from it," he told his disciple Eugène Boré in later years.

However many reasons Lammenais had for disapproving of the Papacy's political attitude, and even of Rome's treatment of his own case, it surely argues not consistency but extreme instability for one and the same man to assume the role of herald of Christianity and later to abjure Christianity altogether and to take refuge as he did in a vague Mazzinian blend of deism, pantheism and idolatry of the People. Or, to put it differently, what glaring contrast is there between the Lamennais of the middle years translating the *Imitatio Christi* not without adding to each chapter his own devout meditations, and the Lamennais of the closing years of his life, who, as far as one can judge, has turned his mind away from Christ! Had he been really firm in his belief, he would have been prepared to go on suffering for it rather than disavow it. "If, after all, you should have to suffer in the cause of right, yours is a blessed lot." (I Peter iii. 14.) But Lamennais, though endowed with signal moral courage, was not cut out to be a martyr. I have quoted his words to Eugène Boré about the abyss that he had always seen at his side and from which he had turned his eyes away. "But," he added significantly "when I felt myself treated with such injustice and contempt, I had the courage to plumb it."

The vagaries of his mind and of his heart, which must be regarded as the keynote to his personality, were reflected also in his frequent change of profession. He had started as a teacher, had then assumed the priesthood, next acquired fame as the author of profound politico-religious works, afterwards became a journalist (albeit of the highest order) and ended as a political pamphleteer. In a sense, however, the special pleading of the pamphleteer had always been discernible in his writings. Blondel has rightly said of him, "Lamennais almost always thought against someone."

The final impression that fascinating and harrowing figure

leaves in my mind is that of a deeply unhappy genius. More than any of his contemporaries he embodied Romanticism, that latest European-wide movement of ideas and sentiments. The brilliant and sometimes ecstatic style; the inspired and almost prophetic vision; the yearning for a faith and the religious frustration; the optimism regarding the fate of mankind paradoxically combined with the sombre mood of *Weltschmerz*; the propensity for medita-tation marred by an incurable restlessness of mind; the stirring promise and the disheartening unfulfilment—the whole gamut of Romantic *leit-motivs* are present in Lamennais, many of them carried to their extreme and revealing the forcefulness and depth, and, at the same time, the inner disharmony of a movement that was so fervently longing for harmony without ever achieving it.

PART FOUR

Romantic Enchantment

CHAPTER FIFTEEN

The Cult of the Ego

IF the Abbé de Lamennais may be regarded as the epitome of religious Romanticism, his Breton compatriot, the Vicomte de Chateaubriand, certainly deserves his reputation as the wizard of Romantic enchantment in the widest sense of the word.

Like Lamennais, Chateaubriand too was born at St. Malo, the date of his birth being 1768. In his youth Chateaubriand also passed through an irreligious stage when he fell under the spell of philosophical works of the Enlightenment which he had discovered in his father's library at the Château de Combourg. He was further alienated from Christianity by his contact in Paris with so-called *esprits forts* such as Parny, Ginguené and above all Chamfort. It was in keeping with the decadent *ancien régime* that Chateaubriand, during his period of unbelief, never hesitated to join the Knights of the Order of Malta. Noble birth and the inconvenience of a slight tonsure was all that was required for the purpose. As late as 1797, five years before the publication of *Génie du Christianisme*, he was still as far removed from the faith as ever. This is borne out not only by passages of his first work, the *Essai historique sur les Révolutions*,[1] published in London in 1797, but more unequivocally in some marginal notes he jotted down in a confidential copy of the *Essai* soon after its publication. Concerning Christianity, he there says bluntly: "Personne n'y croit plus." In later years Chateaubriand denied, somewhat disingenuously, that the *Essai* had been imbued with the spirit of unbelief, but truthfulness about matters relating to himself was hardly among his distinctive virtues. In fact, far from being on the religious plane merely a book of doubt, as he afterwards claimed, the *Essai historique sur les Révolutions* contained, in the words of a discerning critic, a foretaste of nihilism.[2] While engaged on this work, Chateaubriand in his exile in London had to contend with emotional as well as financial distress; moreover, his health was dangerously impaired. Yet it is hard to avoid the impression that the root cause of his despair lay precisely in his nihilistic mood. In describing, in his *Memoirs*, his state of mind when he tried to be an *esprit fort*, he says significantly, "Eventually one thing crushed me: the groundless despair which I carried at the bottom of my heart."[3] This typical *Weltschmerz* attitude found its literary expression in the figure of René, conceived by Chateaubriand during that darkest period of his life. All the characteristics of un-redeemed *Weltschmerz* are present in René: the introspection, the misanthropy and quest for solitude, the unbounded craving of the soul as well as the perpetual dissatisfaction, the *ennui* and resultant melancholy, the disgust with life and the attempted flight—to past civilizations, to nature, to the New World, or even to suicide. For René, in the sickness of his soul, feels a strong urge to put an end to a life which has lost all meaning for him. True, René's *Weltschmerz* had been anticipated in Rousseau's *Rêveries d'un Promeneur Solitaire* as well as in Goethe's *Werther*, both of which were familiar to the author of *René*. Nor can it be denied that in some of its details the story deviates from the life of the author. For example, the incestuous love between René and Amélie was in all probability not based on autobiographical fact, great though Chateaubriand's affection was for his sister Lucile who had been his first congenial companion. René's "confusion of sentiments"—a device stemming from Rousseau's *Confessions*—was, it is generally held, a purely imaginary ingredient of the story. However, essentially there cannot be the slightest doubt that René is a Romantic self-portrait.

At the very end of the story, and it would seem almost as an afterthought, religion is recognized to be the only remedy for the spiritual malady whose symptoms the author had been describing with so much sensitivity. A priest, Father Souël, addresses the hero of the story in these words:

> I see a young man infatuated with illusions, satisfied with nothing, withdrawn from the burdens of society, and wrapped up in idle dreams. A man is not superior because he sees the world in a dismal light. Only those of limited vision can hate

men and life. . . . Presumptuous youth, you thought man sufficient unto himself. Know now that solitude is bad for the man who does not live with God. It increases the soul's power while robbing it at the same time of every opportunity to find expression.

By the time the story of *René* was thus given a religious twist, Chateaubriand was well advanced on his return to the Christian faith. While still in London, he had at Easter 1799 completed a short manuscript containing Christian apologetic reflections. At first he had envisaged a purely aesthetic defence of the "touching beauties" of Christianity which he would have entitled *De la religion chrétienne par rapport à la poésie*. Later he widened its scope in an endeavour "to reconstruct religion from its ruins", as he himself put it. Yet it would not be unfair to say that the most successful part of the story lay in the enchanting panorama which Chateaubriand painted of the outward splendour of the Church. The introductory section, on Christian dogma and doctrine, at any rate, is by far the weakest part of *Génie du Christianisme*. Of greater importance is the attack it contains on the spirit of the eighteenth century with its stoic code of morality as preached, for example, by Vauvenargues. By and large, the religion of *Génie du Christianisme* is the typical "religion du cœur et de l'imagination". It is significant that according to Madame Hamelin the reaction among women readers of the book was: "Quoi, c'est là le christianisme; mais il est délicieux!" The timing of the publication could hardly have been more fortunate, for April 1802 happened to be the very month of the Concordat concluded by the First Consul. Napoleon's own persecution of the Church lay as yet in the future, and the former anti-religious wave that had swept France during the Revolution had obviously receded. Churches in Paris and other parts of the country which had been closed, or had served as club headquarters, stores, or prisons, were now being reopened. Many who had previously not shown much sympathy for Catholicism, now began to sympathize with the steadfast priests and laymen who had suffered so terribly under the Revolution. Needless to say, the author of *Génie du Christianisme* played heavily on these emotions.

Many years after the event, Chateaubriand asserted in his *Memoirs* that his *Génie du Christianisme*, far from producing only a temporary stir, had exercised a profound impact on his contemporaries. Though this claim may seem exaggerated, it must be admitted that his book helped to undermine people's anti-religious prejudices. To quote his own words, "men permitted themselves to examine any system, however absurd it might seem to them, even though it were Christian".[4] But as for the majority of those who, influenced by *Génie du Christianisme*, felt nostalgic for the beauty of the Christian cult, this, was to all intents and purposes, as far as they were prepared to go. Their attitude is perhaps best depicted in Chateaubriand's words written, on a journey to the south of France, while he was travelling down the Rhône in the autumn of 1802:

> The author of this article cannot resist an image drawn from the circumstances in which he finds himself placed. At the very moment at which he is writing these words he is descending one of the greatest rivers of France. On two opposite mountains stand two ruined towers; at the top of these towers are fastened little bells, which the mountaineers ring as we pass. This river, those mountains, those sounds, those Gothic monuments, divert the eyes of the spectator for a moment, but not one stops to go whither the bell-tower calls him. Thus the men who today preach morality and religion in vain give the signal from the top of their ruins to those whom the torrent of the age carries with it; the traveller is amazed at the grandeur of the ruins, at the sweetness of the sounds that issue from them, at the majesty of the memories that rise above them, but he does not interrupt his journey, and at the first turn in the stream all is forgotten.[5]

But what about our preacher of morality and religion? Did he himself go all the way along the road back to religion on which he had erected so many alluring signposts? Or can we agree with those critics who grant the real sincerity of Chateaubriand's approach to religion but yet maintain that it was essentially superficial? Was Veuillot justified in saying: "Chateaubriand avait la sensation chrétienne, il n'avait pas le sens chrétien"?

There is, first of all, the glaring discrepancy between the

preacher's sermon and his life. "Is a book sufficient for God? Is it not my life that I ought to offer Him? And is that life, pray, true to the *Génie du Christianisme?*,"[6] Chateaubriand muses in remorseful retrospect. It is indeed ironic to reflect that, having been married for some years, he finished this work of apologetics in which the sacrament of marriage was extolled while living with his mistress Madame de Beaumont. Perhaps his decision of 1792 to marry Céleste Buisson de la Vigne might itself serve as an illustration of the disharmony in his character: on the one hand, he despised money in typical aristocratic fashion, and yet this marriage was, from his side, entered into for purely financial reasons. The confrontation of Chateaubriand's life and *œuvre* reveals other contradictions. For example, he was—or pretended to be—enamoured of death, but nevertheless lived to see his eightieth birthday, thus doubling Leopardi's life span. More important, the man who could write of himself: "Il n'est pas ici-bas chrétien plus croyant et homme plus incrédule que moi," obviously never experienced the inner tranquillity of unshakeable faith any more than did Lamennais. André Maurois has written of Chateaubriand that he always oscillated between faith and doubt.[7] This view is certainly tenable, but probably nearer the truth is the interpretation put forward by Emile Faguet that Chateaubriand invented, and presumably himself experienced, the modern spiritual phenomenon of *demicroyance*, a state of mind in which faith and dreams become almost indistinguishable.[8] Religion then ceases to be reality in the full sense of the word, but instead partakes of the nature of Romantic escape from reality into the imaginary, or at any rate half-imaginary, world of Romantic enchantment.

Chateaubriand was fully at home in the world of Romantic enchantment—indeed, he discovered some of its unexplored regions—particularly the enchantments of the past; he also enriched others, as we shall see later. He shared the melancholy attitude to nature. In a characteristic passage from the *Memoirs*, entitled 'My Autumn Joys' he wrote: "A moral character is attached to autumn scenery: those leaves which fall like our years, those flowers which fade like our days, those clouds which flee like our illusions, that light which fails like our intelligence, that sun which cools like our love, those streams which freeze like our life, bear a secret relation to our destiny." [9] The immensity of the ocean, the superhuman grandeur of the American landscape, and in particular the sublime chaos of the Niagara Falls, offered a novel background for nature worship. Exoticism and idyllic primitivism, again, appear in enticing new colours and hues in his stories of *Atala* and *Les Natchez*, where, apart from the concluding sections of the *Mémoires d'Outre-Tombe*, his harmonious poetic prose reaches its highest degree of perfection. Jean-Jacques Rousseau, with his fertile imagination, had already extolled uncivilized man. Explorers and scientists, from first-hand knowledge, had described him in a more realistic way. Chateaubriand, possessing some and claiming a greater amount of first-hand experience, idealized or romanticized him. Even in his *Voyage en Amérique* (1826), narrative and imaginary portrayal of the 'ideal savage' of North America are inextricably interwoven.

And yet, Chateaubriand's life itself, without any trappings of the imagination, might well be likened to a magic fairy tale. The quest of the highly sophisticated scion of an old European aristocracy for the savage way of life, his "emigration from the world", to use his own descriptive phrase, is but one element of that story. Another magic touch: here if anywhere was a man who came to know both sides of life in a lifetime. Compare, for instance, his seven years' exile in London, where symbolically the outlook from his attic in New Road (near Tottenham Court Road) was on to a cemetery, and his triumphant return to London many years later as Ambassador of France under the Bourbon Monarchy. There were times, during his emigration, when he had dined on a little bread, hot water and a bit of sugar. A quarter of a century later, the culinary display at his diplomatic banquets in Portland Place was such that gastronomy has immortalized two dishes invented for the purpose: the luscious beafsteak à la Chateaubriand and the delicious Pudding à la Chateaubriand, later renamed 'Pudding Diplomate'. When, some years before the Bourbon Restoration, Empress Elizabeth of Russia financed his long desired journey to the Holy Places, thus showing her recognition of the illustrious author of *Génie du Christianisme*, Chateaubriand's thoughts may well have wandered back to the last months of 1791 when, owing to the Revolution, he had already lost most of his property, and, wishing to return from America, had to persuade the captain of a sailing ship to take him back to Europe on trust. Chateaubriand, like so many restless Celts, had a passion for travelling. Among the adventurous aims of his voyage to North America had been his hope to discover the North West passage, though this plan soon had to be dropped.[10] During the period of his forced inactivity his ceaselessly active mind travelled back to the past.

Rises and falls followed each other in quick succession. Politically the zenith was reached when Chateaubriand was appointed Foreign Minister of France under Louis XVIII. Some ten years later, the former Foreign Minister, on his way to the exiled King Charles X in Prague, was refused entry into Bohemia by the custom house officials at Haselbach on the Bavarian–Bohemian frontier, and had to wait several anxious days in the Bavarian border village before he was graciously permitted to proceed on his journey.

Nietzsche argued later in the century that the stupendous advance historiography had made since the beginning of the century was perhaps to some extent due to the crumbling of rigid social hierarchies, and the resultant rapid rises and falls on the social scale which historians were liable to experience like everyone else, but which would prove an especially enriching experience for the historian's mind.[11] Here, indeed, is a case in point. Chateaubriand's chequered career between the *ancien régime* and the last years of the Bourgeois Monarchy helped him to rise, intellectually, *au-dessus de la mêlée*, and it was from that vantage point that he surveyed the momentous historical events of his life-time in the *Mémoires d'Outre-Tombe*. As for the French Revolution, in the early *Essai historique sur les Révolutions* he had already declared that its outbreak had been inevitable, a detachment of view which contrasted with the far more negative attitude of most of the leading French *émigrés* whom he had met in London, like Malouet, Montlosier or Mallet du Pan. In the *Memoirs*, the unbiased analysis of the main causes of the Revolution is resumed. Aristocracy, we are here told, passes through three successive stages: at first there is the glorious age of superiority; this is succeeded by the age of privilege, during which the aristocracy degenerates; finally, during the age of vanity it dies out.[12] And yet, as has been shown in an earlier part of this study, Chateaubriand by no means idealized democracy either. If he had lost faith in the kings and nobles of the decadent *ancien régime*, this did not imply that he had much confidence in the people, that upstart sovereign of the post-aristocratic age. In his own country where, since the July Revolution, this shift of the political centre of gravity had proceeded further than elsewhere, he observed with deep apprehension the complete disappearance of respect for authority of any kind: "Nothing more exists," he stated in the *Memoirs*, "authority of experience and age, birth or genius, talent or virtue: all are denied, contested and despised." In the same final section of the *Memoirs*, written in the early 1840s, he called the world of that time "a world without consecrated authority".[13] It is interesting to compare this diagnosis with that made by Bossuet concerning the Reformation which, in his view, was characterized by "a secret disgust for anyone who had some kind of authority".[14]

In the *Mémoires d'Outre-Tombe* which occupied him at intervals for the last forty years of life, the three dimensions of time are blended in a panorama of unusual breadth of vision. Past and present, whose interconnexions are shown in every single chapter, indeed preponderate, but the third dimension, or, as it might be called, the third act (for Chateaubriand's approach has a strong dramatic flavour) is not left out. The greatest invention of the nineteenth century, the railways' "enchanted chariots" as he called them in 1825, had just come into being. The next steps would be the construction of the Suez and Panama Canals and a tremendous acceleration of the means of transport and communication. He predicted that one day, perhaps in the coming century, men would lunch in Paris and dine in Peking. This trend towards ubiquity and its subjective corollary, the shrinking of our globe, would eventually bring about the desire for space travel and the colonizing of other planets. In the meantime, the standards of living on this earth would and should indeed be bettered, for he fully endorsed Lamennais's grim diagnosis of the misery in which the contemporary proletariat had to live. However, technological and material progress would not be accompanied by a corresponding cultural and moral improvement. Moreover, in his opinion there existed the danger that mankind might altogether lose its belief in eternal life, and this in turn would of necessity lead into the desert of spiritual nihilism. His warning, at the end of the *Memoirs*, is emphatic: "Do not deceive yourselves: without the possibility of attaining all, without the idea of eternal life, there is nothingness everywhere."[15] Should man once lose his hold on religion, human liberty itself could not survive. "La liberté est chrétienne," he had reflected in 1829. With freedom gone, he feared man's individuality would suffer a substantial diminution, and we might all turn into hard-working bees busily occupied in common in producing our honey.[16] A somewhat Orwellian picture, a hundred years or so before the conception of *Nineteen Eighty-Four*.

At the root of the modern crisis that threatened to engulf the whole world lay, so Chateaubriand concluded, a formidable idolatry: the self-idolatry of man.[17] While Chateaubriand made this prophecy, independently of each other Ludwig Feuerbach in Germany and Auguste Comte in France conceived the grotesque idea of a completely anthropocentric religion of humanity where mankind would take the hallowed place of the supernatural deity. In some of their aspects, the French Revolutionary cults may even be said to have anticipated this trend of thought.

Chateaubriand quite clearly diagnosed the fatal modern tendency of self-idolatry. But so complex was the nature of this great Romantic—and of the movement to which he belonged—that both tended to exaggerate the very worship of self which Chateaubriand here condemned. For did not Chateaubriand follow Rousseau, whom he secretly admired, in making a literary cult of his own person by means of exhibiting his ego—though, also in the manner of the master, not always quite truthfully? To be sure, a person writing his memoirs cannot find it very easy to hide his light under a bushel, and myriads of lesser men than the Vicomte have in the meantime treated us to intimate memoirs, sometimes not even waiting till the end of their lives. However, during the early part of the nineteenth century, the degree of egocentricity exhibited in Chateaubriand's literary work, and not only in the posthumously published *Memoirs*, was decidedly novel. Barely concealed in *René*, it shines forth in the *Essai sur les Révolutions*, in *Les Natchez*, in the *Itinéraire de Paris à Jérusalem*, and to some extent also in *Les Martyrs de Dioclétien* and the *Vie de*

Rancé, for even in dealing with Church history Chateaubriand cannot refrain from somehow occupying the centre of the stage. At the same time he was aware of the great contrast between his own age and that of the seventeenth-century founder of the Trappist Order. "The man who repents," he wrote of Rancé, "is immense; but who would nowadays wish to be immense without being seen?" This was much more to the point than the excuse he had previously offered for the egocentricity of his *Essai sur les Révolutions* when he said: "The ego makes itself felt with all those writers who, persecuted by their fellow human beings, have spent their life away from them."

The egocentricity of his literary work was matched by the personal selfishness of the "roi des égotistes", as Stendhal—that other egomaniac—has dubbed him. This trait of his character was especially marked in his attitude towards women. Mention has already been made of his loveless marriage and of his affair with Madame de Beaumont. The latter was succeeded by a galaxy of charming and some illustrious ladies who were all attracted by that insatiable man: Delphine de Custine, Natalie de Noailles, Claire de Duras, Cordélia de Castellane, Hortense de Allart and others. With the one and notable exception of his "guardian angel", Juliette de Récamier—the "Merveilleuse" as she was admiringly styled—they were all made unhappy by his incapacity for real love. So similar was their emotional fate that it would almost seem as though they had all subconsciously been yearning for a broken heart.

Looking back on his long, eventful life, Chateaubriand claimed in the 'préface testamentaire' to his *Memoirs*, that he had exercised a triple influence on his age: in the fields of religion, politics and literature. His ephemeral role on the political stage does not concern us here. On the religious plane, his influence—though by no means negligible—was certainly less marked than that of the Abbé de Lamennais. However, his impact on the literature of his country and beyond was indeed profound. The debt of the French Romantics to Chateaubriand was summarized by Théophile Gautier: "In the *Genié du Christianisme* he restored the Gothic cathedral; in *Natchez* he rediscovered the greatness of Nature . . . and in *René* he invented melancholy and modern passion."

Lamartine, Vigny, George Sand, Musset, Thierry—all tried to emulate his example, and young Victor Hugo's highest ambition was in his own words "to be Chateaubriand or nothing". Referring to the young generation of writers in France, in 1831, the Enchanter wrote, not without irony, yet with unconcealed pride: "Les romantiques—mes fils."[18] Was Chateaubriand justified in arrogating the rights of paternity also in respect of Lord Byron's most characteristic creations? Were *Childe Harold* and *Manfred* inspired by *René*? And if that be the case, what right had the author of *René* to denounce the nefarious effect of "Byronism" as he did?[19] These are problems to which we now have to turn.

Towards the end of the nineteenth century there appeared in Cracow a book written by a renowned historian of comparative European literature under the title *Byron i jego wiek*[20] (*Byron and his Age*). While opinions on Byron's literary merit vary widely, it is clear that the stamp of this arch-Romantic on his age was due partly to his extraordinary personality. Perhaps no other Romantic, with the exception of Chateaubriand, embodied so many aspects of Romanticism, and none displayed quite to the same extent as Byron that Romantic attitude *par excellence*: the preoccupation with, and parading of, the self.

Byron's forebears were as wild as they were distinguished. On his father's side the line could be traced back to the Byrons (or Buruns) of Normandy who had accompanied William the Conqueror into England. Another ancestor, much nearer in time, was vice-admiral John Byron, known in the Navy as 'Hardy Byron' or 'Foulweather Jack' who married a Cornish-woman, thus adding a Celtic admixture to the blood of his grandson. The eldest male offspring of this union, Byron's father, known as 'mad Jack', was a profligate and ne'er-do-well of the same type as Nikolaus Lenau's father. And again, as in the case of the Austrian poet, it is hard to avoid the impression that with Byron too, however much heredity may have helped to produce his genius, it must at the same time have imposed a heavy and almost insufferable strain upon his nervous system. Byron himself surmised that his all too frequent morbid depression of spirit was hereditary. "There was always madness in the family," he remarked. The violence of his passions seems to have come down to him through that channel, and not only from the paternal side where, but to mention one more instance, his uncle, the "wicked Lord Byron", had killed a relation in a fit of rage. However, his Celtic-Scottish mother (who could boast James I of Scotland among her ancestors) also used to allow wild hysterical tempers to run away with her. Byron's burden of nervous irritability was further aggravated by the physical handicap of a deformed foot, which made him limp and often caused him considerable pain, especially when an illiterate quack made vain attempts to cure him. More serious were the psychological repercussions of this. "Everyone knows me—I am deformed,"[21] are words he uttered in his youth, and later, in one of his dramas, the poetic laments occurs:

> . . . with all Deformity's dull, deadly
> Discouraging weight upon me like a mountain.[22]

On yet another occasion he remarked: "That foot has been the bane of my life."[23]

As if to compensate for these hardships, nature had endowed him over-abundantly in many ways. His facial beauty, well preserved in the pencil sketch by Holmes for a miniature in 1815, was not only recorded by fascinated women. Coleridge described his appearance thus: "So beautiful a countenance I scarcely ever saw —his eyes the portals of the sun—things of light and for light—and his forehead so ample and yet so flexible, passing from marble smoothness into a hundred wreaths and lines and dimples correspondent to the feelings and sentiments he is uttering." Coleridge also remarked upon Byron's charming smile which he called the Gate of Heaven. A somewhat unusual witness, the dreaded Ali Pasha of Yanina, whom Byron visited in 1809, admired his visitor's small ears, curling hair and little white hands. Others recorded the impression made on them by his low, flexible and melodious voice.

To heredity Byron also owed his exalted station in society and the pecuniary resources that went with it. Born in 1788, his father's death occurring three years later, he was still a child when after the uncle's death he succeeded to the peerage. It was in 1789 that George Gordon became the sixth Lord Byron. At Harrow,

Byron (portrait by T. Phillips)

George Sand (portrait by E. Leygue)

where he made some lasting friendships, his strong histrionic talent made him conspicuous. His gay and extravagant mode of life at the unreformed University of Cambridge was typical for a young man of the upper class, though some of his escapades struck his contemporaries as unusual: notably his introduction into Trinity College of a tame bear who, he declared, should sit for a fellowship. The story of the monk's skull used as a drinking cup by Byron and his convivial cronies at the inherited, half-ruined estate of Newstead Abbey, is characteristic of his youthful bravado. While a Cambridge undergraduate and, still more, after his un-earned academic graduation, he spent much time and money in London where he became immersed in the restless yet empty high life of the fashionable world which he so savagely depicted some years later in *Don Juan*. Looking back at his early years in town he observed: "I was at this time a mere Bond Street lounger —a great man at lobbies, coffee and gambling-houses: my after-noons were passed in visits, luncheons, lounging and boxing—not to mention drinking."[24] Dandyism and a notoriously dissolute erotic life complete the picture of his dissipations. All his passions, and he had many, seem to have arisen at an unusually early age. As he himself came to deplore, he thus anticipated life,[25] and at the age of nineteen he had already had more than enough of it:

> Worse than adversity the Childe befell,
> He felt the fulness of satiety.

The quotation comes from his semi-autobiographical Spenserian poem *Childe Harold's Pilgrimage*,[26] published in 1812, soon after his return from a long voyage to Portugal, Spain, Sardinia, Malta, Constantinople, Athens, and the countries of the Near East. Be-fore setting out on his travels, Byron, always an avid reader, ac-quired a considerable knowledge of the recent history of the Le-vant.[27] Among many other adventures he swam the Tagus and even emulated Leander of legendary fame by swimming across the Hellespont from Sestos to Abydos. The journey—he had been on his travels for two years—refreshed his tired senses. Greece in particular had appealed to him as "a country replete with the brightest and darkest, but always most lively colours of his memory".[28] The Romantic poem, consisting so far of but two

cantos, made him famous overnight. His earlier lyrical efforts had
not found much favour, least of all among the leading critics on
whom he took bitter and rather foolhardy revenge, in the satirical
poem *English Bard and Scotch Reviewers*. Now however there was
added to his many attractions that of being the fashionable poet.
Half a dozen exotic Eastern Tales, culminating in *The Corsair*,
followed in quick succession. Fame brought more temptation in its
wake, especially when Byron was appointed to the committee of
Drury Lane Theatre in London. At this time he really sank so
low as to become "the very slave of circumstance and impulse"[29]
that dragged him along through "sin's long labyrinth". This tempestuous wave of debauchery did not cease at the time of his
marriage to the well-endowed blue-stocking Anne Isabella Milbanke early in 1815.

Contemporaries and posterity alike have argued—and are still
arguing—about the causes of the shipwreck of this marriage which
ended in legal separation fifteen months later. It is an established
fact that an incestuous relationship between Byron and his half-
sister Augusta[30] (who had married her first cousin Colonel Leigh)
was the root cause of it. It is equally certain that the hapless
Medora Leigh, born in April 1814, was an offspring of this
union. What is not clear is whether or not the relationship persisted into the period of Byron's married life. Certainly, he hinted
as much to his wife, but he may not have spoken the truth. In conversation and correspondence, as in his published work, he indulged in wild self-accusation, prompted by many motives, among
them, very obviously, a strain of perverted pride. Lady Blessington, who had many conversations with him, emphasized this point:
"He claimed admiration not only for his genius, but for his defects,
as a sort of right that appertained solely to him."[31] In the same
vein Byron told Medwin in 1822: "You will see my confessions in
good time and you will wonder at two things—that I should have
so much to confess, and that I should have confessed so much."
He was referring to his memoirs, the manuscript of which he had
entrusted to his friend with the request to publish it after his death.
In the event, Moore, strongly urged by several of Byron's friends,
including the publisher John Murray and most emphatically by
Augusta Leigh, reluctantly agreed to go against the expressed

wish of his friend by allowing the embarrassing document to be destroyed. One of the few who had read the manuscript, Lord Rancliffe, declared in a letter to Byron's faithful friend John Cam Hobhouse that it was not fit for publication.[32]

The following lines taken from one of the Eastern poetic tales, *Lara*, epitomize Byron's peculiar feeling of pride, here attributed to the hero of the story:

> Too high for common selfishness, he could
> At times resign his own for others' good,
> But not in pity—not because he ought,
> But in some strange perversity of thought,
> That swayed him onward with a secret pride
> To do what few or none could do beside;
> And this same impulse would, in tempting time,
> Mislead his spirit equally to crime;
> So much he soared beyond, or sank beneath,
> The men with whom he felt condemned to breathe
> And longed by good or ill to separate
> Himself from all who shared his mortal state.[33]

Yet by themselves boastfulness or pride would not explain Byron's astonishing exhibition of his faults. Mingled with them there appears to have been an equally distinct feeling of remorse, and the paradoxical product of it all was what Byron's wife acutely diagnosed as "remorse without repentance". The deeper significance of that typically Byronic frame of mind can be seen in the survival of a genuine religious sentiment of remorse in a secularized form, or rather in a kind of irreligious vacuum. This can be illustrated from *Manfred* (though one must beware of identifying Byron too closely with his fictional heroes). Manfred's stirring lament would seem to throw much light on Byron's own predicament:

> The innate torture of that deep despair,
> Which is remorse without the fear of hell
> But all in all sufficient to itself
> Would make a hell of heaven—can exorcise
> From out the unbounded spirit the quick sense

Of its own sins, wrongs, sufferings, and revenge
Upon itself; there is no future pang
Can deal that justice on the self-condemn'd
He deals on his own soul.[34]

Here, clearly, one can see the repudiation of the traditional idea of
Christ sitting in judgment, and its substitution by the judgment
of the sinner's own mind or conscience. Christ's redemption of
sin, the power to forgive sinners, and consequently the sacrament
of penance, consisting of the tripartite process of confession, contrition and absolution by the priest, have ceased to be realities of
faith, and yet Manfred feels an irrepressible urge for expiation.
Unable to repent, his sensitive conscience—elsewhere Byron calls
man's conscience "the Oracle of God"[35]—refuses him self-
absolution, and it is for this reason that Manfred insists that he
has been and will hereafter be "his own destroyer". Thus the
spirit's formidable incantation[36] is fulfilled:

> I call upon thee! and compel
> Thyself to be thy proper Hell!

This was almost exactly Byron's own situation. He was sceptical
about Christianity, with which he had first come into contact
under the singularly uncongenial shape of Scottish Calvinism.
Unable or unwilling to repent and to reach a state of contrition,
he was yet seeking ways and means of psychological self-mortifica-
tion and ended up by becoming, in Goethe's words, 'ein ewiger
Selbstquäler' (a perpetual self-torturer).[37] Feeling a strong urge
to confess but spurning a Christian confession, he confessed to his
friends, to chance acquaintances, to his contemporaries, to posterity. Contemptuous of his fellow humans, he yet unburdened his
heart to all of them to an extent to which the history of ideas and
sentiments prior to the Romantic era offers no parallel. Only the
case of Jean-Jacques Rousseau, significantly the great precursor
of Romanticism, can afford any comparison at all. Stendhal, who
met Byron in Milan in 1816 and afterwards corresponded with
him, remarked: "Lord Byron greatly resembled Rousseau in the
sense that he was constantly occupied with himself and with the
effect he produced on others."[38] True, Byron himself took great

pains to disprove his resemblance to Rousseau. Characteristically, however, in the passage concerned, the first person singular occurs no less than twenty-seven times on the space of two pages.[39]

It was because Byron followed the lead given in Rousseau's *Confessions* in taking so perverse a delight in self-reproach and in the obsession with his own self that his *œuvre* lies in the tradition of Continental far more than of English Romanticism. Rousseau—Chateaubriand—Byron, the three great egocentrics, form a logical sequence, whereas Byron, viewed against the background of English Romanticism, must seem a freak, for English Romanticism, as Louis Cazamian has rightly remarked, does not consist in the triumph of the self.[40] This is not to maintain that a considerable degree of egocentricity was unknown in Romantic England. The very subject matter of Wordsworth's *chef d'œuvre*, *The Prelude*, with its characteristic subtitle, *Growth of a Poet's Mind*, is proof to the contrary. As for Byron, it is the excess of one who "was always in extremes", his almost pathological preoccupation with his own self and indiscreet exhibition of guilt that links him with Rousseau and some of the Continental Romantics. Perhaps this was one of the reasons why even after his death Byron was appreciated more on the Continent than at home where no place could be found for him in the Poets' Corner at Westminster Abbey.

Rousseau, Chateaubriand, Byron and their emulators are chiefly responsible for that overriding intimacy that exists between writers and their public. What glaring contrast is provided by the Elizabethan age where Shakespeare is hidden from our view in almost total anonymity. Since, however the appeal of Romantic literature of the type described lies in part precisely in the self-revelations and glimpses it affords into the artist's soul, the historian must not be so fastidious as to dismiss those glimpses as irrelevant. In a well-known essay on Byron Viscount Morley adopted this attitude when he suggested that the stories of Byron's libertinism were irrelevant. Had Morley been describing a less self-conscious epoch there would have been more force to his argument. In the circumstances, it is somewhat anachronistic to discard essential biographical details, for it was surely of the very essence of that age that the private lives of writers and artists in general ceased to be private. In this particular case, Morley, writing mainly for an English public, was right only in so far as he protested against the tendency prevailing in some Victorian circles to dismiss Byron as a great poet simply on account of his personal failings.

One half of Lord Byron's adult life was spent away from Britain. As soon as the separation from his wife was settled he moved again to the Continent, this time never to return. After a journey through the Low Countries and the Rhineland and an eventful tour through Switzerland where the Alpine scenery of the Jungfrau region inspired him to his loftiest poetry, most of the rest of his life was lived in Italy, which was obviously more congenial to his impulsive temperament than either England or Scotland. Stendhal noted that in the new surroundings Byron "yielded naturally to his emotions, as though he had all his life been an inhabitant of the South. . . . The more he lived among the Italians, the more happy and good-natured he became." At first, however, his time in Venice was marked by wild debauchery in which Byron and his valet Fletcher followed in the fabulous footsteps of Don Giovanni and Leporello. To Venetians who heard the rumours of his exotic orgies it seemed that the old adage was still true: An Englishman italianate is the Devil incarnate. If the mild epithet 'good-natured' could ever be applied to Byron—Claire Clairmont, the mother of his natural daughter Allegra, might have had her doubts—this must have been after his departure from the lagoons. And as for happiness, at the best of times a somewhat relative and elusive frame of mind, this must especially seem so in our case. For Byron, though at times turning to the exuberant mockery of *Don Juan*—a fitting enough subject, as we have seen— still often indulged in the gloomy *Weltschmerz* that permeates the last two cantos of *Childe Harold's Pilgrimage* and, to an even greater extent, *Manfred* and *Cain*.

In the two last works, as in the forceful and markedly autobiographical tragedy *Sardanapalus*, scepticism, pessimism and spiritual revolt are as prominent as in Nikolaus Lenau's dramas, e.g. *Faust* and *Die Albigenser*, which owe so much to Byron. And yet, just as Lenau was by no means an exponent of nihilistic *Welt-*

schmerz, so neither was Byron.[41] Ruthless and morbid though he was in psychological introspection and his exhibition of the darkest side of his nature, he was still not a nihilist. According to Lady Blessington he was sceptical but not an unbeliever: that is to say not an out-and-out atheist.[42] Thomas Medwin arrived at the same conclusion and so did the Methodist James Kennedy who, in 1823, held long conversations with him in Greece on the very subject of religion.[43] Kennedy concluded that Byron felt a final inability to believe without reservations and yet had deep-rooted religious instincts. The accuracy of this conclusion was confirmed by Lady Byron herself: after exhausting his powers of reason, wit and ridicule in trying to refute the argument of religion, he would often say with violence: "The worst of it is, I do believe."[44] Kennedy's further observation that Byron felt uneasy in his unsettled notions on religion is also borne out by independent testimonies, among them by that of Pietro Gamba (Teresa Guiccioli's brother): "As for the incomprehensible mysteries of religion", says Gamba, "his mind floated in doubts which he wished most earnestly to dispel, as they oppressed him." Clearly, Byron shared the characteristic Romantic yearning for a faith, and seems at times to have felt strongly attracted to Catholicism.[45]

Unlike Leopardi, Byron for all his scepticism always clung to the belief in a God and creator, and in the immortality of the human soul. Pantheistic conceptions which abound in his work do not seem to have influenced his own religious outlook. "So completely isolated a man," it has been suggested with regard to his egocentricity, "cannot be a successful pantheist."[46] Byron's misanthropy was not the intransigent misanthropy of Schopenhauer. At times he showed the same overweening intellectual pride and contempt for the whole human race, to whom he almost preferred the many animals kept in his strange household. Shelley, who came to know him well in Switzerland and Venice, wrote of him:

> The sense that he was greater than mankind,
> Had struck, methinks, his eagle spirit blind,
> By gazing on its own exceeding light.[47]

Thus, Shelley explains, Byron derived "from a comparison of his extraordinary mind, with the dwarfish intellects that surround him, an intense apprehension of the nothingness of human life".[48] In marked contrast to Schopenhauer and other misanthropes, however, Byron's complex character contained a strong element of charity among its redeeming features. There are many witnesses to his compassionate and lavish acts of generosity to the poor, and his ungrudging support of deserving causes. Well might contemporaries be puzzled by the chameleon-like character of the man they found so difficult to portray. Did not Byron say of himself

> . . . I almost think the same skin
> For one without—has two or three within.[49]

No word can describe this Protean trait of his nature better than the one he coined himself: mobility. It found an outward expression in his continuous craving for movement and frequent change of scenery. In the course of the seven years between his departure from England, in 1816, and his last journey to Greece, in 1823, he had as many as seven homes: namely, Lake Geneva, Milan, Venice, Ravenna, Pisa, Montenero near Leghorn, and Genoa.

> But there are Wanderers o'er Eternity
> Whose bark drives on and on,
> And anchor'd never shall be.[50]

A comparative calm, before the final storm, set in towards the end of his residence in Venice when he met the young Italian Countess Teresa Guiccioli, who seems to have reminded him in many ways of Augusta.[51] Now that the Countess's papers have been published, we know that Byron's last attachment was also the deepest and helped to bring about that partial change of his personality for the better. Teresa, unhappily married to a husband forty years her senior, certainly exerted a mellowing influence upon her illustrious *cavalier servente*. That astounding satirical poem, *The Vision of Judgment*, where in Goethe's opinion Byron came to the height and limit of his powers, was written during this period, and so was much of *Don Juan*, which was his greatest achievement. Even so anti-romantic a writer as T. S. Eliot has commended the last cantos of *Don Juan* for their unparalleled satire upon English society.[52] It lies in the nature of things that this aspect appeals more to foreigners.

Don Juan contains, apart from Romantic ingredients, such as enchantment of the past and of exotic countries with a liberal dose of picaresque adventure, also a high degree of *esprit*: probably a further reason for Byron's relative unpopularity with the English who, for all their distinct sense of humour, have for some time past fought shy of *esprit*, which thus has tended to become monopolized by Irishmen and Frenchmen. *Esprit* can best be displayed in prose,[53] and this is why Byron's lasting literary merit as a stylist lies perhaps in his letters, which elicited the highest praise from so critical a judge as John Ruskin.[54] The letter offers, of course, the widest scope for self-revelation. A master of improvization, Byron must have been a dazzling talker if we are to judge by the impressive evidence compiled in the American volume *His Very Self and Voice: Collected Conversations of Lord Byron.*[55] The somewhat impressionistic style as well as the metre in which *Don Juan* is cast, the conversational *ottava rima*, allows us occasional glimpses of that brilliance. The flippant asides, irritating as they are, also seem to be in character. Yet he was by no means always flippant. "His more serious conversation is a sort of intoxication," wrote Shelley, and added, "men are held by it as by a spell."[56]

It was the political side of Byron's life that came increasingly to occupy the last years of his crowded life. Political theorists, with a propensity for neat classification, might find it somewhat baffling to classify Byron's case. Georg Brandes, the Danish critic, was probably right when he declared that Byron's approach to politics was largely based on emotional grounds. Intensely proud of his noble origin, he yet repeatedly avowed republican ideas. Tending to see merely the oppressive side of monarchy, he yet felt no attachment to democracy, which he considered an aristocracy of blackguards.[57] Had the French Revolution not shown that mobs too could turn oppressors? Thus he could write to Hobhouse in 1820: "Pray don't mistake me: it is not against the pure principle of reform that I protest, but against low, designing, dirty levellers who would pioneer their way to a democratical tyranny."[58] Byron's hatred of the oppressors, in whatever land, undoubtedly exceeded his sympathy for the oppressed. There was, as E. H. Coleridge has pointed out, a Coriolanus-note of revenge in his attitude, and Sir Walter Scott was not far off the mark when he suggested that Byron's pleasure in displaying his wit and satire against individuals in office had much to do with his political views. The social ostracism which clung to his name since the days of his separation from Lady Byron may also have enhanced his radicalism. However, the world searching for a hero cannot be expected to scrutinize his motives all that carefully. What mattered was that revolutionary movements all over the world had Byron's outspoken sympathy, and those of Italy and Greece even his active support. Thus this English Lord came to be regarded as the standard-bearer of radicalism.

The lure of the Greek War of Independence proved, after some hesitation, irresistible. Some of his distant ancestors had taken part in the Crusades, and the awareness of this may well have been a contributory factor. Shortly before embarking for Greece, it is true he still toyed with the idea of emigrating to South America where a whole continent was in turmoil. The element of unrest clearly attracted that restless man. But an adventure of such magnitude might have meant starting a new life, and for such an enterprise a man who had lived life too fast had not sufficient mental resources. In his own metaphor, he had squandered his whole summer, while it was May.[59] It has been said of him that when he sailed for Greece he was already in emotional capacity 'un uomo finito'.[60] This, among other reasons, was why he returned to his early love, the fair Isles of Greece, in order, though for a brief spell only, to recapture his youth. And then?

> If thou regretst thy youth why live?
> The land of honourable death
> Is here:—up to the field and give
> Away thy breath!
>
> Seek out—less often sought than found—
> A soldier's grave, for thee the best;
> Then look around, and choose thy ground,
> And take thy rest.[61]

The lines are from Byron's poetic epilogue, in some respects his finest poem, composed in Missolonghi on the morning of his thirty-sixth birthday. Before three months had elapsed, the rest for which he had longed was granted to him. Complex in his desires to the last, he had at the same time been hoping for a "dashing exit".[62] This second hope was not quite fulfilled, for although he sought personal danger, he died not on the battlefield but, as fore-shadowed in his own presentiment, on the bed of disease from the after-effects of a severe rheumatic fever contracted in the marshy climate of the Ionian isthmus. Instead of the enemy's lance, the lancet of the doctors, and the inevitable leeches, accelerated the end.

While still at the crest of his life, the great self-torturer had posed the mournful question so revealing of his inner predicament:

What Exile from himself can flee?[63]

Now, on Easter Monday 1824, that flight too had been accomplished. A simple epitaph in the Certosa cemetery in Ferrara had made a great impression on him some years back. It consisted of no more than the name of the deceased and the two words 'implora pace'. It had been his wish that this should one day be his own epitaph.

Lord Byron's posthumous impact was prodigious, and lies partly outside the scope of this study. Although the enthusiasm for Byron's personality caught on all over Europe, the appeal of the poet whom Goethe hailed as the herald of world literature varied from nation to nation, in that each picked out that part of Byron's *œuvre* most congenial to itself. What, for example, fascinated the French most of all was what they described as Byron's 'inquiétude métaphysique',[64] his intrepid search for knowledge, and preoccupation with the problem of human destiny, expressed in that daring mystery-play *Cain*, or in the following lines from the final canto of *Childe Harold's Pilgrimage*:

Yet let us ponder boldly—'t is a base
Abandonment of reason to resign
Our right of thought—our last and only place
Of refuge; this, at least, shall still be mine:
Though from our birth the faculty divine
Is chain'd and tortured—cabin'd, cribb'd, confined,

And bred in darkness, lest the truth should shine
Too brightly on the unprepared mind,
The beams pour in, for time and skill will couch the blind.

Ten years after Byron's death the French Romantic composer Hector Berlioz composed a symphony entitled 'Harold en Italie'. In the Germany of the Goethe period, Manfred's *Weltschmerz*, which had been somewhat anticipated in Goethe's *Faust* (Part One),[65] created the deepest impression, later intensified by the stirring music written for the dramatic poem by Robert Schumann. In Spain, the cynicism and egocentricity of *Don Juan* was emulated by the 'Spanish Byron' José de Espronceda in his weird masterpiece *Diablo Mundo*. In Bohemia, the sombre and more melancholy hues of Byron's Eastern tale *Lara* left their impact on the outstanding Czech Romantic work, the dramatic poem *Máj* (May) by Karel Hynek Mácha. Finally, in Italy, Poland, Russia and the Balkans, as well as in the politically minded Germany of Heinrich Heine and the Young Germany movement, it was the radical impetus of Byron's work that had the greatest effect. We find it epitomized in Giuseppe Mazzini's prognostication of 1835: "The day will come when Democracy will remember all that it owes to Byron."[66] Even the official English attitude to Byron has mellowed with time: in April 1959 a newly executed copy of Thorvaldsen's marble statue of the poet was unveiled in the gardens of the Villa Borghese in Rome by Queen Elizabeth the Queen Mother.

One name stands out among Byron's Russian admirers and emulators, Mikhail Lermontov, the only genuine and at the same time significant Russian Romantic. Though the Russian poet was born in Moscow, his origins were not entirely different from those of Lord Byron, for one of his ancestors was Captain George Learmonth, a Scottish adventurer who in the early seventeenth century had entered the Russian service. Lermontov's life, almost ten years shorter than Byron's, was hardly less tempestuous. A petty nobleman by birth, destined for one of the crack regiments of the Tsar, the young man soon indulged in the frivolous life so characteristic of Russian high society of that period. He satirized the circles in which he was then moving in his melodrama *The Masked*

Ball. Despite a somewhat unprepossessing appearance the young poet fancied himself in the role of a Don Juan. More absorbing still was his desire to emulate his English paragon in every way. Sharing "Byron's soul and sounds", as he himself put it, he fervently aspired to share also his fate. Of Byron's poetry, *The Prisoner of Chillon* and the *Bride of Abydos* had the greatest influence on him.

The fascination exerted on the English poet by the Levant, and Greece in particular, was matched by Lermontov's enthusiasm for the exotic scenery of the Caucasus which he extolled in a sublime manner. Having visited Georgia in his childhood he was exiled there in 1837 and again three years later. Both his poetic tales *Mtsýri* (The Novice) and *Démon*, as well as his masterpiece, the novel *Geroý náshego vrémeni* (*A Hero of Our Time*), are set in the Caucasus. His sense of rhythm and keen eye for wild and colourful scenery are distinctive features of his poetry from which in our century Alexander Blok and Boris Pasternak have drawn inspiration.

Like Byron, Lermontov too regarded himself in a state of war with the society that surrounded him. For the stifling régime of Tsar Nicholas I and the social strata that supported it he had nothing but contempt, as was obvious from his *Ode on the Death of Pushkin*. This rebellious poem caused his first transfer to Georgia. Again, as in Byron's case, Lermontov's protest did not remain confined to the realm of politics. The note of metaphysical defiance that characterizes *Manfred* and *Cain* and reaches a climax in Vigny's *Eloa*, recurs in Lermontov's *Démon* and, most strikingly, in the sarcastic poem *Blagodarnost* (Gratitude) where the poet addresses God in these words:

> For all, for all, my thanks to Thee I offer
> For passion's martyrdom that no one knew,
> For poisoned kisses, for the grief I suffer,
> Vengeance of foes, slander of friends untrue,
> For the soul's ardour squandered in waste places,
> For everything in life that cheated me—
> But see that now and after such Thy grace is
> That I no longer must give thanks to Thee![67]

This acid cynicism born of the deepest unhappiness came at times dangerously near to spiritual nihilism, as, for example, on the occasion when life seemed to him to consist but of "empty and meaningless jesting". But there also existed a brighter, or at any rate less gloomy, side to his personality, for, to judge by his poem *The Angel*, Lermontov too experienced a yearning for "the music of heaven". More evidence may be found in *A Tale for Children*, which Gogol interpreted as an attempt on the part of Lermontov to exorcize the demoniac element in his nature,[68] but above all in the poem entitled prayer:

> When life's oppressive hour is mine
> And in my heart griefs crowd,
> A prayer of wondrous power is mine
> That I repeat aloud.
>
> Blest is the strength that flows to me
> In concords of sweet sound;
> Past reckoning it blows to me
> Divine enchantment round.
>
> Doubt, like a burden, leaping then
> Far from the spirit flies;
> From words of faith and weeping then
> How light, how light we rise![69]

Where Lermontov resembles Byron most strongly is in his marked self-analytical approach that characterizes his novel, the first psychological Russian novel, *A Hero of Our Time*, which contains some of the best prose in the language.[70] Pechorin, the hero of the story, who is an officer serving in the Caucasus, dissects his own character in the most merciless manner. Again, hero and author are almost interchangeable, for the critic Belinsky was undoubtedly right when he called Pechorin a subjective projection of Lermontov.[71]

This theme links Byron and all his followers—the Europeans that is, who maintained the tradition of introspection and self-depiction inaugurated by Rousseau, developed by Chateaubriand, and further enhanced by Lord Byron. We may assume that this was in Goethe's mind when in the allegorical Helena scene in the Second Part of *Faust* he made Byron the representative of modern poetry.

Yet, lest it should be thought that Goethe's admiration for Byron and all he stood for in literature was unqualified, we must remember what Goethe said to Eckermann on 29 January 1826: "All epochs that are in retrogression and in a state of dissolution are subjective. . . . Our whole contemporary period is a retrogressive one, for it is subjective. This you can see not merely in its poetry, but also in its painting and many other things besides."

CHAPTER SIXTEEN

Romantic Love and Friendship

ROMANTICISM would not have been among the great all-embracing movements of ideas and sentiments if it had not also profoundly affected the mutual relationship of the sexes. Real changes in human sentiment may be rare, but that one of these took place during the Romantic period there cannot be the slightest doubt.

Before probing into the more distant past, the Romantic attitude in this respect has to be contrasted with that of rationalist Enlightenment. The rationalists, as we have seen, believed in the equality and interchangeability of human beings. If taken to its logical conclusion, that attitude was bound to lead to a movement for female emancipation as advocated by Condorcet in France, William Godwin's wife Mary Wollstonecraft in England, and Theodor Gottlieb von Hippel in Germany. Equality of education, equal political rights, no discrimination as regards professions: such were the aims of the rationalist reformers. Since they were almost exclusively concerned with the rational faculties of human beings, it escaped their attention that women might possess intuitive faculties peculiar to their own sex. Let women's intellects develop along male lines—so ran the argument of these sex levellers—and within a few generations women will have caught up with men, and Equality, that rationalist ideal *par excellence*, will be established also in this important sphere.

On the Romantic side there existed a far greater awareness of the characteristic differences in the minds of men and women. Friedrich Schlegel and others, for example, maintained that women had a greater propensity for poetry and religion.[1] A rationalist would probably have denied or minimized this difference; at best he would have deplored it, at least as far as religion was concerned. Not so the Romantic. For him the variety of human attitudes was a desirable and indeed most salutary phenomenon. According to him, each of the two sexes had its own peculiar approach to the world of spiritual and intellectual values. Moreover there was a sense in which each sex was right. Closely bound up with this idea was the theory of the incomplete nature of the two sexes each of which needed to be complemented by the opposite sex. That is what Coleridge meant when he declared that a great mind is androgynous. This view, which can be traced back to Plato's *Symposium* as well as to some of the Gnostic sects, is highly characteristic of the Romantics where we find it expressed in the writings of Friedrich Schlegel and Fichte, and again in George Sand's novels *Lélia* and *Evenor et Leucippe*. Nikolaus Lenau summarized it tersely in a letter to his beloved Sophie: "Who has genius? can woman have it? Fatuous question. Man and woman have it conjointly."[2]

The idea of the complementary character of the two sexes found its fullest elaboration in Schopenhauer's metaphysics of sexual love. According to the philosopher, all sexuality is partiality. This partiality or onesidedness is more decidedly expressed and present in a higher degree in one individual than in another. Manliness and womanliness admit of innumerable degrees. The partners complement each other ideally if, for example, the particular degree of *his* manliness corresponds exactly to the particular degree of *her* womanliness, so that the one-sidedness of each exactly cancels that of the other.[3] Schopenhauer thus to all intents and purposes anticipated Otto Weininger's law of sexual attraction propounded in *Geschlecht und Charakter* (1903) which runs as follows: "For true sexual union it is necessary that there come to-

gether a complete male (M) and a complete female (F) even although in different cases the M and F are distributed between the
two individuals in different proportions."

What were the deeper reasons for the acceptance of this view
among the Romantics? It has been observed that Romantic men
often possessed a feminine trait and that, conversely, Romantic
women tended to become more masculine in their minds.[4] If this
kind of *rapprochement* really took place at that period, as it seems
to have done, it would appear that the time must have been highly
propitious for a mutual re-orientation of the sexes. Nor should this
trend be confused with the above-mentioned levelling of the sexes
advocated by the rationalist champions of women's emancipation,
the main point of contrast being that whereas the rationalists
postulated, to all intents and purposes, that women should ape
men, the Romantics of both sexes made a genuine effort to fathom
the character of the opposite sex.

Where the Romantics differed most fundamentally from the
attitude of the preceding century was in their conception of love.
What they envisaged was nothing less than a perfectly harmonious
union between man and woman. This implied, above all else, that
the sexual impulse and spiritual love were no longer to be disso-
ciated as they had tended to be during the previous epoch when, to
quote but one example, Goethe had found spiritual stimulation in
the company of Charlotte von Stein, but had kept the unsophisticated Christiane von Vulpius, whom he later married, as "the
treasure of his bed" (*Bettschatz*). Friedrich Schlegel's daring
novel *Lucinde* and Shelley's *Rosalind and Helen* both present the
new Romantic point of view, expressed again in a letter of Adam
Mickiewicz to the American writer Margaret Fuller:

> The time will come when the inner beauty, the inner life of
> the soul will be the first and foremost attribute of a woman.
> Without this inner beauty a woman cannot even physically be
> attractive.[5]

In order to complete the harmony between the lovers, it was
further postulated that they be intellectually congenial, a point
strongly emphasized by Friedrich Schlegel and later by George
Sand. Such exquisite harmony, it was further assumed, could be

attained only with one particular partner.[6] There was some speculation as to whether, in some mysterious way, those who fulfilled
these exacting Romantic requirements might not have been predestined for each other. And might not this union survive death?[7]
Of all Christian expectations, the promise of the resurrection of the
dead thus assumed a special significance.

The quest for the absolute, so characteristic of the Romantics, is
clearly reflected in their conception of love. Complete satisfaction
of the senses, the lofty emotion of spiritual love, a fruitful inter-
change of ideas coupled with a comrade-like bond of friendship—
all these the Romantics expected of love, and yet they demanded of
it still one more quality: a feeling of religious fulfilment. Like some
of the other Romantic enchantments, the enchantment of love, when
carried to an extreme, did not remain always this side of idolatry.
The resulting fusion between love and religion is epitomized in
one of Lenau's love letters. "This love for you," he wrote to
Sophie, "is no longer in me; I am in it. It is my God."[8] A like confusion between sacred and profane love prevails throughout a
great deal of Romantic thought, as for example when Corinne,
the heroine of Madame de Staël's novel, declaims: "Love, supreme
power of the heart, mysterious enthusiasm that encloses in itself all
poetry, all heroism, all religion!"

However, it would be erroneous to suppose that the idolization
of love is a specifically modern phenomenon unknown to earlier
centuries. C. S. Lewis, Father M. C. D'Arcy, Denis de Rougemont and others have shown that this Romantic trend was anticipated in Western Europe as early as the twelfth century.[9] Love as
an ennobling passion was certainly the keynote of the knightly
Troubadour poetry in Provence, and closely bound up with it was
the new deferential and indeed chivalrous attitude shown to the
fair sex. Significantly it was in the twelfth century that the most
powerful piece on the chessboard, formerly the vizier, received the
title of Lady or Queen. This is not the place to discuss the origins
of the medieval cult of love, as it has sometimes been called.
Suffice it to mention that a powerful stimulus would seem to have
reached Provence from Islamic Spain where women enjoyed a far
higher status than in modern Islam.[10] Gnostic eastern influences
also seem to have been at work—which is not surprising in an age

during which the traffic of ideas was greatly fostered by the crusades. Whatever its origins, Troubadour love, or *Minnedienst*, no doubt differed considerably from the traditional Christian ideal of love. For one thing, the Troubadour never sang the praises of his own wife.

The impact of the new conception of love was as lasting as it was widespread. It is well to remember that the Renaissance—with Pierre de Ronsard's *Amours* sonnets and Shakespeare's *Romeo and Juliet*—marked a second crest of the wave. The subsequent ebbing was probably in part due to the Reformation, for, as Max Scheler has pointed out, Protestantism, in sharp contrast to the Renaissance, deflated the emotional relationship between the sexes.[11] Romanticism, by re-intensifying that emotional relationship, proved thus once more to be an intrinsically anti-Protestant movement.

In the cool intellectual climate of the Enlightenment passionate love had found only a few literary champions: notably Jean-Jacques Rousseau, of whom Lord Byron remarked that he "threw enchantment over passion". True, the Abbé Prévost's *Manon Lescaut* (on which Puccini's opera is based), Richardson's *Clarissa*, and Goethe's *Sufferings of Young Werther*, all helped to pave the way for the Romantic idolization of love, but Rousseau's *Nouvelle Héloïse* had by far the greatest impact on contemporaries and posterity alike. But even Rousseau, for all his anticipation of Romantic love, did not yet dare to recognize it as the supreme value. For *La Nouvelle Héloïse* ends by upholding the sanctity of marriage. Thus the untrammelled cult of love did not make its appearance until the advent of Romanticism. Yet even then there was initially something distinctly esoteric about that cult. Its adherents, Madame de Staël and the young Friedrich Schlegel, and later George Sand and Victor Hugo, were all convinced that the passion of true love was confined to an *élite* whose superiority lay in the fact that they were capable of experiencing the emotion of love in a deeper and more intensive manner than most of their fellows. As George Sand put it in a famous letter to Lamennais, "Strong characters, great souls animated by faith and goodness, are sometimes dominated by passion which seems to come from heaven itself."[12] Victor Hugo voiced the same conviction when he compared passionate love to the natural phenomenon of lightning which never strikes lower objects. So, it was believed, vulgar souls never experienced what the Romantics described as '*la grande passion*'. The marked anti-egalitarian note that characterizes so many aspects of Romantic thought is again clearly visible.

An even more characteristic feature of Romantic love, and a notably un-Christian one, was its hedonism. "Happiness," young Shelley proclaimed, "is the object of all human unions."[13] This is why so large a premium was set on the fleeting moments of bliss as well as on the ideal of perfect personal compatibility or harmony. In that prototype of the Romantic love story, young Friedrich Schlegel's semi-autobiographical *Lucinde*, the marriage between Julius and Lucinde rests upon the ideal of mutual joy and happiness which has replaced the traditional Christian idea of marriage with its emphasis upon the responsibilities of husband and wife. In this respect, the Romantics' deviation from Christianity has been most glaring, for whereas the sacramental character of the Christian marriage, concluded as it is "for better or for worse", vouchsafes its indissolubility, the hedonistic facet of Romantic love all but sanctifies its impermanence. And, indeed apart from some notable exceptions, it could be shown that marriages relying exclusively upon the foundations of Romantic love have proved to be built on shifting sands.

Romantic attacks on the indissolubility of the marriage bond varied in intensity. Few contemporaries were as impetuous as young Shelley, who declared that the system of marriage was hostile to human happiness.[14] In his assault on marriage Shelley unwittingly reveals the precarious and ephemeral character of Romantic love when he writes: "Love is free: to promise for ever to love the same woman is not less absurd than to promise to believe the same creed." Shelley even drops the term 'marriage' altogether and instead asks himself the question: "How long then ought the sexual connection to last?" His conclusion foreshadows the matrimonial chaos of our own days. "A husband and wife," he writes, "ought to continue so long united as they love each other: any law which should bind them to cohabitation for one moment after the decay of their affection, would be an intolerable tyranny and the most unworthy of toleration." In his own short

life Shelley certainly acted on these words. The result was an in-
extricable tangle of emotions involving Harriet (his first wife),
Jane, Claire, his second wife Mary, and Emilia Viviani. Some of
the other Romantics, if less outspoken on the problem of matrimony, were hardly more restrained in their erotic relationships.
The one who was least restrained of all, Victor Hugo, in his poem
Amour echoed Shelley:

> Est-on maître d'aimer? Pourquoi deux êtres s'aiment?
> Demande à l'eau qui court, demande à l'air qui fuit,
> Au moucheron qui vole à la flamme de nuit,
> Au rayon d'or qui vient baiser la grappe mûre!
> Demande à ce qui chante, appelle, attend, murmure!
> Demande aux nids profonds qu'avril met en émoi!
> Le cœur éperdu crie: Est-ce que je sais, moi?[15]

Among Romantic women, Baroness Dudevant, who assumed
the pen name George Sand, was the foremost spokesman, as well
as practitioner, of Romantic love. A fervent apostle of Rousseau's
cult of love and untiring champion of "the sacred rights of love"
which she propagated in several of her novels—e.g. *Indiana*,
Valentine, *Horace* and *La Marquise*—George Sand firmly believed
that in certain circumstances love might grow so irresistible that
the marriage binding one of the lovers must be dissolved. Once
marriage had become desacramentalized and profane love sancti-
fied in its place, it was only consistent that George Sand should go
further and advocate legislation that would grant the rights of
divorce in marriage. Her novel *Jacques* boldly argues that in future
the laws would have to be adjusted to fit human emotions and not,
as hitherto, emotions subordinated to law. In this context it is
worth noting that divorce had already been legalized in revolutionary France in 1792, but abolished during the Restoration in 1816.
George Sand's reasoning, in 1837, in favour of a new divorce law—
paraphrased a thousand times since then—was significant: "I
can find but one remedy," she wrote to Lamennais, "for the bar-
barous injustice and endless misery of a hopelessly unhappy
marriage. That remedy is the right to dissolve such a marriage with
liberty to marry again." Looking towards the future, George Sand
in a millenarian mood characteristic of the 1830s forecast that one

day Romantic love would cease to be the cult of the few, for, as she put it, "as human beings progress, their love will become more worthy of enduring interest and mutual intensity, so that the power of love will increase in proportion to the development of intelligence". Thus she arrived at her somewhat startling conclusion: "The increasing need for a divorce law arises from the higher order of attraction between the sexes."[16]

As for George Sand's own life, after her unhappy marriage to Casimir Dudevant, her love affairs though no doubt of the highest intensity cannot be said to have been particularly enduring. The list, as is well known, includes, apart from several *dii minores*, such Romantic celebrities as Alfred de Musset, Prosper Mérimée, Pierre Leroux, and Frédéric Chopin. In *Lucretia Floriani*, which is something of a Romantic self-portrait, George Sand makes a disarming comment upon the last passion of her heroine:

> To such rich natures the last love always appears to be the first, and so much is certain that, if such feelings can be measured according to the height of enthusiasm, she had never loved so much.

To attempt any final verdict upon the complex phenomenon of Romantic love would not be an easy task. True, the indictment, as we saw, is formidable enough: for how could it be denied that Romanticism in various ways helped to undermine the institution of matrimony, that cornerstone of Christian society? In about 1870, Georg Brandes rightly forecast that novels such as *Indiana*, *Lélia* or *Jacques*, despite their small artistic value, would continue to produce the profoundest of social repercussions.[17]

However, the counsel for the defence would be in a position to plead that there is also another side to the case. And indeed it is equally undeniable that some marriages have been greatly enriched by the Romantic intensification of love. Though anything but a safe basis for a marriage, Romantic love can add passionate lustre, and in some cases even blissful harmony to it. Once again, the two-edged character of Romanticism is clearly revealed.

The fervour of Romantic love was all but matched by the intensity of Romantic friendship. Few human beings can live for long in isolation. Age-old social communities had broken down; perhaps it thus became all the more imperative to fall back upon those older social bonds. As in every renaissance, the generation that redis-covered their charm and blessing experienced the exhilarating feeling of breaking new ground. Great indeed is the number of friendships related to us by mythology and history previous to the Romantic era. Nevertheless, when we peruse the correspondence of the first Romantic generation in England or Germany, we begin to wonder whether anyone living before their time could ever have experienced friendship with so much passion. It might, it is true, be argued that this impression is based on an illusion. In a fairly advanced, or even late, stage of a civilization, emotions tend to become more conscious, the inner self is watched and exposed to an increasing degree, and consequently more is made of feelings that must always have existed in men's hearts. Yet when all allow-ances are made it still remains true that the Romantics almost desperately clung to the ideal of friendship, even though in reality they did not always remain faithful to their particular friends. But often they did: indeed the very close friendship that united the scholarly brothers Jakob and Wilhelm Grimm was life-long and undisturbed. And Charles Lamb's undying loyalty to Coleridge, whom he remembered as his "fifty years old friend without a dis-sension", obviously weakened his determination to live on after the latter's death in July 1834: before the year was out, Lamb too passed away. Brothers were often very close to each other. Apart from the brothers Grimm, Friedrich von Hardenberg (Novalis) and his younger brother Erasmus, the painter Philipp Otto Runge and his brother Daniel,[18] or Félicité and Jean-Marie de la Mennais spring to mind.

The brothers Lamennais, both of them priests, were not only joint authors of several works on religious history, but also co-founders of a religious order, the Congrégation Saint-Pierre. Félicité's apostasy from the Church caused his elder brother the most poignant sorrow. In spite of the fact that any advances made to Félicité might endanger himself, he never tired in his attempts to win his brother back—though all his efforts proved abortive in the end.[19]

Equally intensive was Schleiermacher's friendship with Novalis.

Other great friendships, such as that between Friedrich Schlegel and his brother August Wilhelm, or that between Coleridge and Wordsworth, "twins almost in genius and mind", as the latter put it, did not remain untarnished, but, while they lasted, proved signally fruitful. It is well to remember that the Romantic movement proper dates from the spiritual unions which found their first literary expression in the *Athenaeumsfragmente* and the *Lyrical Ballads*, both published in 1798. The pedantic, pseudo-scholarly attempt to count and disentangle the respective contributions to these proto-Romantic works misses the point altogether. For, even though it can be proved that Wordsworth wrote most of the *Lyrical Ballads*, it is more than likely that he would not have written any of them had it not been for the stimulating influence of Coleridge, for it has rightly been said that it was through his friend that Wordsworth first came to understand himself and his poetic aims. Within one year, the *annus mirabilis* from 2 July 1797 to 2 July 1798, when the two minds were most frequently in touch with each other, Wordsworth achieved even more than his share of the *Lyrical Ballads* (except for *Tintern Abbey*, written just after): parts of the *Prelude* and the *Excursion* were also written then. In the *Prelude*, which is dedicated to his friend, Wordsworth has immortalized the bond that united him and Dorothy to Coleridge:

> But thou art with us, with us in the past,
> The present, with us in the times to come:
> There is no grief, no sorrow, no despair,
> No languor, no dejection, no dismay,
> No absence scarcely can there be for those
> Who love as we do.[20]

Other notable joint Romantic works were the *Herzensergiessungen eines kunstliebenden Klosterbruders* by Tieck and Wackenroder, the miraculous story of the *Uhrmacher Bogs* by Görres and Clemens Brentano, or in another medium the famous fresco paintings of the Casa Bartholdi and the Villa Massini in Rome, a joint effort by the painters Cornelius, Veit and Schnorr von Carolsfeld, who, with others, organized themselves along the lines of a medieval guild in the Roman monastery of San Isidoro.

Co-operation did not always, or even in the majority of cases, manifest itself in the shape of joint authorship. In most cases it was confined to discussion and mutual criticism of works or ideas in the state of preparation. The Romantic movement was particularly rich in organs for this purpose. Indeed, small literary or philosophical groups or *cénacles*, as they were called in France, flourished it seems more than at any time before or since. As often as not, these gatherings of friends united men from different artistic or intellectual fields and sometimes from several nationalities. A famous meeting place in Germany was the picturesque castle of Giebichenstein near Halle, perched on a rock high above the river Saale, where the composer Reichardt assembled a galaxy of Romantic poets and artists, often for days on end. Equally memorable was the circle of young friends who, between 1819 and 1826, regularly met during the winter months in the Viennese inn 'Zur Ungarischen Krone'. Of Franz Schubert, the heart and soul of this circle, the poet Bauernfeld later said: "Through Schubert we all became brothers and friends." Among the composer's intimate friends, the painter Moritz von Schwind also deserves to be mentioned: his gifts, like those of some of his fellow Romantics, were ambivalent, for music meant hardly less to him than the visual arts. Foremost among the international centres of the movement was Madame de Staël's château at Coppet on Lake Geneva where the brothers Schlegel, Constant, Sismondi, Oehlenschläger and others foregathered for weeks and months on end.

In the French *cénacles* as elsewhere conversation, in the true sense of the word, unlike those highly entertaining yet equally irresponsible fireworks of Voltaire or the Abbé Galiani, was indulged in on a lavish scale. To the reign of wit, said Emile Deschamps, had succeeded that of a warm heart. Never since the Renaissance had intellectuals conversed with each other so much for the purpose, not of exhibiting their *esprit* nor of pursuing truth by rational argument and counter-argument, but of inspiring each other in the never-ending art of revealing truth. For the most part the conversations themselves are unfortunately lost to us. Their very length takes our breath away in this age when most of the elaborate talking, if not thinking, is done for us through the media of mass communication, so that the great Wordsworth scholar Ernest de Selincourt, as early as 1947, had to arrive at the sad conclusion that "with the rise in the standard of physical comfort social intercourse has tended to degenerate".[21] In 1802, the young Dane Oehlenschläger made the acquaintance of the Norwegian Henrik Steffens. A conversation on the topic of German Romanticism ensued which went on for sixteen hours.

Hardly less than the art of conversation, the art of letter writing was enlivened and enriched by the Romantics, for the discussion had to be carried on even at times when the partner was far away. In Germany, the letters written and received by A. W. Schlegel's wife Karoline (who later married Schelling), are typical examples. In the English language no one has written livelier letters than Lord Byron. It was such literary exchange on an international level that helped to transform Romanticism into a European intellectual movement, a process greatly intensified by the emergence of what Goethe called *Weltliteratur*: a growing number of translations of significant literary works of all ages into one or several other languages.

CHAPTER SEVENTEEN

Nature Mysticism

THE name of William Wordsworth, the foremost Romantic prophet of Nature, will always be associated with the lake and village of Grasmere in Westmorland. True, his childhood and adolescence, during which, to quote his own words, his soul had a fair seed-time, were spent more towards the periphery of the Lake District, at his birthplace, Cockermouth, his mother's home Penrith, and at school at Hawkshead, all celebrated in his great autobiographical poem. But it was the central part of the Lakes, where he settled in his thirtieth year just before Christmas 1799, that became the Wordsworth country *par excellence*. In his *Guide to the Lakes*, first published anonymously in 1810, Wordsworth attributes the superiority of that region, as compared to the most attractive districts of Scotland and Wales, to the concentration of interest as well as its unity. As for the comparison to the Alpine scenery, he points out that three thousand feet is enough to produce the effect of magnificence. What he cherished most in the Lake scenery was its "tranquil sublimity".

Grasmere in particular always remained for him "a haunt of pure affection", ever since he had first set eyes on it on one of his rambles from Hawkshead. In *The Recluse* his abiding attachment to Grasmere is explained:

> Nowhere else is found
> Nowhere (or is it fancy?) can be found
> The one sensation that is here; 'tis here,
> Here as it found its way into my heart
> In childhood, here as it abides by day,
> By night, here only; or in chosen minds
> That take it with them hence wher'er they go.
> 'Tis but I cannot name it, 'tis the sense
> Of majesty and beauty and repose
> A blessed holiness of earth and sky,
> Something that makes this individual Spot,
> This small Abiding-place of many Men,
> A termination, and a last retreat;
> A centre, come from wheresoe'er you will,
> A whole without dependence or defect,
> Made for itself and happy in itself,
> Perfect contentment, Unity entire.

Wordsworth's enthusiasm for the place was shared by his sister Dorothy, who described the view from Allen Bank in these words: "Wherever we turn there is nothing more beautiful than we see from our windows, while the treasures of Easdale lie as it were at our door." It was in Easdale, beside the Easdale Beck, that Wordsworth composed thousands of lines. Another favourite hermitage was the little island on Grasmere. Alone, or in the company of Dorothy or one of his friends, he indulged in frequent rambles and walking tours during which, travelling very light indeed, he sometimes covered as much as forty miles a day. Just before settling at Grasmere, Wordsworth and Coleridge, who had previously done a great deal of walking in the Quantock Hills and the Wye Valley, in less than three weeks criss-crossed the whole of the Lake District in almost every direction, but already nine years earlier Wordsworth's walking tour through the Alps had been on an unprecedented scale. Fritz Strich's characterization of the Romantic human type as the *Wanderer an sich*[1] decidedly applies to the two English poets.

This Romantic *Wanderlust* was certainly not motivated by the quest for establishing records of physical endurance. The main motive behind it was no doubt the poet's desire to imprint on his soul a variety of vivid and lasting impressions. At the present age, when most people no longer allow themselves time and leisure for long rambles and rather prefer to cover hundreds or thousands of miles a day by means of high-speed locomotion, the substitute device of the photographic camera is brought in to supply a mechanized record of the fleeting impressions gathered in the course of the journey. Nevertheless, our age is by no means devoid of Romantic tendencies—only of an entirely novel kind. Perhaps one way of illustrating the contrast might be to compare the reactions towards faster transport on the part of two highly sensitive writers. Whereas Nikolaus Lenau, in the 1830s, complained that his impressions tended to become blurred on a steamer trip round one of the Salzkammergut lakes,[2] the French aviator Antoine de Saint-Exupéry in his novels a hundred years later created a kind of aeronautic neo-Romanticism based on his spiritual experiences in the cockpit during his daring flights.

To return to the idyllic days of the early nineteenth century: "I love a public road," Wordsworth exclaimed in *The Prelude* in 1805. How blissfully undisturbed was the pedestrian in those days is brought home to us by his description of the delight of

> . . . wandering from day to day
> Where I could meditate in peace.

Naturally he did not like to be disturbed in his musings, and therefore, despite his love for simple folk, he did not often stop to talk to the local dalesmen he met on his walks, which could not fail to make him rather unpopular in those quarters.[3] What his soul needed on such occasions was the company of a truly congenial friend, or better still solitude.

Nature Mysticism

There are two sides to Nature, we are told in *The Prelude*, emotion and calm, both of which satisfy deep human cravings:

> From Nature doth emotion come, and moods
> Of calmness equally are Nature's gifts;
> This is her glory; these two attributes
> Are sister horns that constitute her strength.[4]

The poet's main emphasis, however, is on the state of tranquillity so conducive to the act of contemplation. In passing we may note that the question for repose on the part of the Romantics helps to explain their predilection for the autumnal season. Wordsworth's contemplation and meditation were invariably focused on preceding moments of vision in which he had beheld Nature: visions which he now relived as it were on a sublimated or transfigured plane. In his poem *The White Doe of Rylstone*, he claims to have received "authentic tidings of invisible things", and thus to have gained access to regions beyond sense. If one were to use the language of mysticism one might describe those supreme moments when Wordsworth became ecstatically conscious of the beauty of the universe, as well as of the 'holy calm' at the very centre of things, as a kind of beatific vision. And indeed, great Christian mystics like St. Teresa of Avila or St. John of the Cross also found Nature conducive to meditation. But is it really justifiable to use the analogy of mysticism? Did Wordsworth in his most solemn meditations on Nature and the Universe really find release from self as the great Christian mystics did, or did he lack the forgetfulness of self indispensable for that act of total self-abandonment? While Basil Willey (although by no means an unqualified admirer of Wordsworth) inclines to the former view, and Dean Inge included Wordsworth among his *Studies of English Mystics*, Albert Gérard, the French historian of English Romantic poetry, strongly favours the latter. As regards the earliest and most 'mystical' version of *The Prelude*, the French critic writes: "The poet does not submerge his individuality, passively and humbly, to the divine influx; rather it is his own individuality that appears to him deified—and it is here, no doubt, that he comes near to Rousseau." [5] The French critic even speaks, somewhat harshly of Wordsworth's "prétentions mystiques". Which of these interpretations is correct can never be fully established, but on balance Gérard's view, with some qualifications, would seem to be more in keeping with the known features of Wordsworth's personality.

Whether or not Wordsworth had genuine mystical experiences, he certainly came to be preoccupied with the interaction of the mind of man with Nature, and contributed much towards the elucidation of the psychological problems involved. In particular, the psychology of the poetic process was greatly enriched by the intimate revelations of *The Prelude* whose title should have been *The Growth of a Poet's Mind*. This was perhaps of greater significance than the fact that, as a truly original poet of Nature, he was the first to evaluate in his poetry an impressive array of natural sights and sounds that had hitherto not been celebrated in verse.

It is perhaps worth noting in this context that Ludwig van Beethoven's *Pastoral Symphony* (1808) was almost contemporaneous with the original version of *The Prelude*, which was written in 1805. The analogies between those two works are astounding. I am not here concerned so much with the rather raw, though ever popular, imitation of bird songs—the nightingale, quail and cuckoo—towards the end of the second movement of the symphony, a feature which according to the composer was merely intended for a joke.[6] Of far greater significance is the composer's musical rendering, in quavers or semi-quavers on the lower strings, of the murmur of the brook which, it seems, he had acoustically observed some five years earlier while his outward sense of hearing was still acute.[7] What Easdale, Grasmere or Rydal Water meant to Wordsworth, the secluded Wiesental valley, now named after the composer, close to Heiligenstadt in the wooded surroundings of Vienna, was to Beethoven. Here we may picture him roaming for hours on end, or sitting in the fork of some favourite tree, his musical sketch-book under one arm, brandishing the other and singing to himself in a loud voice.[8]

The prevalent mood of the *Pastoral Symphony*, and especially of its incomparable second movement and the finale, closely resembles the blissful sentiment of tranquillity which is reflected in large sections of *The Prelude* or, for that matter, *The Excursion*. Wordsworth's Westmorland dalesmen find their counterpart in the Austrian shepherds and country musicians whose efforts Beethoven often watched with amusement at the tavern of 'The Three Ravens' in his beloved Upper Brühl near Mödling. In the Allegro of the fourth movement a fearful tempest bursts upon the revels of the country-folk, and indeed the composer no less than the poet runs through the whole gamut of emotions conjured up by Nature's everchanging moods. More important still: both works, the *Pastoral Symphony* no less than *The Prelude*, are the fruit of meditation based upon previous moments of vision or acoustic impressions (or indeed both). That is why Beethoven significantly added this sub-title to his symphony:

> Recollection of country life; the expression of sentiment rather than painting.

As for Wordsworth, so for him too, Nature was fully alive: "Woods, trees and rock," he noted, "give the response which man longs for." And on another occasion: "Every tree seems to say Holy, Holy." Beethoven's affection for Nature in all her forms was intense. The English pianist and composer Charles Neate, one of the founders of the Philharmonic Society, who lived in intimate friendship with Beethoven in Vienna for eight months in 1815, remarked that he had "never met anyone who so delighted in Nature, or so thoroughly enjoyed flowers or clouds or other natural objects". Perhaps it is not surprising to find that Beethoven also held unorthodox views on religion which strongly resembled those of Wordsworth during his pre-Anglican era. Taken all in all, the poet's nature worship was matched by the composer's *Naturfrömmigkeit* which, it is believed, was not uninfluenced by the remarkable *Betrachtungen über die Werke Gottes im Reiche der Natur* [9] (1772) by Christoph Christian Sturm, the earliest of the German Protestant *Naturprediger*.

To return to Wordsworth: nature fascinated him in all her different moods, which, under the influence of the English climate, tend to change more rapidly than anywhere else in Europe. This sturdy man really seems to have enjoyed all kinds of weather,[10] not excepting gales, which inspired this exultant passage in *The Excursion*:

> Oh what a joy it were, in vigorous health,
> To have a body . . .
> And to the elements surrender it
> As if it were a spirit!—How divine
> The liberty for frail, for mortal, man
> To roam at large among unpeopled glens
> And mountainous retirements, only trod
> By devious footsteps; regions consecrate
> To oldest time! and, reckless of the storm
> That keeps the raven quiet in her nest,
> Be as a presence or a motion—one
> Among the many there; and while the mists
> Flying, and rainy vapours, call out shapes
> And phantoms from the crags and solid earth
> As fast as a musician scatters sounds
> Out of an instrument; and while the streams . . .
> Descending from the region of the clouds,
> And starting from the hollows of the earth
> More multitudinous every moment, rend
> Their way before them—what a joy to roam
> An equal among mightiest energies;
> And haply sometimes with articulate voice,
> Amid the deafening tumult, scarcely heard
> By him that utters it, exclaim aloud,
> 'Rage on, ye elements! let moon and stars
> Their aspects lend, and mingle in their turn
> With this commotion (ruinous though it be)
> From day to night, from night to day prolonged!'[11]

The same desire for identification with elemental Nature was shown by the painter Turner, who, in his old age, had himself lashed to the mast of a ship so that he could experience to the full the ferocity of a snowstorm at sea. This is how his painting *Snowstorm with a Steamship*, which is now in the National Gallery, originated.

Wordsworth believed in the sacredness of all living things;

Lermontov (copy by V. G. Pévrov of a portrait by Zabolotsky)

Beethoven (portrait by Gorbunov)

moreover, there were times when all things seemed to him to be alive:

> To every natural form, rock, fruit or flower,
> Even the loose stones that cover the high-way,
> I gave a moral life, I saw them feel,
> Or link'd them to some feeling: the great mass
> Lay bedded in a quickening soul, and all
> That I beheld, respired with inward meaning.[12]

In another passage of *The Prelude* he tells us how he felt the sentiment of Being spread "over all that moves, and all seemeth still", and in the same poem he refers to the "pulse of Being"[13] and thus echoes an idea of Plotinus that had probably reached him through Coleridge.[14] Once again Neo-Platonism and Romanticism proved to be kindred outlooks on life.

An equally striking analogy exists between Wordsworth's intellectual attitude on the one hand and Bishop Berkeley's philosophical idealism on the other. For, like Berkeley a hundred years before him, Wordsworth too refused to accept the mechanical materialism of eighteenth-century science.[15] He believed that science had transformed "this beauteous world" into a mere laboratory of unrelated studies. Moreover, the scientist's dry mathematical approach had left no room for the imagination, and worst of all their materialism had led to the denial of the human soul. To the cold abstraction of science Wordsworth opposed his own vivid and concrete experience. Coleridge, Novalis and other Romantics adopted a similar attitude to modern science. In *L'ultimo canto di Saffo*, Leopardi deplored the fact that Nature had been reduced to an "object of study". And Keats, who so greatly admired Wordsworth, in his poem *Lamia*, poured scorn on Isaac Newton for having ungoddessed the rainbow:

> For the sage,
> Let spear-grass and the spiteful thistle wage
> War on his temples. Do not all charms fly
> At the mere touch of cold philosophy?
> There was an awful rainbow once in heaven:
> We know her woof, her texture; she is given
> In the dull catalogue of common things.

> Philosophy will clip an Angel's wings,
> Conquer all mysteries by rule and line,
> Empty the haunted air, and gnomed mine—
> Unweave a rainbow, as it erewhile made
> The tender-person'd Lamia melt into a shade.

Shelley saw Wordsworth as a healing power against the spirit of natural science. It is against the eighteenth-century background of mechanical materialism and shallow Deism, in which the God of Nature had been little more than an intellectual abstraction, that Wordsworth with his revivification stands out as a champion of spirituality. We may conjecture that this was in Cardinal Newman's mind when he numbered Wordsworth among the harbingers of the spiritual awakening of his time. On the other hand, Coleridge called Wordsworth a 'semi-atheist', a judgment based on the undeniable fact that in Wordsworth's earlier—and poetically glorious—years Christianity meant very little to him.

Anglicanism never vitally gripped his imagination: the dry latitudinarianism prevalent at Cambridge in his student days had no appeal for him, and that he had nothing but scorn for the compulsory attendance at College Chapel is shown in the first version of *The Prelude*, where he mocks at the College authorities:

> be wise
> Ye Presidents and Deans, and to your Bells
> Give seasonable rest; for 'tis a sound
> Hollow as ever vex'd the tranquil air;
> And your officious doings bring disgrace
> On the plain Steeples of our English Church
> Whose worship 'mid the remotest village trees
> Suffers for this.[16]

Nor was Wordsworth at any time influenced by the Evangelical revival. Until 1805, his religion consisted essentially in the worship of Nature. Even in *The Excursion* the finest parts are not those which are specifically Christian, but rather those in which he was still able to draw upon the intensity of his experience as a worshipper of Nature.[17] Time and again it had been Nature that, in a cathartic manner, had revived and restored his weary soul, as is described in *The Prelude*:

> it is shaken off,
> As by miraculous gift 'tis shaken off,
> That burthen of my own unnatural self,
> The heavy weight of many a weary day
> Not mine, and such as were not made for me.[18]

Moreover, it was Nature to which he had fled to soothe his *Weltschmerz* in the early 1790s: Nature, and Nature alone, had filled the spiritual void created by the shipwreck of his hopes in the French Revolution as well as by his disillusionment with Godwin's philosophy, and last but not least personal vicissitudes. Significantly, Nature—or the Universe, to which he also attributed infinite wisdom—almost invariably appeared to Wordsworth in the shape of a beneficent goddess. If Coleridge was too severe when he called his friend a 'semi-atheist', he was far nearer the mark when he referred to Wordsworth's "vague, misty rather than mystic, confusion of God with the world", a trait which he regarded as unhealthful.[19] It is hard to avoid the impression that Wordsworth evaded the challenge of definite questions of belief. For all his dedication to the causes of Nature and Poetry, there is something non-committal about his religious emotions.

From about 1805 onwards, Wordsworth seems to have sensed the inadequacy of his religious attitude. The death by drowning of his beloved brother John, in the February of that year, brought him closer to Christianity, and some of his friends, notably Sir George Beaumont and the Quaker Thomas Clarkson, were working in the same direction. Henceforth he came to include more and more Christian thought and sentiment in his poetry. His Christianity, however, did not carry nearly as much conviction as his naturalistic religion had done. His Christian poetry is decidedly inferior to the poetry of the *Lyrical Ballads* and the early *Prelude*. Not only was his creative power largely spent, but theological difficulties were pressing on his mind. For one thing, he found himself unable to reconcile the Divine prescience with accountability in man.[20] More disturbing still were his recurring doubts about personal survival. Six years before his death, he declared in a melancholy vein: "The spirituality of my nature does not expand and rise the nearer I approach the grave."

It was Wordsworth's poetic nature-worship, and not his Christian poetry, that made a deep and lasting impression on contemporaries and posterity alike. According to Shelley, who worshipped at the same shrine, the religion of Nature was of all religious systems the one that was immortal. Matthew Arnold, like Shelley before him, spoke of Wordsworth's healing power, and John Morley extolled the last half of Book IV of *The Excursion* as "real religion". Haydon's portrait of Wordsworth musing upon Helvellyn, which is now in the National Portrait Gallery, made Elizabeth Barrett Browning compose a sonnet in which Wordsworth appears as

> poet-priest
> By the high altar, singing prayer and prayer
> To the high Heavens.

John Ruskin's and Leslie Stephen's mystery of mountains, so characteristic a trait of their writings about the Alps, is yet another legacy of Wordsworth. Many others too, but in particular Germans and Austrians in the late nineteenth and early twentieth centuries, often confused the exhilaration of mountain-climbing with the fervour of religious experience. Basil Willey suggests that in England the Wordsworthian faith, or habit of mind, became during that period the most considerable alternative or rival to orthodox Christianity.[21] This would probably not be true of other European countries where that role fell rather to nationalism, but even there some of those who had lost God in church rediscovered Him in what Wordsworth called "the solemn temples" of mountains. In the midst of the most impressive mountain scenery in Europe, at Montenvers, near Chamonix, above the Mer de Glace, nature enthusiasts as far back as 1795 even erected a so-called 'Temple de la Nature'.

Nature worship, reminiscent of, and indeed influenced by, Wordsworth did not remain confined to this side of the Atlantic. Among its American exponents, Henri David Thoreau, the author of *Walden*, deserves our special attention. He belonged to the so-called Transcendentalists, a group of American writers centred round R. W. Emerson whose outlook on life, with its marked opposition to the Enlightenment, shared many of its features with the European Romantic Movement. Coleridge, Carlyle, but also Wordsworth, undoubtedly influenced the American movement.

Thoreau's name immediately conjures up that of his birthplace, Concord, a large village formerly named Musketaquid or 'Grassground River'. This is where, in April 1775, the first shot was fired in the American War of Independence. Although in the New World in general, Nature, in the words of an English traveller, "has outlined her words on a larger scale" than in Europe, the quiet beauty of the New England landscape round Concord, with its lakes, woods and hills, would seem to bear resemblance to the Wordsworth country. The English poet's above-mentioned *Guide to the Lakes* finds its parallel in Thoreau's plan to depict the natural history of Massachusetts, a region he rightly regarded as a highly favoured centre for natural observation. In his masterpiece, and especially in his copious *Journals* (published posthumously in 1906), Thoreau proved to be one of the best interpreters of American fauna, flora and weather. Few could equal his intimate knowledge of nature's calendar or the sensitivity of his ear for what he called "the music of the seasons".

Like Wordsworth, Thoreau had been fond of outdoor life ever since his boyhood and was also a redoubtable walker. He tells us that he never felt well unless he could spend at least four hours a day sauntering through the woods and over the hills and fields.[22] In a characteristic digression he reminds his readers that "to saunter" is etymologically derived from "idle people who roved about the country, in the Middle Ages, and asked charity, under pretence of going à la Saint-Terre, till the children exclaimed, 'There goes a Saint-Terrer', a Saunterer—a Holy-Lander." Thoreau believed that "it required a direct dispensation from Heaven to become a walker". "The chivalric heroic spirit which once belonged to the Rider," he remarked, "seems now to reside in, or perchance to have subsided into, the Walker—not the Knight, but Walker Errant."

Perhaps he did not travel quite as light as Wordsworth or Coleridge, for according to Emerson he carried under his arms an old music-book to press plants, and in his pocket his diary and pencil, a spyglass for birds, a microscope, jack-knife and twine. On his rambles he wore a straw hat, stout shoes and strong grey trousers to brave the fiercest of shrubs and to climb a tree for a hawk's or squirrel's nest. Thoreau, who was of mixed French and Scottish origin—his paternal ancestors hailed from Tours—was short, firmly built, fair complexioned, with strong, serious eyes and a grave expression, his face in later years covered with what Emerson described as "a becoming beard".[23] His remarkable physical prowess, which lasted until the age of forty, stood him in good stead when after an inconclusive attempt at schoolmastering he worked as a surveyor and later when he became, in his own words, "a self-appointed inspector of snow-storms and rain-storms". Although he did not always spurn human company, on his long walks he preferred solitude even more emphatically than Wordsworth. "My desire," he wrote, "to commune with the spirit of the Universe . . . is perennial and constant." Moreover he pretended to be a mystic: "I am a mystic, a Transcendentalist, and a natural philosopher to boot." In the best Wordsworthian tradition he declared the earth to be "all alive and covered with feelers of sensation", and in his first book, *A Week on the Concord and Merrimack Rivers*, described the sense of Being that allied him to the whole Universe. The doctrine of pan-psychism and the sentiment of empathy are indeed among the outstanding features of his outlook on life. Like several of the English Romantics, he deplored the fact that science had left no room for delight amidst all the wonders of Nature. Though an acute and careful observer of Nature, he felt "that it is not the fact that imports, but the impression of the fact on your mind".

In his religious outlook Thoreau was decidedly not a Christian. Hindu mysticism had a stronger appeal for him, but by and large it was the Wordsworthian type of Nature worship which he accepted for himself. As for Wordsworth, so for him, the serenity of Nature provided an antidote to disillusionment and despair. The pantheistic element was more marked in Thoreau, but even he was conscious of "the greater Benefactor and Intelligence that stands . . . over the human insect".[24]

His yearning for wild, untamed nature was immense. "In wildness," he proclaimed, "is the preservation of the world." And again:

> When I consider that the nobler animals have been extermin-
> ated here—the cougar, the panther, lynx, wolverine, wolf, bear,
> moose, deer, the beaver, the turkey etc. etc.—I cannot but feel
> as if I lived in a tamed, and as it were emasculated country.

And he added melancholically:

> Is it not a maimed and imperfect nature that I am conversant
> with?

In the very recent past the wilderness—of which he was catch-
ing the last glimpse—had been undisturbed, but now Nature was
already fighting a losing battle against the artifices of civilization, and in true Romantic fashion Thoreau's sympathy was on
the side of the lost cause.[25] The wild and primitive character of
large regions of the United States had appealed to the English
landscape painter Thomas Cole, who emigrated to Ohio in 1819;
in Europe, he felt, man had gone too far in domesticating the elements.[26] But now America was going the same way—only much
faster. Complaining that the axe was always destroying his forest
Thoreau exclaimed:

> Thank God, they cannot cut down the clouds!

> All kinds of figures are drawn on the blue ground with the
> fibrous white-paint.

New York, not surprisingly, horrified him:

> I walked through New York yesterday and met no real and
> living person. . . . When will the world learn that a million men
> are of no importance compared with one man?

The Romantic reaction to mass civilization is epitomized in this
outcry. Naturally, Thoreau showed much interest in the indigenous Indian tribes and their relics. The virtual extermination of the
'noble savage' was a matter of deep concern for him, as it had been
for Lenau,[27] or for the painter George Catlin, who, in 1841,
brought out his book on *The Manners, Customs and Conditions of
the North American Indians.*

The highlight of Thoreau's life was his symbolic retirement to the edge of Walden Pond. True, the withdrawal from the world was only temporary and lasted for little over two years. At the age of thirty—when Wordsworth had only just settled at Dove Cottage—Thoreau had already returned to civilization. Nor had his seclusion at Walden been either remote or completely isolated, for the Pond was within easy walking distance from the village. Many visitors made the pilgrimage to Walden, where this modern Diogenes lived in a one-roomed cabin, built almost single-handed, and so small that even a single visitor had to sit on a chair outside the door of the sanctuary. For much of the time, though, the hermit was undisturbed and could indulge in the closest communion with Nature and the Universe. Nevertheless, it seems that Thoreau's retirement was prompted primarily by his desire to write *Walden*, and present in the form of a day-to-day autobiographical sketch his ideas about Nature and modern civilization, which in his view had created so many unnecessary desires and demands.[28] Not even in his wildest moments did Thoreau cherish the hope that many of his fellow citizens would, even temporarily, abandon civilization to turn into ascetic and celibate nature worshippers like himself. He held to the typical Romantic postulate that each man should follow the lead of his own emotional impulses.

Rather late in his comparatively short span of life he joined in the battle against slavery, whose final abolition he did not live to see. Extreme physical exertion or exposure to the elements made him succumb to an attack of tuberculosis in the spring of 1862, and he lies buried, with his friends Emerson, Hawthorne and the Alcotts, in the beautiful Sleepy Hollow Cemetery at Concord.

His impact is hard to assess. Mahatma Gandhi, for one, gained inspiration from *Walden*. But although this book, in all its eccentricities, was widely read, late nineteenth-century America was too buoyant in its expansionism to be seriously disturbed by Thoreau's warnings. But perhaps the super-civilization of the United States may yet experience something like a Thoreau renaissance.

CHAPTER EIGHTEEN

Metaphysical Intoxication

'PHILOSOPHIA ancilla theologiae' had been the old saying current at a time when theology was still revered as the Queen of the sciences. With the gradual undermining, and eventual collapse, of so many hierarchies, that subordination of philosophy too came to an end. During the Age of Enlightenment, theology was scorned, and the crown passed on to rational and scientific philosophy. To prove this point one need only consider the small space given to theological problems in Pierre Bayle's *Dictionnaire* or the *Grande Encyclopédie*. The Romantic Movement gave rise to a new situation. It was then that new irrational philosophies sprang up which boldly, or surreptitiously, encroached upon theological territory. In Protestant Germany especially, the *mystique* that had previously attached to transcendental religion now came to be usurped by a hybrid brand of metaphysics. It was that state of affairs which Nietzsche had in mind when he described German philosophy as "a cunningly camouflaged theology".[1] A more recent critic has spoken in this context of a "Revelation without a revealing Deity".[2]

The philosopher Georg Wilhelm Friedrich Hegel, the "theologian *malgré lui*" as he has been called, obviously springs to mind. Yet although Hegel must be regarded as the most influential metaphysician of his time, he did not, or not quite, belong to the Romantic Movement. A decidedly anti-Romantic feature of his thought was that he tended to glorify the present as "the fruitful moment or καιρος given to his generation that it might consummate the work of earlier periods".[3] Thus we are left with the three great German Romantic metaphysicians, Fichte, Schopenhauer and Schelling. Fichte's subjectivist excesses, so characteristic of early Romanticism, have already been touched upon in an earlier chapter of this study. We have also, not without a sensation of dizziness, followed Schopenhauer on his flight of fantasy, which, among other weird ideas, made him postulate the existence of a transcendental yet non-divine Will-to-live. However, it was Friedrich Wilhelm Joseph Schelling, the most all-embracing if also most abstruse of those three thinkers who undoubtedly was cast for the role of the Romantic philosopher *par excellence*. At the beginning of the present chapter our attention will be focused mainly on one aspect of Schelling's mind: namely, his self-intoxication through metaphysical speculation. It will be well to bear in mind that Russia as well as Germany had those who craved for this kind of intellectual stimulant.

Whereas Hegel attempted, and partially succeeded, to construct one single philosophical edifice, Schelling, with characteristic restlessness, conceived six or seven metaphysical systems, each of them on a grandiose scale. The earliest of them, his so-called *Naturphilosophie*, is of special interest to the student of European Romanticism in that it offers some striking analogies with ideas voiced during the same decade (1797–1806) by Wordsworth.[4] In a similar vein, Schelling, in his lectures at Jena, launched an all-out attack upon the mechanistic science of the eighteenth century. In that campaign he was strongly supported by other German Romantics, notably Novalis and August Wilhelm Schlegel. But Goethe too, engaged as he was in a philosophical battle against some of Newton's ideas, welcomed young Schelling as an ally. It was not until 1817, the tercentenary of the Reformation in Germany, that Goethe openly turned against Schelling's efforts to re-introduce outworn religious ideas "under a mystical-pantheistic and abstruse philosophical cloak".[5]

As to Wordsworth, so to Schelling, everything in Nature seemed to be alive. The inorganic he regarded as the extinguished product of a lower form of life, a kind of petrified intelligence. In a dazzling aphorism he called Nature 'das werdende Ich', the self which is in the process of becoming. In other words, Nature was to be understood as the embodiment of a process by which the spirit tends to rise to a consciousness of itself. In passing we note that similar ideas, albeit with markedly Christian overtones, came to be expressed in our time by the daring Catholic thinker Pierre Teilhard de Chardin in his remarkable book *The Phenomenon of Man*.

Nor can it be denied that Schelling's writings on *Naturphiloso-*

phie, as indeed most of his later works, contain brilliant flashes of intuition. The very attempt to integrate modern scientific knowledge and the new type of philosophy was in itself awe-inspiring. However, the groundwork for that Herculean venture of the mind proved to be lamentably inadequate. After all, even an exceedingly precocious young man of twenty-one years of age could hardly be expected to master all the mathematics, physics, chemistry and medicine of his day in a matter of two years, as the young genius confidently believed he had done in the course of his studies at Leipzig University (1796–8). Small wonder that he had to take refuge in bold and sometimes fantastic hypotheses to conceal his lack of detailed knowledge, or, for that matter, of available evidence. With the painstaking progress of experimental physics he had little patience, and this is why he announced his intention to provide "wings for our slow-moving physics". The flight on which his mind embarked with the help of those wings unfolded before him an *a priori* vista of Nature to which he felt man was entitled because of the assumed affinity between nature and spirit.

While still at Leipzig, Schelling published his *Ideen zu einer Philosophie der Natur* (1797). Next he tried out his new ideas in a spectacular course of lectures at Jena,[6] and brought out his pantheistic treatise *Von der Weltseele* which was in keeping with the prevalent emotional approach to religion. Finally, at the ripe age of twenty-four, he presented the world with his pretentious *Einleitung zu einem Entwurf eines Systems der Philosophie*. All through these writings he makes great play, in a manner sometimes referred to as logical manipulation, with notions such as 'attraction' 'repulsion', 'polarity', 'excitability' and so forth, without taking the trouble to give anything like a clear-cut definition of those terms. Some years ago, an eminent Polish philosopher of science, Leo Chwistek, rightly chided the obnoxious tendency, on the part of Hegel as well as of the German Romantic philosophers, to exploit the vagueness of concepts for purposes of their own.[7] As far as Schelling was concerned, the higher his imaginary wings carried him into the rarefied atmosphere of abstraction and speculative intuition, the more dimly he perceived reality until he almost lost sight of it altogether. However, and this is what matters, he still continued to pontificate about it.

The branch of science which was most adversely affected by the impact of Schelling's *Naturphilosophie* was undoubtedly medicine. Here the wanton play with supposed analogies—as for example between gouty nodes and flower buds—but above all the high-handed neglect of empirical investigations, had truly disastrous effects. In Kieser's *System der Medizin*, published at Halle in 1817, of 130 pages devoted to general diagnosis, only twenty-four related to practical observations; the remaining 106 were given to theories about the meaning of various symptoms in relation to the general nature of disease. The author of the textbook, who was professor of pathology at Jena, took his cue from Schelling's emphasis on the polarity of such opposites as male and female, or of positive and negative electrical charges. Kieser thus arrived at the somewhat vague conclusion that health represented a balance of positive and negative spheres of life. Disease was supposed to result when some cause aroused the negative principle, and so disturbed the normal equilibrium between those mystical biological principles. On at least one occasion, Schelling's confidence in his medical proficiency was partly responsible for the death of a patient, Auguste Böhmer, daughter of Caroline, who later became Schelling's wife. Nevertheless, Landshut University two years later (1802) conferred upon him the honorary degree of doctor of medicine.

Indirectly, however, the system of thought known under the name of *Naturphilosophie* exacted a far heavier toll when German medical men, between about 1810 and 1840, fell under its spell and began to treat some of the patients under their care no better than quacks or charlatans might have done. This at any rate was the verdict of so eminent a scientist as Justus von Liebig, who, in the 1840s, went so far as to call the *Naturphilosophie* "the black death of our century". Later on other leading scientists, such as Helmholtz and Heinrich Hertz, were to reach the conclusion that under its impact German medical science had fallen behind English and French standards of the time.[8] The explorer Alexander von Humboldt had to warn German chemists to fight shy of the type of "chemistry in which you do not wet your hands". Even in the realm of botany the pernicious influence of Schelling's excessive speculation made itself felt. As for German medical science, it would appear that it did not recover from its Romantic aberration until the late 1840s. Doctors and medical researchers outside Germany seem to have remained immune.

And yet, for all its aberrations and dangers, Schelling's impetuous *Naturphilosophie* obviously bears the mark of originality and genius. The contrast between youthful achievement and later frustration is again reminiscent of Wordsworth. Despite their occasional flashes of brilliance, Schelling's later pronouncements, both in his lectures and posthumously published writings, are signally lacking in spontaneity. As early as 1806, Friedrich Schlegel remarked perspicaciously: "Schelling certainly has excellent talents, but he belongs to those men who are quickly burnt up and extinguished, and whose best part is their fire of youth." Indeed, five or six years later Schelling, by then in his late thirties, was to pass through a crisis which affected his literary productivity in such a way that, from 1812 onwards, he never published another work. Perhaps it was not so much the fact that Schelling was prematurely "burnt up" that was at the bottom of the crisis, but rather his peculiar method of philosophizing which had so greatly relied both on intuitive flashes of thought as well as on hasty construction of abstract edifices. To maintain such an intellectual process at the same fever pitch would clearly become increasingly difficult with the advancing years.[9] But is that not another way of saying that a certain brand of Romanticism on the one hand, and middle age on the other, are incompatible notions?

In matters of religion, Schelling's attitude, oscillating as it did between faith and unbelief, was again typically Romantic. Born as the son of a Protestant parson in the small Swabian town of Leonberg and brought up, together with his seniors and friends Hegel and Hölderlin at the renowned Tübingen Stift, he soon developed a strong antipathy towards the Christian religion. At the age of twenty, he scornfully dubbed the Gospels "the dust of antiquity", a satirical venom that became even more marked in his long and bitter poem *Epikurisch Glaubensbekenntnis Heinz Widerporstens* (1798). His return to Christianity was slow and tortuous. Hindu mysticism provided a bridge when, in 1807, he fell under the spell of Friedrich Schlegel's enthusiastic treatise *Ueber die Sprache und Weisheit der Indier* which was to leave its mark on

Schelling's own *Philosophische Untersuchungen über das Wesen der menschlichen Freiheit* (1809). It is not easy to specify the date at which he again became a Christian, but some evidence points to the year 1809, when Schelling was thirty-four. The death in that year of his beloved wife Karoline, to whom he had been married since 1803, intensified his craving for survival after death, as was shown by the meditations contained in his imaginary conversation entitled *Clara, oder über den Zusammenhang der Natur mit der Geisterwelt*. However, the most potent single factor operating in the direction of Christianity was probably the impact made on his mind by the Renaissance mystic Jacob Boehme, to whose thought he had been introduced by Franz von Baader soon after his removal to Munich in 1806. Even previous to this was the deep interest he had shown in the theosophical writings of the Swabian pietist Friedrich Christoph Oetinger. Schelling's approach to Christianity always remained vague, undogmatic and highly emotional. Nevertheless, his reputation as a Christian philosopher increased steadily, and it was on that score that, in 1827, he was called to the newly founded University of Munich, and again fourteen years later to Berlin University. It was on the occasion of his inaugural lecture there that he posed the rhetorical question: "Shall the great and glorious movement of German philosophizing which started with Kant and bore so much that was great . . . end with the destruction of all great persuasions?" He hastened to declare his resolution that this must never be allowed to happen.

Schelling's intellectual quest for totality had by now reached its apex. Already in his *Vorlesungen über die Methode des akademischen Studiums*, delivered at Jena in 1802, he had stressed the interdependence of all branches of knowledge and had warned his students not to become bogged down in over-specialized studies. What they must never lose sight of was what he called "the totality of knowledge". At that time he had himself, as we have seen, made the brave attempt to encompass both philosophy and science. In the meantime, his return to Christianity had brought about a shift of interest from science to religion. By now the distinction between philosophy and theology had become blurred for him. It has been said of Schelling that, like his Romantic fellow-metaphysician Coleridge, he too longed to know metaphysically the Spirit of God.

When in 1816 he was invited to return to Jena and to take up a chair of philosophy there, his impatience with the artificial barriers between the faculties, and perhaps also his own dictatorial aspirations, made him reply that he would willingly accept on condition that he was also appointed, *honoris causa*, to a professorship of theology. It was largely due to Goethe's official intervention in his capacity as minister of Saxe-Weimar that Schelling's request was refused. Two years later Schelling accepted a call to Erlangen University where he stayed till 1827. While at Erlangen, but especially during the subsequent years at Munich and Berlin, he embarked on what must appear a rather over-ambitious synthesis of the two spheres of faith and knowledge. This applies to his *Philosophie der Mythologie* and the *Philosophie der Offenbarung* no less than to *Die Weltalter* which he had hoped would be his *magnum opus* and which inevitably remained a torso. The canvas of *Die Weltalter* is the widest imaginable. It encompasses the whole history of the Divine consciousness with the inclusion of that which came before the world and that which will be there after its end. All these writings clearly fall between two stools: their philosophy is flabby if not abstruse, and their theology full of theosophical speculation and on the whole heterodox even though it is announced as the very fulfilment of Christianity. In a characteristically grand sweep the entire history of Christendom is traced from the Catholic Church of Saint Peter via the Protestant Church of Saint Paul to the philosophical Church of Saint John the Evangelist, i.e. the Church of the Future of which Schelling poses as a kind of prophet. There is also in Schelling's later teaching a marked element of Gnosticism, as Jacob Burckhardt, then a student at Berlin University, was perhaps the first to point out when he wrote in the summer of 1842: "Schelling is a Gnostic in the proper sense of the word. Thence the uncanny, monstrous and shapeless in this part of his doctrine. I thought that at any moment some monstrous Asiatic God on twelve legs would come waddling in and with twelve arms take six hats off six heads. In the long run even the Berlin students will not be able to put up with this frightful, half-sensuous form of perception and expression."[10] Perhaps it was not surprising that Frenchmen like Benjamin Constant, who put so high a store by intellectual lucidity, found

Schelling's philosophy repulsive. Another Frenchman, Charles de Sainte-Foi, who visited him in Munich in 1831, even went so far as to call it "the last word in human aberration".

In the most important monograph on Schelling, written in 1954, on the occasion of the centenary of the philosopher's death, Karl Jaspers, after scrutinizing the questionable character of the very kernel of Schelling's philosophy, professes that his affection for Schelling is not greater than his antipathy towards him.[11] It would be less than honest were I to conceal the fact that my own antipathy outweighs my feeling of admiration. However, what I do admire in Schelling is twofold: in the first place, his attempt, however quixotic, at counteracting the atomization of knowledge, and secondly his realization of the fact that the loss of metaphysical reflection would be an unmitigated disaster. To quote his own words, from one of his Berlin lectures: "Without metaphysics, not only is there no philosophy, but also no religion, no art—all that would be lost if one altogether despaired of metaphysics."[12] On the other hand, there can be no doubt that Schelling's own high-handed and pseudo-prophetic use of metaphysics was largely responsible for producing an intellectual climate in which metaphysical systems have become suspect if, indeed, they are not held in utter disrepute. However, the intellectual climate is not immutable.

Romantic pseudo-prophets did not remain confined to Germany. But whereas in that country they tended to don the academic gown of the professor, would-be prophets elsewhere appeared in the guise of men of letters. The Scotsman Thomas Carlyle, who spent most of his long life in England, is a case in point. His debt to German Romantic metaphysicians was frankly acknowledged by him.[13] The fact that, in spite of his indebtedness, he believed himself essentially to be the enemy and destroyer of Romanticism need not detain us here. True, he was in many ways out of tune with the great English Romantics, but in the wider European context he should most certainly be regarded as a Romantic *malgré lui* in much the same way as Friedrich Nietzsche.

Like his German paragons, of whom he admired Fichte most,

Carlyle also encroached upon theological territory, and more important still, his mind too was imbued with secularized Protestant doctrine. For although in the course of his studies in Edinburgh his faith in Christianity was corroded and all but destroyed by the sceptical and empiricist doctrines of the eighteenth-century philosophers, Carlyle never entirely emancipated himself from the gloomy Calvinism of his youth. His early loss of faith is forcefully depicted in *Sartor Resartus*, which, while purporting to be the spiritual autobiography of a weird German professor by the grotesque name of Diogenes Teufelsdröckh, is in reality largely autobiographical. "For a pure moral nature," Carlyle's mouthpiece declares, "the loss of religious Belief was the loss of everything." And he continues: "To me the Universe was all void of Life, of Purpose, of Volition, even of Hostility: it was one huge, dead, immeasurable Steam-engine, rolling on, in its dead indifference to grind me limb from limb. Why was the Living banished thither companionless, conscious?" Carlyle himself, no less than his imaginary German metaphysician, even contemplated suicide, from which, we are told, he was held back by a certain 'aftershine' of Christianity.

Having thus poignantly experienced the darkness of nihilism, Carlyle's soul was fervently longing for a spiritual rebirth. For a considerable time his yearning remained vague and nebulous, and like many of his contemporaries he felt nostalgia for past ages when men had still been imbued with a living faith. It was from that sentiment that there arose the historical portrait, included in *Past and Present*, of Abbot Samson of St. Edmunds, the medieval English prelate. Previous to this he had already attributed all great events to what he chose to call 'heroes', in whom he saw the successive embodiments of divine revelation. This conception was most probably influenced by Fichte's *Grundzüge des gegenwärtigen Zeitalters*[14] as well as by the Calvinist doctrine of 'the elect'.

In his lectures on *Heroes, Hero-Worship and the Heroic in History*, delivered in London in 1840, "transcendental admiration of great men" (the expression is Carlyle's) clearly emerges as an *ersatz* religion, for Carlyle refers to it as "the most solacing fact one sees in the world at present". Strange though it may seem, the appeal of Carlyle's new 'religion' was considerable.[15] Who then were his heroes? The list strikes one as rather heterogeneous. Some of them were religious figures, such as Mahomet, Luther, John Knox, and, oddly enough the Nordic mythical deity Odin, but admission to Carlyle's Valhalla was also granted to such secular categories as "the hero as poet" (e.g. Dante and Shakespeare), "the hero as man of letters" (e.g. Dr. Johnson, Rousseau, Burns and Goethe), and "the hero as statesman" (e.g. Cromwell and Napoleon). We may note in passing that in the very year of Carlyle's lectures on heroes, French hero-worship of the Emperor received a momentous expression in the transfer of Napoleon's remains from St. Helena to the Dôme des Invalides in Paris. To return to Carlyle, in the long run it was undoubtedly the political men of destiny that exerted the greatest fascination on his mind. In his highly documented biography of the great Puritan hero, entitled *Cromwell's Letters and Speeches*, hero-worship reaches such an intensity that Cromwell must be proved right every time, whether against Cavaliers, Roundheads or Irish. Similarly, in his eight-volume *History of Friedrich II of Prussia called Frederick the Great*, his eulogy of the King necessitates different standards of judgment as applied to Frederick and his opponents: for example, a treaty broken by the King becomes "a kind of provisional off-and-on treaty", and so forth.

The more Carlyle idolized the authoritarian rulers of the past, the firmer grew his conviction that the panacea for the world's ills lay in despotism. With increasing vehemence the sage of Chelsea (for this he had become) fulminated, from his soundproof study, against all those who failed to realize mankind's need for an autocratic ruler. Whereas in his earlier writings, notably in his highly perceptive *Chartism* (1829) but also in *Past and Present* he had sponsored the cause of the poor and had shown as much respect for the mass of people as did Charles Dickens, that sentiment later turned into violent contempt. In the end, the obnoxious idea of the totality of power to be put into the hands of a dictator became an obsession with Carlyle, so that Ernst Cassirer was not unfair when he pointed out that "perhaps no other philosophical doctrine has done so much to pave the way for the modern ideals of political leadership as did Carlyle's later political doctrine".[16] However, with equal justification, Cassirer rejected too close an analogy between Carlyle's thought and the ideologies of Fascism and Nazism. An essential distinction between Carlyle and twentieth-century exponents of totalitarianism lies in the cynicism of the latter and their utter disregard for truth, an attitude deeply repugnant to Carlyle. It is therefore somewhat misleading to go so far as to identify 'romantic authoritarianism' with Fascist and Nazi thought, as T. E. Utley and J. Stuart Maclure have done in a publication entitled *Documents of Modern Political Thought* (1957). For such a terminology does not allow sufficiently for the perversion which nineteenth-century doctrines, however odious in themselves, still had to undergo before totalitarian practitioners were able to make use of them for their own ends.[17]

CHAPTER NINETEEN

National Messianism

POLISH Romanticism has hitherto hardly been touched upon in this study. Yet it is undeniable that Poland contributed more than its share to the European Romantic symposium. If it were our object to study European Romanticism country by country, the three greatest Polish Romantic poets, Mickiewicz, Słowacki and Krasiński, would claim our attention in almost equal proportions. As it is, the present chapter will be focused on Adam Mickiewicz alone, and this for the reason that he, more than any of his contemporaries, may be said to have embodied that highly questionable but peculiarly Romantic concept of national messianism.

This is not to maintain that Mickiewicz did not entertain other Romantic ideals as well. Above all else, his hero-worship, focused mainly on Napoleon I, reached almost the same intensity as that of Carlyle. The sight of the Emperor with his *Grande Armée* (which included some Polish legions) passing through Mickiewicz's birthplace in the summer of 1812 and posing as the liberator of the Poles, filled young Mickiewicz—he was then in his fourteenth year—with great and lasting enthusiasm. Indeed, later on in life he was to become one of the foremost exponents of the Napoleon legend, so much so that he extended his adulation even to Napoleon III. Since mention has been made of Carlyle, it may be pertinent to point out that there existed a further analogy between those two thinkers. For just as Carlyle's political thought, ominous though it was, should not be confused with Fascism or Nazism, so neither should Mickiewicz's fervent patriotism be identified with the ultra-nationalism of the late nineteenth or the twentieth century. For unlike our latter-day chauvinists, he firmly rejected all manner of egoism among nations and always attempted to harmonize the cause of his beloved Polish nation with that of humanity. Despite the fact that in his younger days he had experienced a political trial and subsequent deportation at the hands of the Russians, his attitude towards that nation was by no means intransigently hostile. For he genuinely strove to comprehend all that was alien, and for that reason refrained from wholesale condemnation or contempt.

Yet, for all those provisos, Mickiewicz clearly idolized his own nation, and indeed went so far as to regard them as God's Chosen People. Before examining the positive foundations for his belief, we may legitimately enquire on what grounds the candidature of other modern nations was repudiated by him. Although, in the manner of the Slavophils, he found a great deal that was praiseworthy in agrarian Russia, he was appalled by the fact that in that country an unhampered growth of free human beings was wellnigh impossible. St. Petersburg in particular, where he had been living for some time, struck him as the symbol of an artificial and sub-human element in Russian life. As for the British, they seemed to Mickiewicz totally absorbed in the quest for sea-power, while the Germans—more than one hundred years prior to the *Wirtschaftswunder*—were supposed to be imbued by an exaggerated *Brotsinn,* as he called it, which obviously implied an almost exclusive preoccupation with their material standard of living, a strange enough comment coming so soon after Madame de Staël's (equally exaggerated) diagnosis of the Germans as the nation of poets and thinkers. Mickiewicz's attitude to France was more complex. He often spoke of the humanitarian mission of the French nation, but was all the more disillusioned with the bourgeois philistinism and materialism of Louis Philippe's monarchy which he castigated as fiercely as did his French confrères. Political disenchantment entered into it, for after their unsuccessful rising against Russia, in 1830–1, a large number of Polish refugees had chosen 'revolutionary' France precisely in memory of Napoleon I and the Polish legions. They had hoped to be able to resume the struggle from France, or at least to await such an occasion as military formations, but the cautious policy of Louis Philippe's régime had frustrated all their efforts. By the spring of 1832 it had become clear that the dream of creating Polish legions on French soil had to be abandoned. The emigrant army henceforward degenerated into a mass of displaced persons. It seemed that the French, for all their revolutionary past, had sadly betrayed their role as champions of humanity.

Although the term 'messianism' as applied to a particular nation was new—significantly it was the Polish mystical philosopher Hoene Wronski who coined it—the concept of a Chosen People evidently goes back to Antiquity when both Persians and Jews claimed that supernatural distinction for themselves. In passing we may note that, at the height of their power in the Middle Ages the Arabs arrogated the same role to themselves. A closer parallel to the Polish claim of the early nineteenth century might be seen in Fichte's exorbitant claims for the German nation[1] made at the time of Prussia's grave humiliation at the hands of Napoleon. Some defeated nations, so it would seem, require an especially potent fillip to sustain their morale.

The Poles seemed to Mickiewicz to be destined for the role of God's Chosen People on more than one ground. In the first place, they had steadfastly clung to their religious faith in an era during which other European nations had turned idolizers of more mundane matters. Furthermore they had, or so he believed, shown themselves to be peace-loving and anxious to work for the ideal of international reconciliation. Their previous constitution might even be regarded as the model for a future world government.[2] For all those reasons, so the argument ran, the Poles deserved a divine reward. However, the crux of the matter lay elsewhere: namely in the supposed analogy between the suffering of Christ and that of the Polish nation. Whereas at the time of the outbreak of the Polish revolt Mickiewicz had looked upon Polish martyrdom as pointless—his poem 'To a Polish Mother' is proof of that—he later came to believe in the mystical ransom of his nation's blood. Once the fantastic Christological analogy was accepted, it was possible to claim that the Polish nation had passed through experiences resembling the Stations of the Cross, and also that Poland's final partition of 1795 might be compared to Christ's first day in the Holy Sepulchre, and the crushing of her revolt in 1831 to the second day. As for the third day, which was to see Poland's resurrection, it was expected in the near future. At all events Poland's agony appeared to the Polish messianists as a momentous step towards the redemption of mankind. If Christ's Passion, Death and Resurrection had made the human individual alive to his own immortality, one of the nations had to experience suffering, extinction and the conquest of death before nations in general became conscious of their own sanctity and immortality. It was Poland's special privilege to have been chosen for the role of martyr among nations. The emphasis on the inevitability of suffering, which we have found to have been a pivotal Romantic concept, could not be illustrated more vividly.

At the time of the outbreak of the revolt in November 1830, Mickiewicz, who had been living in the West since the previous year, happened to be in Italy. Whatever the purveyors of the Mickiewicz legend may or may not declare, the fact remains that he did not hurry back to the battlefield. In point of fact, apart from a brief stay in the province of Poznan in 1831, he never reached Polish territory at all. However, when after a lapse of several months he eventually arrived at Dresden, the gloomy impression of Polish refugees streaming into the city probably accentuated his qualms about his own passivity during the ordeal. Now his patriotic passion became inflamed to fever pitch. Not having taken up his sword, he now took up his pen—with a vengeance—and in an amazingly short space of time produced the most impressive Polish Romantic work, the dramatic poem *Forefathers' Eve, Part III*, which has rightly been termed a national Passion play. The period of his highest creativity was almost as short as Wordsworth's and Coleridge's *annus mirabilis*: it lasted from 1832 to

1834. Before it was over, Mickiewicz also brought out what may be regarded as the Bible of Polish messianism, i.e. the *Books of the Polish Nation and of the Polish Pilgrimage*, one of the finest specimens of rhythmical prose in the language. In content and style not uninfluenced by Lamennais, the *Books* in their turn intensified the Abbé's own fervour and are believed to have left their imprint on his explosive *Paroles d'un Croyant*.

There can be little doubt that, in spite of its Christian inspiration and frequent allusions to Christianity, the national messianism or "religion of the fatherland" preached in the *Books of the Polish Nation and of the Polish Pilgrimage* was to all intents and purposes a substitute religion. The relapse from world religions to narrower types of national religions, or religions of nationalism, had already begun, although the most sinister stages of that development lay as yet in the future.

It is characteristic of man's nature to cherish those things most which, at one time possessed, are now irretrievably lost. Uprooted persons often display an especially marked craving for attachment: hence the often vociferous patriotism of exiles. Mickiewicz was a case in point. As far as his fatherland was concerned he knew only very small parts of it, not more than a restricted area of his native Lithuania—the scene of his epic poem *Pan Tadeusz*—and a few districts in Poznan. It should also be borne in mind that by the time of his birth, in 1798, Poland had vanished from the political map of Europe. Moreover, the element of the *déraciné* in Mickiewicz may have been accentuated by his maternal ancestry, for there is strong reason to believe that his mother was partly of Jewish origin.[3] According to his friend Branicki, Mickiewicz informed him: "My father was of Masovian origin, my mother came of a family of baptized Jews named Majewski. I am, therefore, half a Lechite, half an Israelite, and I am proud of it."[4] He strengthened his association with the Jews, firstly by marrying Celina, a girl of Jewish origin and daughter of the renowned pianist Maria Szymanowska, and later by planning the formation of a Jewish legion in the Crimean War. Is it too fanciful to suggest that the Jewish concept of the Chosen People still appealed to Mickiewicz although he regarded the Old Testament as superseded by the New?

George Sand, who came to know him well, commented on his personality in these words: "I have met several men who might be called minor ecstatics, but Mickiewicz is the only great ecstatic I know. . . . He is neither unbalanced nor a poseur. He is a big-hearted man, full of genius and enthusiasm, completely master of himself, and able to maintain his own point of view with poise and logic. But sometimes he is carried away by the nature of his beliefs, by the violence of his elemental instincts, and by the sympathy he feels for the misfortune of his country. . . ."[5]

It was during the early 1830s that Mickiewicz became increasingly conscious of being the spiritual leader of his nation, but the prodigious *élan* of his soul, diagnosed by George Sand, produced in him the yearning for an even more exalted role. There is indeed reason to believe that the "Saviour of our land", alluded to in *Forefathers' Eve, Part III*, was meant to be none other than the poet himself. This was, at any rate, what he intimated to his friend Goszczyński in 1839, not without adding that the idea had not come to him from conceit, as he was fully aware of the sacrifice demanded of such a man. Certain events in his own life appeared to him in the light of mystical portents of his great mission: notably, his birth on the Christmas Eve of 1798, the year the last Polish King died, and also some occurrence during the political trial and persecution in which he had been involved together with other innocent youths.

However, Mickiewicz—like Lamennais—was craving for a more palpable sign from heaven: in other words for a miracle. It is at this point that the tense drama of his life's story for a time takes on the character of tragi-comedy, although even at the present time idolizers of Mickiewicz who like to regard him as the unblemished symbol of their nation may be loath to admit it. For the substitute religions, not to be outdone by Christianity, have their own hagiographies. In the case of Mickiewicz, the facts themselves are only too painfully obvious. As has happened in other cases, his own mystical inspiration dried up, but the feeling of exaltation remained, and as a result the overcredulous man fell a prey to a subtle mystification. There was, to start with, the longed for 'miracle'. His wife Celina had for some time past been affected by a severe mental illness. Now, a short, stocky, bespectacled man by the name of Andrzej Towiańksi who had arrived in Paris from Lithuania contrived by means of hypnotism to cure Celina, or so it seemed. At the same time Towiański pretended to be a clairvoyant The charlatan—for that is what he was—went even so far as to declare that he himself was God's third emissary, after Christ, who had brought mankind the Gospel of love, and Napoleon, who ought to have brought fraternity to the nations but somehow failed in the task. On other occasions Towiański emphasized his role as the Messiah of the Slavs. By the middle of the century, he prophesied, God's Kingdom on earth would be inaugurated with the help of the three Chosen Nations: namely, the Jews, the French and the Poles. Towiański's teaching, if such it can be called, consisted of an unwholesome cocktail of ideas distilled from Catholicism, Christian as well as Hindu mysticism, and Bonapartism, with a liberal seasoning of age-old Lithuanian superstitions. It did not take the Vatican long to repudiate 'Towianism' as a heresy. Mickiewicz, however, completely succumbed to the Lithuanian magus's spell and became one of his leading apostles. During Towiański's absence from France he even undertook to take over the temporary leadership of the sect, whose following was not inconsiderable. Worse still, from 1842 onwards he increasingly confused the two spheres of scholarship and mysticism in his Paris lectures on comparative Slavonic literature: an interesting parallel to Schelling's lectures in Berlin held at the same time. What eventually decided Louis Philippe's government to terminate his lecture courses was that, besides extolling Towiański and his ideas, he had also shown himself to be a fervent exponent of the Napoleon cult. Some Polish *émigrés*, on the other hand, never trusted Towiański. In fact there was an insistent rumour to the effect that he was a cleverly disguised Tsarist agent. Mickiewicz's poetic rival, Julius Słowacki, openly attacked him in one of his poems, virtually calling him a swindler. Eventually Mickiewicz himself saw the light and, after a long period of hesitation, finally repudiated Towiański. If the whole episode may be taken to prove anything at all, it surely exposes the danger inherent in excessive irrationalism, Romantic or otherwise.

Like Lamennais whom he resembled in so many ways, Mickiewicz henceforward turned to political journalism, and in that capacity championed the cause of the common people, a trend of thought that will be analysed briefly in the following chapter.

During the Revolutions of 1848, Mickiewicz, that Protean figure, once more changed his mode of life, and actively supported the anti-Austrian forces in Italy as Lord Byron had done a quarter of a century before him. Some seven years later, at the height of the Crimean War, Mickiewicz, by now in his late fifties, decided to join the crusade against the Tsar, his nation's age-old enemy. Like Byron, he wished to die fighting: the Crimean War meant to him much the same as the Greek War of Independence had done to his English model. Ironically, however, the Turks, whom Europe had execrated thirty years earlier, were now supposed to be on the side of the angels, and Poles and Turks, who during the second siege of Vienna in 1683 had been fighting for and against the salvation of Christendom, were now cordial allies, with one of the leading Poles, Michal Czajkowski, even going to the length of turning Mohammedan and styling himself Sadyk Pascha.

Mickiewicz, too, found the longed-for repose and died at Constantinople on 26 November 1855: to be sure, not on the battlefield, but as the victim of a disease that bore some resemblance to cholera. Posthumously more fortunate than Byron, Mickiewicz's remains that had at first been brought to Paris were in 1890 removed to the Wawel in Cracow, where they lie side by side with those of the Kings of Poland.

CHAPTER TWENTY

The New Religion of Progress

THE only Romantic destined for a like apotheosis was Victor Hugo, whose body came to rest in the Panthéon in Paris. Unlike Mickiewicz, however, Hugo lived to see his own ultimate triumph when, on 26 February 1881, the day he entered upon his eightieth year, was celebrated throughout France as a national festival, and the people of Paris were marching in procession under the poet's

window. Such triumph had never been experienced by any other
Romantic or for that matter by any artist. Its secret lay less in the
undeniable beauty of Hugo's finest poetry, for example in *Les
Feuilles D'Automne* or *Les Contemplations*, than in the fact that in
his genius Romantic messianism had reached an all but unsurpassable climax. All its various strains were here developed to their
utmost limits and yet were made to appear in harmony with each
other. So great was Hugo's persuasive magic that in his message
French national messianism seemed to be reconciled with the cult
of Humanity and, even more surprisingly, the messianic role
assumed by the artist himself was found to be compatible with the
Romantic legend of the People so fervently championed by him.

In his youth, it will be remembered, Victor Hugo had revealed
his ambition to become "Chateaubriand or nothing". Soon after
the July Revolution of 1830, the poet and dramatist, then in his
early thirties, had already become the acknowledged leader of the
second Romantic generation in France. Like Chateaubriand and
Lamennais, Hugo too had Celtic ancestors, for his mother was
Breton. He was also of partly German origin—a fact which perhaps helps to explain his Romantic exuberance. His life, like that
of his paragon, abounded in contrasts: reduced circumstances
followed by wealth; elevation to the Peerage and favour from the
Court of the Bourgeois Monarchy; afterwards, during the régime
of Louis Napoleon (whom he had ridiculed as Napoléon le Petit),
the barricades, proscription and exile lasting the best part of twenty
years; finally, a solemn return to his fatherland at the very moment
of France's humiliation at the hands of Prussia—such was the
outward setting. As in the case of Chateaubriand, so here too the
contrasts were accentuated by the artist's histrionics. For example,
he would be seen attending the Senate of the Third Republic pur-
posely dressed like an old carpenter or bricklayer. It was in a
similar vein that he insisted that at the funeral his body be carried
on a pauper's hearse, a striking enough contrast to the unprecedented pomp and ceremony by means of which the nation was to
manifest its pride as well as its mourning. One more parallel between the old and the new Enchanter, who had so much in common, lay in their erotic insatiability, but whereas Chateaubriand
might perhaps be described as unusually fickle in this respect,

Hugo—especially in later years—worked himself up into a state of sexual frenzy strongly reminiscent of the youthful Lord Byron. Maurice Barrès has maintained that physical love added considerable vigour to Hugo's genius. The relevance and ethical implications of that statement need not detain us here.

French national messianism differed in character from the Polish variety studied in the preceding chapter. While Polish Romantic imagination, as we have seen, was able to find a parallel between Christ's Passion and the suffering of the partitioned and subjected Polish nation, the French emphasized the role of their nation as the Redeemer of mankind. Just as Christ's message had given rise to the regeneration of man, so France, it was now believed, would set itself, and fulfil, a similar task. As early as February 1793, at a time when the Revolution was threatened from without, the Convention, in a stirring manifesto to the troops, held out this prospect in case of a successful outcome of the struggle: "The nations will embrace each other . . . they will for ever extinguish the torch of War. You will be extolled as saviours of the fatherland, founders of the republic and regenerators of the universe."[1]

When the historian Michelet half a century later took upon himself the task of rehabilitating the French Revolution, for example by dissociating it from the Terror, it was in precisely the same light that the revolutionaries appeared to him. France had acted—and was still acting—as the pilot-vessel of humanity: a blessed state of affairs, since her heart was full of magnanimity and clemency. His *Introduction à l'Histoire Universelle*, Michelet declared revealingly, might have carried the subtitle *Introduction à l'Histoire de France*.

Victor Hugo, whose breadth of vision was wider than Michelet's, also tended to identify the cause of mankind with that of his own country. For him France was the soul of the world:

L'immense cœur du monde en sa poitrine bat.[2]

Although he liked to think of himself as "the patriot of mankind", he was greatly disconcerted when his daughter declared her intention of marrying an Englishman. On the other hand, he never ceased to extol the all-embracing genius of Shakespeare, whom he regarded as a predecessor worthy of a successor like himself. As in the case of genuine religious leaders, so here too temporary withdrawal from mankind greatly intensified such aspirations. Especially during his exile, strong mystical leanings, coupled with an inordinate ego-worship, prompted him to see himself cast for the role of one of God's elect in the same rank as Zoroaster, Moses, Isaiah, St. John the Baptist and even Christ. While Mickiewicz, after all, never went beyond imagining that his own function was that of a new Messiah of the Polish nation, Hugo at times believed himself to be a divinely inspired mediator between mankind and the supernatural deity. Yet somewhere in the innermost recesses of his mind he must have felt unsure of his mission if we are to judge from the poem 'Quatre Vents de l'Esprit' where he thus speaks of himself:

> Je suis presque prophète et je suis presque apôtre.[3]

Separation from the crowd, however prolonged it might be, never engendered in Hugo that sentiment of aloofness so characteristic of the Romantics of the *l'art pour l'art* variety in their proverbial ivory tower. On the contrary, it was precisely at such times that the fate of mankind weighed most heavily with him. As early as 1833 when he was fêted as the rising dramatist of the day, he had already stated in the preface to his drama *Marie Tudor*: "It is only in solitude that one can work for the masses." More than thirty years later, in relative solitude in Guernsey, he thus expatiated on the same idea in *William Shakespeare* (1864):

> The prophet seeks solitude, but not isolation. He unravels and untwists the threads of humanity, tied and rolled in a skein within his soul; he does not break them. He goes into the desert to think—of whom? Of the multitudes.

And in a challenging passage of the same work he pours scorn on "the pure lovers of art":

> Art for art's sake may be very fine, but art for progress is finer still.

The deep contrast between those two Romantic attitudes—yet another antinomy of the movement—is epitomized in his formula which must be quoted in the original:

> Rêver la rêverie est bien, rêver l'Utopie est mieux.[4]

Although Hugo's road to Utopia was not quite as straight-forward as some of his hagiographers have tried to make us believe, his deep concern for social justice is evident already in some of his earliest novels: notably in *Claude Gueux* (1834), which is based on actual events. It was then that he began to voice his conviction that vice and crime are caused by misery and destitution, and that they would disappear once those social evils were rooted out—a naïve enough optimism if viewed from the vantage point of our own affluent and crime-ridden age. In *Les Misérables* (1862), the theme of society's responsibility for wickedness and crime is resumed. Indeed, the appalling degradation of human nature as a result of the conditions in which the contemporary proletariat was con-demned to live can never have been depicted more poignantly than in that work, which Tolstoy, the arch-enemy of *l'art pour l'art*, regarded as the greatest of all novels. Nor is it at all likely that Hugo's fervent social compassion was but a literary theme, as some left wing politicians and other critics have suspected. If the most detailed entries in his diary may be taken at their face value, Hugo's generosity towards a large number of unfortunate persons must have been at least equal to that of Lord Byron. Nor did he spare himself the effort of intervening on behalf of victims of oppression or excessive retribution in almost any land under the sun, thus acting as the spokesman of mankind's conscience in much the same way as Zola was to act at the height of the Dreyfus crisis.

To return to *Les Misérables*, it is worth remembering that the anarchist Proudhon, who thought that all Romantic books should be thrown into the fire, yet expressed his admiration for that book which, as he put it, had something that could hold crowds in a new and compelling way. It is certainly true that the reader of *Les Misérables* is spellbound by the plot, in which, it has been claimed, Hugo "rises to the most sublime discovery of the detective genre".[5] Nevertheless, this aspect in itself could hardly have sufficed to make a man like Proudhon perceive in the novel "signs of an original literature to come".[6] The deeper reason for his admiration lay surely in the fact that *Les Misérables* furnished the most elo-quent example of that idolization of the People that was so marked a feature of Romanticism after 1830. Although worshippers of the People were not confined to France—Mickiewicz, Mazzini, and the brothers Grimm are proof to the contrary—yet that country most decidedly took the lead. Here again Lamennais, after his rupture with Rome, had blazed the trail which was soon followed by Leroux, George Sand and, most notably, Michelet, who, on the eve of the Revolution of 1848, brought out his panegryic entitled *Le Peuple*. In much of this literature, the People, an ill-defined layer of society, were credited with such virtues as innocence, courage, faith, love and readiness for self-sacrifice. Or, to quote from Victor Hugo's first speech in the Legislative Assembly on 9 July 1849: "The people has the instinct of truth just as it has the instinct of justice, and once it has calmed down, the people becomes the personification of good sense."

Closely linked with his exalted concept of the People was Hugo's belief in a glorious future for mankind and the eventual triumph of truth and justice and harmony on earth. While he was at work on the all-embracing *Légende des Siècles*, that Bible of Progress, as it has been called,[7] there appeared to him, in 1859, a vision of the twentieth century symbolized by a strange machine, the so-called *aéroscaphe*, a cross as it were between an airship and a spacecraft. But technological progress, here rightly predicted, was only the setting for a more comprehensive advance. In fact, an enchanting vista of harmony and bliss opens before the poet's eyes:

> Où va-t-il ce navire? Il va, de jour vêtu,
> A l'avenir divin et pur, à la vertu,
>   A la science qu'on voit luire,
> A la mort des fléaux, à l'oubli généreux,
> A l'abondance, au calme, au rire, à l'homme heureux;
>
> Il va, ce gloire navire,
> Au droit, à la raison, à la fraternité,
> A la religieuse et sainte vérité
>   Sans impostures et sans voiles,
> A l'amour, sur les cœurs serrant son doux lien,
> Au juste, au grand, au bon, au beau . . .
>   Vous voyez bien
> Qu'en effet il monte aux Etoiles.[8]

Thus the wheel had turned full circle, or so it seemed. European Romanticism had begun with enthusiastic expectations of human progress but had soon become disenchanted and gloomy about the prospects for mankind. After 1830 a powerful second wave of secular enthusiasm affected the movement, and the resulting new Romantic religion of Progress all but dominated it in its final stages. Several of the ingredients of Romanticism, as analysed above, went nto the making of the new religion. There was, above all, an unbridled emotionalism; there were the prophetic postures, the exceedingly vague yet emphatic message, and the intoxicating effect of oratorical and poetic phrases about the secularized Christian virtues of Love, Fraternity and Compassion. The mixture, duly advertised as a religion, was not lacking in followers. As for Hugo's part, a student attending the revival of *Hernani* in Paris in 1867 probably spoke for many when he remarked to Paul Meurice: "Monsieur Victor Hugo is our religion."

However, the new religion in its turn also met with biting scepticism and unbelief. Thus Edmond de Goncourt, after visiting Victor Hugo in the Rue de la Rochefoucauld in 1872, noted in his *Journal*:

> There was, deep down in me, a feeling of irony, when I thought of all the mystical, sonorous, empty mumbo-jumbo by means of which men like Michelet and Hugo pontificate, seeking to impose themselves on their environment, as though they were Augurs having the ear of the Gods.[9]

Indeed as far back as 1843, Heine, the renegade Romantic, had savagely satirized Pierre Leroux's dreams about the future:

> He would build a mighty bridge of one arch resting on two pillars, one of which is the Materialistic granite of the last century, the other the visioned moonshine of the future, and to this latter pier he gives as support some as yet undiscovered star in the Milky Way. . . . Method is here wanting. He has only the ideas, and in this respect a certain likeness to Joseph Schelling cannot be denied, only that all his ideas refer to the enfranchisement of humanity, and he, far from patching up old religion with philosophy, rather bestows on the latter the garments of a new religion.[10]

Perhaps we should once more ponder the fortunes of the ideal of Progress in the development of Romanticism and ask ourselves

Schelling (portrait by Carl Begar)

Liszt (photograph of 1886)

again: had the wheel really come full circle or was the appearance somewhat deceptive? In other words, was the optimism of those later Romantics as untarnished by doubt and misgivings as had been the case during the initial stages of the movement? The answer, I think, can only be in the negative. For the new promises of heaven on earth, if studied more closely, reveal an overtone of hope against hope, and even of defiance. Most important of all, the problem of human suffering, re-emphasized only so recently, still loomed too large to be brushed aside. Victor Hugo for one was fully aware of it when he wrote:

> Do away with poverty and destitution we can, but do away with suffering we cannot. Suffering, we profoundly believe, is the law of this earth until some new dispensation. . . . The quantity of fatality that depends on man is called Penury and can be abolished; the quantity of fatality that depends on the unknown is called Sorrow and can only be contemplated in fear and trembling.[11]

One final word: our crucial theme throughout the present study has been that of the relationship between European Romanticism in many of its various shapes on the one hand, and Christianity on the other. Seen in this light, the new Romantic religion of Progress, with its strong emphasis on charity, would appear to have been of all the Romantic enchantments the one least unlike Christianity.

CHAPTER TWENTY-ONE

Redemption through Music

I T was a Romantic—none other than E. T. A. Hoffmann—who called music the most romantic of all the arts. And indeed music must be regarded as the most congenial romantic enchantment. The unprecedented intensity of musical life in Romantic Europe is but an outward proof. Varied and manifold are the inner links between music and the Romantic spirit. Thus it is not without significance that Jean-Jacques Rousseau, the great harbinger of the movement, was also a musician, and that Friedrich Nietzsche, the involuntary heir of Romanticism, showed so profound an insight into music.

At the outset it should be noted that in the Romantic era music and poetry were brought into a more intimate alliance and indeed were blended in the Romantic art form *par excellence*, the German *Lied*, where for example Wilhelm Müller's verse and Schubert's music appear in perfect harmony with each other. Old and unsophisticated folk-songs were now rediscovered and revived, an endeavour partly stimulated by patriotism and nostalgia, though its main impulse lay in the desire to penetrate into the mysterious depth, or, as we would say, the subconscious regions, of a nation's personality. The two spheres of music and language were brought nearer to each other also in a different way, through the conscious effort on the part of certain poets and men of letters at developing what one might call a musical style of writing. Suffice it to mention but three examples, chosen almost at random: Novalis, Shelley and Lamennais. At times the Romantics even anticipated Symbolist exploits by making the spoken word all but assume the function of music. Thus some of Ludwig Tieck's dramas have aptly been described as "operas of sheer word-music". Even the spoken everyday language was sometimes tested by musical standards. Jan Kollár, for example, the champion of cultural Panslavism, suggested the adaptation of the Czech vernacular—which he considered to have become harsh and unmelodious—to the softer Slovak speech, which had better preserved the old full vowels.

The Romantic enthusiasm for music can be accounted for in several ways. In the first place, Romantic emotionalism hailed music as the art that probes more deeply than any other into the depth of human emotions. Tieck's young friend Wackenroder put it in a suggestive phrase when he wrote in his *Phantasien über die Kunst*: "Music teaches us to feel our own feeling." Robert Schumann placed music "among the highest organs of art which have characters and symbols for every emotional state". Or, to quote George Sand's more effusive panegyric: "It has been rightly said," she wrote, "that the object of music is the awakening of emotion. No other art can so sublimely arouse human sentiments in the innermost heart of man. No other art can paint to the eyes of the soul the splendours of nature, the delights of contemplation, the character of nations, the tumult of their passions, and the languor of their sufferings as music can. Regret, hope, terror, meditation, consternation, enthusiasm, faith, doubt, glory, tranquillity, all these and more are given to us and taken from us, thanks to her genius and according to the bent of our own."[1] In some Romantic circles instrumental music was regarded as the ideal medium that could express the otherwise ineffable. Besides, it was with the aid of music that the typical Romantic quest for infinitude could be gratified. Novalis and Schopenhauer even delved into the intriguing problem of the relationship between music and the world of numbers. Furthermore, it was claimed— by Friedrich Schlegel—that music constituted as it were the only universal language in existence.

To other Romantics, however, music was far more than a medium of communication, more even than an art, however exalted. For them music partook of the very essence of religion: for some, indeed, it virtually became a religion. In the course of the Romantic search for spiritual re-integration many different substitutes for religion were tried as we have seen; it is not surprising that music came to be one of them.[2] This aspect of musical history has been seldom examined.

Evidence for Romantic quasi-religious music-worship is fairly widespread. For Wackenroder in his youthful enthusiasms, symphonies such as those of Haydn and Mozart made the art of music "a veritable deity for human hearts". For Ludwig Tieck music constituted "the last mystery of faith, the fully revealed religion". For Bettina von Arnim, man's attitude to music was tantamount to religion. George Sand called music "that divine tongue". Such utterances, which could easily be multiplied, may be vague, but their general direction is unmistakable. In this chapter our attention will be focused on three representative figures who may be said to have embodied the Romantic cult of music.

Our first example is that bizarre character Ernst Theodor Amadeus Hoffmann, born in Königsberg in East Prussia in 1776. He has come down to posterity chiefly as the writer of gruesome, and at times even surrealistic, stories, some of which later came to be known all over the world through Offenbach's opera *Tales of Hoffmann* (1881). His versatility was astounding. For many years he served conscientiously in the stiff-necked Prussian provincial administration, though a lighthearted prank entailed his exile into one of the less desirable provinces. When, owing to the collapse of the Prussian State after Jena, his appointment came to an abrupt end, he changed his profession with the greatest ease and became *Kapellmeister* and officially appointed composer at the court theatre in Bamberg. Although he composed, among other things, a fairly successful opera, *Undine*, which was acclaimed by Weber, he left his mark on the world of music mainly as a critic. In this sphere his contribution was of the highest significance, so much so that he is regarded as one of the originators of modern musical criticism. Hoffmann was also among the first to show a profound understanding of Beethoven and all he stood for. But this was not all: Hoffmann was a kind of artistic Jack-of-all-trades, versatile as architect, draughtsman and even cartoonist. For six whole years, spent at Bamberg and later with the Seconda theatrical company at Leipzig and Dresden, Hoffmann lived the colourful life of a *bohémien*. It is all the more astonishing that in 1814 he found his way back to outward respectability. As though nothing had happened to estrange him from the monotonous world of by-laws and files, he resumed his career as *Kammergerichtsrat* in the Prussian capital and, despite some vicissitudes, clung to it till his death in 1822. But Hoffmann the *bohémien* had not yet played out his role; very far from it. He only withdrew from his day-time routine into the protective darkness of a lurid night-life. In the Jekyll and Hyde existence of Hoffmann's last eight years, both his roles were pursued with equal intensity. Rarely can such a double existence have been led with equal intensity. Assiduous and, it seems, highly competent work in the administration during office hours was followed, more often than not, by uproarious drinking bouts in Lutter and Wegner's famous wine cellar. It was on one of those hilarious occasions that Oehlenschläger, on a visit to Berlin, saw Hoffmann, "a burlesque fantastic gnome", clad in a white apron like a chef, mixing 'Kardinal' from Rhine wine and Cham-

pagne. In the Prologue and the often omitted Epilogue to Offenbach's *Tales of Hoffmann* we catch glimpses of this exuberant side
of his nature. Though these excesses undermined his constitution
and ultimately led to his death at the age of forty-six, that double
life obviously stimulated Hoffmann to reach the utmost limit of his
achievement, which lay in the *genre* of the scurrilous, grotesque or
macabre novel and short story, e.g. *Serapionsbrüder*, *Prinzessin
Brambilla* and finally *Meister Floh*. It was this part of Hoffmann's
œuvre that had the greatest impact, notably on Edgar Allan Poe,
Gogol, and above all in France. When Gérard de Nerval for the
first time looked across the Rhine, he burst into the cry: 'Le pays
d' Hoffmann!'

This is not the place to assess Hoffmann's contribution to
literature, tempting though it would be to follow him into that
sphere where dreams and reality merge. What matters in our context is his complex attitude to music. Our endeavour to understand
it is greatly helped by the fact that Hoffmann has created for us the
figure of *Kapellmeister* Johannes Kreisler into whom he projected
so much of his own personality. Even though Kreisler, the half-
mad musician, may be a self-caricature rather than a self-portrait,
the evidence is extremely valuable. What it proves is that Hoffmann, though magically attracted by music, was at the same time
highly conscious of the dangers inherent in its idolization. Just
as to his imaginary Kreisler, so to himself, music had often served
as an intoxicating drug; or rather it had taken hold of his entire
being and had threatened to destroy the peace of his soul. Where-
in lay music's tremendous power? Hoffmann's answer is that "it
conjures up from the depth of harmony those mighty spirits who
stir up fear, horror and hopeless yearning in man's soul".[3] In another context he speaks of the "demoniacal misuse of music".[4]
Viewed in this light, music would appear as a highly pernicious
enchantment.

Yet, according to Hoffmann, it was equally true to say that
music possessed strong soothing and healing powers. Indeed, there
was a sense in which one might speak of the soul's redemption
through music. Hoffmann took great pains to resolve the seeming
paradox by insisting that only ecclesiastical or religious music
could have that salutary effect.[5] It was this kind of music, and this

kind alone, that appeared to Kreisler as "the angel of light which has power over the evil demons". In an effort to escape from those demons Kreisler takes refuge in a monastery where he can live a contemplative life and where, above all else, he finds a congenial *milieu* for the religious music he composes. In passing we may note the Romantic *leit-motiv* of the return to Catholicism. Hoffmann, who had been deeply impressed by a visit to the Capuchin monastery in Bamberg, wrote in a like vein also in his novel *Elixiere des Teufels*. To return to Kreisler: it is surely also in keeping with the general trend of Romanticism that his return to the faith is only half-hearted. The refuge the weary *Kapellmeister* seeks proves to be only a temporary one, and before long an indefinable urge for freedom makes him change his mode of life once again. What might have been Kreisler's fate had Hoffmann been able to complete the story it is impossible to say. As it is, the work has remained a torso. All we know is that the third and final volume was meant to show us the eccentric Kreisler in a state of transfiguration, his impassioned search for harmony accomplished. A discerning critic, Werner Bergengrün, has made the interesting suggestion that it would have transcended the potentialities of epic art to bring about this solution; only music might, in his opinion, have been equal to the task.[6] However that may be, the figure of Kreisler exerted a remarkable fascination upon Robert Schumann. Kreisler's name occurs in the title of several of his compositions. Schumann too was yearning for redemption through music—without ever attaining it.

Hoffmann himself had already composed liturgical music and had greatly fostered the renewal of interest in, and reverence for, the church music of the sixteenth-century composer Palestrina and some of his successors. Yet the wild, Romantic type of music continued to haunt his overwrought imagination and made him long for the divine harmony which only religion could offer. In a profound treatise, entitled *Gespräche der Serapionsbrüder*, he expresses the hope "that music may once again start off on its flight to the world beyond which is its true home land". Is it surprising then that Hoffmann, torn as he was between the wildest excesses of demoniac music and the sublime raptures of divine music, should at times have despaired of reconciling those extremes? Was one side of his character not always a *Doppelgänger* of the other? And if this be so, is it surprising that in his prose Hoffmann has drawn for us so convincing a picture of the anguish felt by a man who can no longer distinguish between himself and his double?

Hardly less marked are the contradictions in the character of Franz Liszt. Four cities—Paris, Weimar, Rome and Budapest—symbolize, as it were, contrasting facets of his personality. The French metropolis deserves pride of place, for although Liszt was born in a Hungarian village and received his first musical education in Vienna, where he saw Beethoven and Schubert, it was in Paris that he became the supreme pianist of his age. Not only did he develop a new technique of playing: he was also the first pianist ever to give piano-recitals without the aid of any other musician, and the first pianist to perform his programme by heart. It was also in Paris that Liszt as a young man attended a concert given by that gaunt, Hoffmannesque figure, the violin virtuoso Niccolò Paganini, whom henceforth he emulated in many ways. Soon Liszt too began to dazzle his audiences by what contemporaries described as demoniac or, as some would have it, diabolical qualities of his playing. It was said of Liszt, as it had been said of Paganini, that he mesmerized his audiences. Thus the stage was set for the Romantic cult of the virtuoso, which, alas, was destined to outlive Romanticism. It may be of interest to note that among the earliest critics of that cult was Liszt's compatriot Lenau.[7]

At the tender age of twelve, in 1823, Liszt the prodigy had arrived in Paris, which throughout the heyday of French Romanticism was to remain his centre of gravity until he abandoned his career as a virtuoso in the year of the Revolutions. During that quarter of a century the young artist who soon lost the faith of his childhood succumbed to various Romantic enchantments, his celebrated love affair with the Comtesse d'Agoult being the most spectacular of all. Yet it was music that cast the stronger spell upon him. There can be no doubt that Liszt, who had lost the religion of his childhood, tried to raise music to the status of a faith. In one of his letters to a friend there occurs the revealing passage: "Music is certainly not a pleasurable art for me, but it fills a void which without it, remains gaping in my soul."[8] Music's role as a substitute for religion can rarely have been formulated more poignantly. If music was the new religion, the artist was its high priest or prophet, and might even hope to become its Messiah. Liszt eagerly absorbed these bold ideas when they were first expressed by Lamennais during the last stage of the Abbé's amazing spiritual Odyssey.

The small but famous town of Weimar, where, after 1848, Liszt spent the next dozen years or so, gave him the widest scope. In retrospect he recalled that on arriving he had dreamed of a new period for Weimar comparable to that of the Grand Duke Karl August. Wagner and he were to have been the leading lights in the new dispensation, as in former times Goethe and Schiller. Before going to Weimar Liszt abandoned his career as vagrant virtuoso and was thus in a position to concentrate fully on his task. His post as *Hofkapellmeister* and director of the opera enabled him to build up an orchestra after his own liking as well as to enrich the musicians' unusually large repertoire by the addition of his own and later Richard Wagner's compositions, which at that time still met with determined opposition in many quarters.

As to Liszt's own music, it is nowadays almost impossible to form an independent judgment of it. For, whereas the major part of his work is hardly ever performed—1961, the 150th anniversary of his birth, was an exception—we are treated to the same few bravura pieces so frequently that they have become hackneyed. Contemporary informed opinion was strongly divided, even among those who in general sympathized with the Master. For example, what is usually regarded as the acme of Liszt's achievement as a composer, his symphonic poem *Faust*, was enthusiastically received by Wagner and found favour with Tschaikovsky. On the other hand, two of Liszt's *protégés*, the composer Peter Cornelius and the conductor Hans von Bülow, were highly critical. The latter, who had at first expressed admiration for it, came to dislike it intensely, for it now seemed to him "unmusic, quack music, anti-music".[9] Liszt himself seems to have sensed that although he was obviously possessed of a great flair for originality —especially in the sphere of harmony—he was lacking in that almost boundless creativity that characterizes the immortal composer. Probably this feeling, rather than disappointment with the authorities, was at the bottom of his resignation and departure from Weimar in 1860.

Rome was his headquarters for the following six years. True, the path that led him to the Eternal City had been somewhat tortuous, but now that he had arrived just under the age of fifty, he amply made up for it—or so it seemed. Liturgical compositions, including oratorios, began to flow from his pen. Moreover, he took the four Minor Orders and was known to don the black silk cassock of an Abbé. He also became a member of the Third Order of the Franciscans for laymen and women, and even received the honorary title of Canon of Albano. It would seem that music, in the sense in which he understood it before his return to the faith, had proved an insufficient spiritual substitute which could never vouchsafe the redemption of his soul. Christianity, or more precisely Catholicism, could not be dispensed with. That much was beyond doubt. What still remained uncertain was how much religion could mean to him. The note of ecstasy that characterizes some of his liturgical music would seem to suggest that, in the manner of that other Romantic Abbé, Liszt tried to whip himself up into a state of religious frenzy—the parallel with Lamennais at work on his *Essai sur l'Indifférence* is striking. One of the leading experts on Romantic music has shrewdly remarked that Romantic ecstasy, to which not only Liszt but also Berlioz and others had recourse, is foreign to genuine church music.[10]

Liszt's state of indecision between religion and an all too wordly world became manifest during the last stage of his life, the years from 1869 till his death in the summer of 1886. This was the period of his *vie trifurquée*, during which he used to divide his time between Budapest, Weimar and Rome. His links with Rome, to be sure, were not of an exclusively ecclesiastical nature. Princess Caroline zu Sayn-Wittgenstein who in 1848 had escaped from Russian Poland in order to live with him was now resident in Rome, whither she had moved in the first place in order to secure an annulment of her unhappy marriage to the Prince. This Pius IX was unable to grant. The astonishment at the Pope's decision on the part of some of Liszt's biographers is a measure of their profound ignorance of ecclesiastical law. It is true, the Princess herself had been taken by surprise, but after this setback she became extremely devout and spent the last twenty-six years of her life compiling a gigantic literary work, in some twenty-four volumes, under the laborious title *Causes intérieures de la faiblesse extérieure de l'église*. Her spiritual bond with the Abbé Liszt remained unbroken.

The pull exerted by Budapest was of a different kind. Although Liszt could never speak fluent Magyar he remained emotionally attached to his native land and, during the Hungarian Revolution of 1848–9, had even become something of a Magyar nationalist. Twenty years later he agreed to pass henceforth two or three months of each year at Budapest, where he would give tuition as well as advice concerning the best method of setting up an Academy of Music, which was at length opened at the end of 1875. Liszt also strongly emphasized his indebtedness to Gypsy musicians whom he had often heard in his youth. Their rhythms had an echo in his *Hungarian Rhapsodies*. However, his claim to have Gypsy blood in his veins was probably no more than a pose. A Gypsy ancestor, real or imaginary, could serve to shock the Philistines, those mortal enemies of the Romantics. Besides, to be of Gypsy origin added lustre in an age that showed so marked an interest in the exotic.

Though only at intervals, Weimar now came back into its own. Just as half a century earlier poets and men of letters from all over Europe, and even from the United States, had flocked to that town to pay homage to Goethe in his old age, so leading musicians from many parts of the world now came to Weimar to pay their respects to Liszt. Like the venerable Olympian, the Abbé Liszt too always remained susceptible to female charm. Again, after Goethe's fashion, the more he advanced in years, the more he appreciated youth in the opposite sex. At sixty Liszt fell in love with the Russian baroness Meyendorff who was half his age. Some time after that he went through a new rejuvenating love affair, this time with a wild Cossack damsel aged nineteen who at one stage threatened to kill him. All through these and other episodes he kept up his esoteric correspondence with Princess zu Sayn-Wittgenstein who, despite her preoccupation with the *magnum opus*, could not but feel alarmed at the rumours that penetrated as far as her cell. Unlike Goethe, who had done so little to encourage or assist the younger generation, Liszt was generous enough to advise and teach the most gifted young pianists always free of charge. His pupils belonged to many different nationalities and, needless to say, to both sexes. One of his young and attractive women pupils, the American Miss Amy Fay, has left us this vivid description of the Master: "He is tall and slight," she wrote, "with deepset eyes, shaggy eye-brows, and long iron-grey hair. . . . His mouth turns up at the corners which gives him a most crafty and Mephisto-phelian expression when he smiles."[11] Oddly enough, the same note had already been struck by the historian Gregorovius, who met Liszt in Rome in 1862. The entry in his Journal reads: "Mephistopheles disguised as an Abbé. Such is the end of Love-lace."[12] At times the disguise, if such it be, must have worn dan-gerously thin, as for example on the occasion when Liszt, during his Roman period, composed his *Mephisto Waltz*. The episode that piece of descriptive music is meant to portray centres round the devil who seizes the violin and by his playing intoxicates the audience to such an extent that they completely abandon them-selves to love-making.

Liszt one day described himself as "half Gypsy and half Fran-ciscan". While the first half of that statement probably referred to his nomadic life rather than to his origins, the aspiration to a life modelled on that of St. Francis of Assisi is not easy to reconcile with Liszt's prolonged abode at the marvellous Villa d'Este at Tivoli. However, there are degrees of sincerity. It is perhaps legi-timate to surmise that so complex a personality at times experi-enced a genuine yearning for a higher spirituality than was given to him to attain.

Right at the end of his life, in 1886, Liszt once more visited London and Paris, where his public piano recitals, given after an absence of forty years, turned into a great personal triumph. The general impression was well summed up by the French composer Saint-Saëns: "At his instrument, Liszt was the incarnation of all the flourish of the Romantic age." Liszt died and was buried at Bayreuth, the town of the Wagner festival, where on the eve of his death he had attended a performance of *Tristan und Isolde*. The greater musician—and even more problematical character—whose admirer and prophet he had been, had predeceased him in 1883.

Whereas the earliest Romantics dealt with in this study were born round about the year of Napoleon's birth (1769), the last to be included in our pen portrait gallery is Richard Wagner, born at Leipzig on 20 May 1813, not far from the site where a few months later Napoleon was to be defeated in the Battle of the Nations. The problem whether the great composer still belonged to the main current of European Romanticism, or whether he should be included among its illustrious heirs (as Nietzsche, no doubt, ought to be considered) is a moot point, for either view is perfectly tenable. As I hope to show, all the main characteristics of Romanticism are to be found in Wagner's personality no less than in his work, so that viewed from this angle he does indeed appear to be one of the figures of the movement. Moreover, in some ways, as will be shown, his achievement, notably in *Tristan und Isolde*, may be regarded as the very climax and fulfilment of Romanticism, so long as this term is understood in its wider European, as distinct from its merely German, connotation: for it is clear that attempts at squeezing Wagner into the narrower framework of German Romanticism are doomed to failure.[13] Besides, Richard Wagner may be said to have achieved Romantic fulfilment also in the sense that through the powerful medium of his *Musikdrama* Romanticism reached a wider public than could have been reached by means of literature alone. On the other hand, there is also a shrill, hyper-ecstatic and excessively histrionic element in Wagner that would suggest not so much an intensification as a perversion or even a travesty of Romanticism. But, by whatever reckoning, we cannot fail to discern in Wagner and his *œuvre* that note of dissonance which so often throughout this study we have discovered right at the core of Romanticism.

It is in keeping with the highly controversial character of Wagner and all he stood for that even the question of his origins is shrouded in mystery. What look like well attested prosaic facts have probably been invented for the purpose of mystification, and conversely what might at first sight appear as fiction is, more likely than not, the full historical truth. At any rate, the late Ernest Newman, author of the monumental *Life of Richard Wagner* in well over two thousand pages, regarded it as highly probable that Richard's father was not the police actuary Carl Friedrich Wagner, but the remarkably versatile actor and playwright Ludwig Geyer, who, like Hoffmann, worked with the Seconda theatrical company and who married Richard's mother in August 1814.[14] What is certain is that Richard Wagner himself in later life believed in the possibility of Geyer having been his father. Whether or not Nietzsche was right when he hinted at Geyer's (and therefore Wagner's) Jewish origin is hard to assess. But there is mystery on the maternal side as well. It now seems probable that Wagner's mother Johanna was not the legitimate child of the baker Paetz at Weissenfels but rather the natural daughter of Prince Friedrich Ferdinand Constantin of Weimar, the only brother of the then reigning Grand Duke Karl August (the patron of Goethe).[15] Prince Constantin had exceptional musical gifts which, as so often happens, emerged again—if our surmise be correct—in the next generation but one. The Prince's notoriously wild mode of life was yet another trait bequeathed to his grandson. The latter's exorbitant tastes and fantastic extravagance would also point to his partly aristocratic extraction. It seems that Richard Wagner the incorrigible spendthrift was a throwback to a typical prince of the Rococo period. In an earlier chapter of this study Romanticism, in some of its aspects, has been called the swan song of the nobility. If Wagner's music, in its turn, may be regarded as the swan song of the Romantic Movement, his noble ancestor's share in it was perhaps not insignificant. Though it would be something of an understatement to say that the composer's political ideas were flexible to a degree, yet he repeatedly emphasized that the German aristocracy, or at any rate the more enlightened among the German princes, would have to play their part in the regeneration of Germany as he envisaged it. The fear—which had been felt already by the early Romantics—lest European culture be swamped by the uneducated masses, was also present in his mind. Another typical Romantic reaction was Wagner's negative attitude to bourgeois industrialism and mechanization. Not only did he never cease to inveigh against the soulless materialism of the age, but his dislike of large towns certainly influenced him in his choice of a suitable site for his festival theatre. For a time he contemplated Weimar, but in the end he decided in favour of the even smaller town of Bayreuth, despite the fact that all kinds of practical considerations seemed to point to the preferability of the Bavarian capital.

The bewildering complexity of social and political Romanticism was mirrored in the attitude of this extraordinary individual. For, side by side with Wagner the extoller of pre-bourgeois aristocratic tradition, there exists Wagner the revolutionary firebrand. Naturally it is this aspect of his political life, his role during the Saxon insurrection of 1849, that has gained the widest publicity. Romantic humanitarianism, but also the ideas of Ludwig Feuerbach, had undoubtedly made a deep impact on his mind during his three years' stay in Paris from 1839 to 1842 and subsequently in Dresden. But this fact by itself does not fully explain why he plunged headlong into the political agitation as he did. Several other motives spring to mind. For one thing, Wagner's restless character—a parallel to Lord Byron's—may have predisposed him in that direction. However, an even greater weight must be attached to his rootlessness. Even if he was not always conscious of his irregular origins, modern psychological theory would suggest that subconsciously they could have weighed upon him. However that may be, he certainly grew up in a theatrical and *bohémien milieu*. His early career as a musician, though by no means unsuccessful, had been full of vicissitudes. During the six years from 1833 to 1839 he had held posts in as many places, ranging from Würzburg as far as Riga, and at the end had had to stage a highly adventurous flight from Russian Latvia to England and France mainly in order to escape from troublesome creditors. Then followed the three penurious years in Paris which, though fruitful in some ways, must have made Wagner feel more *déraciné* than ever. It seems that he was not even spared the humiliating experience of being committed to prison at the instance of one of his creditors.[16] It is true that in 1843 he was appointed Royal Saxon *Hofkapellmeister* at Dresden, where, in the previous year, his opera *Rienzi* had been successfully performed. However, the more

Wagner saw of the operatic world in Germany, and elsewhere for that matter, the more dissatisfied and rebellious he grew. His plans for the long overdue reform of the Dresden theatre orchestra were not carried out to the full, and more ambitious schemes of his fell on deaf ears. For example, he insisted that the theatre should in no circumstances cater for entertainment. Only works of the highest class should be given, which in his opinion excluded operas such as Flotow's *Martha*. Quite apart from personal idiosyncracies, which also came into it, Wagner's whole conception of what the theatre should aim at differed so radically from the accepted standards of the time that a clash was inevitable. Already during that early period theatrical art, in the form envisaged by him, was in his mind surrounded by a halo of quasi-religious sanctity. The Christianity which he had first met in the shape of Protestantism had never meant much to him. Yet his ardent soul was craving for a faith, and the outcome of it all was a particularly zealous form of art idolatry. This attitude was in Wagner's case inextricably interwoven with an overdose of ego-worship, for the role of the creative artist happened to coincide with that of the high priest, if not the founder, of the new 'religion'. In passing we may observe how Wagner's story here links up with that of Liszt who, at least before his return to the faith, had entertained equally exalted ideas about the function of the artist.

It is not to belittle the ideological reasons for Wagner's revolutionary attitude in 1848–9 if two more personal motives are mentioned here. Indeed the first one is not unconnected with his ambitious artistic plans: his opera *Lohengrin* had been rejected by the theatre management; as second-in-command under the Intendant Lüttichau he was unable to force the issue. His sense of frustration must have been intense. Finally, he had once more become so hopelessly entangled in debts that his well-meaning but shrewd English biographer is forced to conclude: "In 1848 and 1849 he drifted into revolution not merely 'from love of theatre' but from lack of thalers."[17] Wagner's flight after the breakdown of the Revolution proved to be even more hazardous than his escape from Riga ten years previously. He made part of the journey from Dresden in the company of the Russian anarchist Prince Bakunin who, less fortunate than Wagner, fell into the hands of the Saxon police and had to wait for his own escape, from Siberia, until 1860.

For Wagner the thirteen years of his exile, from his thirty-seventh to his fiftieth year, proved in some ways the most fruitful period of his life. To start with, the theoretical foundations were laid on which Wagner's peculiar creation, the *Musikdrama*, was to rest henceforth. Though the Nibelungen saga had attracted him as early as 1848, he only now conceived the idea of writing *Der Ring des Nibelungen* in the form of a gigantic tetralogy, and of creating a special *milieu* for it in the shape of a festival theatre. The score of *Rheingold* was completed fairly quickly, those of *Walküre* and *Siegfrieds Tod* begun. However, the outstanding event of this period was undoubtedly *Tristan und Isolde*, which was embarked upon in 1854 and completed five years later. Significantly, it is also his most Romantic opera. Several of the main strains of Romanticism are woven into its magic web. In the first place we are offered an orgy of Romantic emotionalism, which is here carried to its utmost limits. It has been remarked that almost the whole dramatic action takes place within the souls of the *dramatis personae*. In our century several artists have attempted to expose the unconscious regions of the human personality—notably James Joyce in *Finnegans Wake* (which may be regarded as a cul-de-sac of Romanticism). But the novelist, try as he might—and Joyce's former secretary, Samuel Beckett, has tried very hard indeed—can never completely emancipate himself from language as a rational means of communication. In this respect the composer, as Wagner realized, enjoys a decisive advantage.

Closely bound up with the emotionalism of *Tristan und Isolde* is its apotheosis of Romantic love. Here Wagner's own experiences must be alluded to. As a young man he had married Minna Planer, an attractive German actress. According to his own testimony he had decided on this step in a caprice of passion. Several times the marriage had all but broken down. Wagner's irregular and ultra-bohemian habits had left the household, if such it could be called, on the shakiest of foundations, and even this highly precarious basis disappeared as a result of the two flights of 1839 and 1849. It would have required an almost saintly woman of superhuman powers of endurance to take all these vicissitudes in her stride. Wagner's constantly recurring complaint—his sole reproach against Minna—that she did not love him according to his own conception of love, suggests that he had a romantically exaggerated and fundamentally unrealistic idea of love which Minna could hardly be expected to live up to. Not surprisingly, disharmony set in from the early days of their married life. It grew in intensity when Minna, almost four years older than her husband, was obviously ageing more rapidly. Wagner's attachment to Mathilde Wesendonk eventually brought about the final rupture with Minna.

Mathilde, fifteen years younger than Wagner, was—as so often happened in Romantic circles—the wife of a friend, and indeed Otto Wesendonk, a well-to-do Rhenish industrialist, was one of Wagner's most generous patrons. In later years Wagner contrived to wreck another friend's marriage when he lured Cosima away from Hans von Bülow, whom he used to describe as his *alter ego*. However, Mathilde, unlike Cosima, never left her husband, and thus the relationship between the Wesendonks and Wagner must have been similar to that between Nikolaus Lenau and the Löwenthals.[18] Probably it was just because Wagner's love for Mathilde was denied its ultimate fulfilment that *Tristan und Isolde* turned out to be his greatest masterpiece. If there was ever a case of enforced repression, and artistic sublimation of erotic impulses, this was it. In December 1854 Wagner wrote to Liszt: "Since I have never once in my life enjoyed the real happiness of love I want to erect to this the most beautiful of all dreams a monument on which love will be shown enjoying its fullest satisfaction." Again it was in keeping with the Romantic attitude to love that while the passion lasted Mathilde appeared to Wagner as his 'redemptrice' (Erlöserin). A similar confusion between eroticism and religion prevails in the opera itself. The third characteristically Romantic element in *Tristan und Isolde* is its unredeemed *Weltschmerz*. In the autumn of 1854, Wagner had fallen under the spell of Schopenhauer, whose philosophy greatly strengthened the nihilist tendencies that had been latent in his own nature. To quote his own words: "It was only after reading Schopenhauer that his reason made clear to him what had all along been intuitive in him as an artist."[19] Had he not made the mythical Wotan in the Nibelungen drama yearn for extinction?[20]

We may surmise that Wagner's disillusionment after the break-down of the Revolution of 1848–9 made him even more susceptible to the philosophy of pessimism. The analogy to the disenchantment felt by some of the early Romantics in 1794 and the following years is obvious. However, the emergence of nihilist tendencies in 1800, or 1850 for that matter, can never be fully explained in terms of social and political history. Man's outlook on life and death, though clearly influenced by outward events, is never wholly determined by them. In April 1853 Liszt, who had by now found his way back to Christianity, exhorted his friend to seek solace in the Christian faith. Wagner replied that consolations of that kind were inefficacious in his case. At the beginning of the following year he wrote to Liszt:

> Not a year of my life has passed recently without bringing me *once* to the very verge of a decision to make an end of my life. Everything in it seems so lost and astray! A too hasty marriage with a woman, estimable but totally unsuited to me, has made me an outlaw for life. For a long time the ordinary pressure of circumstances and ambitious plans and wishes to relieve that pressure by winning renown, were able to disguise from myself my real emptiness of heart. The truth is that I reached my thirty-sixth year before I completely realized that terrible emptiness.[21]

Together with his spiritual nihilism—which obviously had deeper roots than the collapse of his hopes in the Revolution—grew his longing for extinction. Thus he could write to Liszt in December 1854:

> I find a last anodyne that alone brings me sleep in wakeful nights—the profound longing of my heart for death, complete unconsciousness, total nihility, a final end to dreaming, the last and only salvation.[22]

The idea of death as an everlasting general anaesthesia, which we have already found in Leopardi and Schopenhauer, could not have been expressed more forcefully.

To return to *Tristan und Isolde*: the opera significantly culmin-ates in the great *Liebestod* duet in which the lovers' ecstatic longing for extinction is fully voiced. The reconciling of the two ideals of love and death (as an eternal sleep) is again typically Romantic. At the turn of the century, Friedrich Schlegel had already coined the aphorism, "Voluptuousness is consummated when it becomes a divination of death, and death when it becomes lust." [23] In Wagner's opera it is boldly assumed that, in the midst of all the nothingness of death, Tristan's and Isolde's love, that 'eternal love', will not and cannot perish. It is further hopefully assumed that death will break down the barriers between the two individuals. The contrast between this conception and that of the real mystics from whom it seems to be derived, is glaring, for whereas the great mystics of the past had fervently hoped for their soul to be united with God, the modern version—or perversion—envisages a union of two human souls, and idolizes that very union.

Finally, there is the new musical idiom of *Tristan und Isolde*. Experts in the history of music have shown that in this opera Wagner's music is most characteristically Romantic, but also shows definite signs of emancipating itself from the hitherto accepted approach to harmony. Apart from Beethoven, whose impact upon Wagner was immeasurable, the Romantic composers Weber, Berlioz, Liszt and to a lesser extent Mendelssohn, Schumann and Chopin had strongly influenced him. Though he was not prone to make grateful acknowledgements, he yet told Bülow: "Since my acquaintance with Liszt's compositions I have become a different sort of harmonist from what I was before." [24] His debt to Berlioz which he never admitted was probably even greater. Already Nietzsche himself pointed out how much Wagner had learned from the French composer's colourful art of orchestration. However that may be, there cannot be the slightest doubt that Wagner, notably in *Tristan und Isolde*, made a highly original contribution to harmony. His most striking innovation consisted in an expansion and development of chromaticism, which, by the standards of the time, could only be regarded as ultra-modern. The medieval theme and the *avant-garde* style of the music (or part of it) form a strange contrast. Past and future compete with each other by offering their magic gifts.

Paradoxically it was during Wagner's exile from Germany, which lasted until 1862, that he became a professed German patriot. Here again his attitude was typical, for as with Romantics in general, so in his particular case, the patriotic attitude extended at first predominantly to the sphere of culture. Thus the exiled composer, in a letter in May 1857, urged Liszt to make the Weimar theatre unique in that the performers should have a genuine German style of their own, instead of the bad mixture of all varieties of style, domestic and foreign, that had been prevalent hitherto. In the same vein he advocated, after his triumphal return to Germany, that a German Music School be established at Munich. When, in 1876, the Bayreuth Festival was inaugurated, he declared this to be a step towards an independent German art. In dealing with the general trend of patriotism in music, Wilhelm Furtwängler, conductor and philosopher of music, has pointed out that it has to be viewed against the background of the secularization of European culture. "In bygone days," he said in his *Gespräche über Musik* (1948), "the Christian religion represented a common soil. Since it was thrust aside, there has remained only the nation— for the composer needs a native soil. Thus, since the eighteenth century, in music nationality has increasingly taken the place of religion, although admittedly without ousting it completely to the present day."[25] No wonder then that Wagner, the free-thinking ex-Protestant, felt the need for that native soil, and this all the more poignantly since his exile from Germany. But here a new paradox comes into view. Whereas his voluminous prose writings abound with patriotic as well as ultra-nationalist sentiments, and patriotic motifs are treated in the texts of several of his operas, Wagner's music itself is far more cosmopolitan than "purely German" in character, whatever the latter term may imply. His indebtedness to Berlioz and Liszt has already been touched upon. Nor, one may surmise, would *wagnérisme*, that well-known phenomenon, have arisen in France in the way it did if his music had really been as Teutonic as he made out.[26]

Characteristically, Wagner's patriotism soon degenerated into an arrogant and aggressive brand of nationalism. Echoing Madame de Staël's impressions—recorded at the height of the Goethe period—he declared that the Germans were "a nation of high-souled dreamers and deep-brained thinkers". Next he arrived at the even more startling assertion that the Germans were "God's own people". Hence there was but one step to the disparagement of the Latin nations to the glory of the German folk. Thus Wagner could write in 1867: "Ever since the regeneration of the German folkblood the German has been the creator and inventor, the Latin the shaper and exploiter."[27] Disparagement was accompanied by threats: in the same article he called for the destruction of the materialistic influence of France. More wounding still was his insult to the French in the poem *To the German Army before Paris*, written during the Franco-Prussian War of 1870, and even more so the farce *Eine Kapitulation*, where, in the worst possible taste, he made merry over the sufferings of the beleaguered and starving Parisians. Wagner's feelings for Paris must have been as venomous as those later harboured by Adolf Hitler against Vienna. As is well known, *Mein Kampf* is full of vituperations against that city. After the *Anschluss* of 1938 Hitler fostered the town of Linz in Upper Austria with the grotesque design that it should one day outstrip Vienna in importance. It seems as though both Wagner and Hitler were trying to get their own back on the great cities where in their younger days they had encountered humiliating setbacks.

Even the final step from nationalism to racialism was already taken by Wagner. Count Gobineau, in the fifties, brought out his baneful book *Essai sur l'inégalité des races humaines* which lent an aura of pseudo-scientific respectability to wild ideas of racial discrimination. The polyhistorian and "universal dilettante", as Gobineau has been called by one of his critics,[28] was certainly responsible for the invention of the Aryan myth, according to which the Aryans,[29] whom he oddly enough identifies with the Teutons, form a racial *élite* destined to rule over the other races. For all his teutomania, the French Count had, it is true, rather a poor opinion of the Germans of his time, whom he considered to be debased by a large admixture of Slav and Celtic blood. Yet such niceties were conveniently overlooked by Wagner and other German racialists, who preferred to see in Gobineau the unqualified champion of Germanism.

Racialist ideologies, the more nebulous the better, were thus eagerly seized upon to bolster up the flattering idea of the *Herrenvolk*. However, they could equally serve the purpose of buttressing anti-Jewish prejudices. Once Gobineau's assumption was accepted that intermarriage has led to the nobler races being tainted by the ignoble, the age-old anti-Jewish bias, which had grown stronger since the emancipation of the Jews, could be transferred to a racial footing. If the Germans could only rid themselves of the Jews, thus ran Wagner's argument in 1880, they might yet hope for a "pure race".[30] But Wagner's anti-Jewish feeling had already existed before he encountered Gobineau and his theories, for as early as September 1849, he had already published his pseudonymous diatribe *Das Judentum in der Musik* (Jewry in Music), which twenty years later he reissued under his own name. Significantly, the intensity of his anti-Jewish outbursts grew apace with his nationalism. In the same measure as he assumed the Teutonic pose, he widened the scope of his attack upon the Jews, on whom, by 1865, he blamed most of the misfortunes and aberrations of the "German spirit".[31] It really seems as though the Germans, with all their bewildering variety of dynastic, religious and other traditions, needed the Jewish bogy for their national unification in the last third of the nineteenth century—that is two generations before Hitler was to use the same device to cement the edifice of the National Socialist régime in Germany and even of his so-called New Order in Nazi-occupied Europe.

Though Richard Wagner himself died six years before Adolf Hitler was born, his second wife Cosima, born in 1837 as a natural daughter of Liszt and the Countess d'Agoult, survived until 1930. Together with her son-in-law Houston Stewart Chamberlain, who married Eva Wagner, the formidable Cosima, for many years in charge of the Bayreuth Festival, kept both the chauvinistic and anti-Jewish flags flying. As might have been foretold, both Cosima and the renegade Englishman whose book *Die Grundlagen des 19. Jahrhunderts* (1899)[32] had glorified the Aryan spirit, later became fervent supporters of the rising Hitler, whose rabid anti-semitism strongly commended him to Cosima. To the conductor Felix Weingartner she once remarked: "No bond between Aryan and Semitic blood is possible."[33] Had racialism of this kind not in the meantime acquired the ghastly associations of the Nazi extermination camps, one might be in a better mood to reflect ironically that Cosima's own mother had owed her birth to the bond between the Vicomte de Flavigny, a French aristocrat, and Marie Bethmann, who belonged to an old Jewish family of money-lenders at Frankfurt-on-Main.[34] In the circumstances it may be more appropriate to pass the verdict that the Wagners, in conjunction with other racialists, helped to lay the ideological foundations for what has rightly been described as the greatest crime in world history. On the other hand, it is absurd to put the whole blame for Nazism on the Romantic Movement, as some historians and publicists have done. Besides neglecting the many other ingredients that have gone into the making of Nazism and such-like modern monstrosities, this overlooks the long and painful process of deterioration and perversion which Romantic ideals underwent between the middle of the nineteenth century and the aftermath of the First World War.[35]

After this short digression into the more immediate past, we must resume the story of Richard Wagner from the completion of *Tristan und Isolde*. On the whole, the early 1860s, though they were not devoid of redeeming features, did not augur well for the composer. In 1861 the production of *Tannhäuser* in Paris, on which months of hard work had been wasted, proved a humiliating failure. Charles Baudelaire was the only critic who predicted that this defeat would not be decisive. True, Wagner was no longer barred from the territory of the German Confederation: a turn of events which he owed chiefly to the good offices of Grand Duke Karl Alexander of Saxe-Weimar,[36] who, if the story of Wagner's descent from Constantin was correct, must have been a relative. For a time the composer took up residence in the inspiring *milieu* of Biebrich on the Rhine, and later staged a large scale concert tour that took him as far as St. Petersburg and Moscow. But for all the German airs he increasingly gave himself, he had yet to conquer the German public. In 1862, on his first visit to Saxony since the Revolution, he had to conduct his newly composed *Die Meistersinger* overture in a half empty hall at Leipzig. A year earlier, his frantic efforts to get *Tristan und Isolde* performed at Vienna had been unsuccessful. Worst of all, in the Austrian capital where he had moved from Biebrich, Wagner, the incorrigible spendthrift, threw himself into Viennese gaiety so energetically that in the spring of 1864 he had to flee once more from his creditors. This time he was almost at his wits' end, though he clung to a kind of intuition which made him believe in a dramatic turn in his fortunes.

And indeed no turn of events could have been more dramatic than the entirely unexpected invitation from King Ludwig II of Bavaria which reached Wagner shortly after his flight from Vienna. Years before, in a preface to the text of his *Der Ring des Nibelungen*, the author, hoping against hope, had posed the question whether some German Prince, with some conception of his duties towards German art, could ever be found who would be prepared to provide the necessary backing for the production of that gigantic *Musikdrama*. These lines young Prince Ludwig (who knew the texts of the Wagner operas by heart) had read in 1863, and in the following May, barely a month after his accession to the throne, he stepped forth, a royal *deus ex machina*, to rescue the *Nibelungen* project and, as we have seen, Wagner himself. It is true, the Wittelsbach dynasty were traditional patrons of culture: Ludwig's father, Maximilian I, had attracted many distinguished poets and scholars to his capital, and Ludwig I had patronized the notable Munich school of painters. However, the young King's enthusiasm for Wagner far exceeded traditional bounds. How can his ardour be explained? Above all else, his was a plain case of the Romantic cult of heroes; but we do well to remember that there were illustrious fellow worshippers at this particular shrine, for even the young Friedrich Nietzsche at first succumbed to Wagner's spell. Among several others there exists also the testimony of the Russian painter Joukovsky (son of the poet). This artist, who came to know Wagner intimately, remarked that he could well understand how the belief in heroes might originate. There was, he asserted, a demoniac element in Wagner's nature, and it was so strong that it seemed predestined to dominate others by inculcating the feeling in them that their hero could achieve the impossible. This demoniac element was observed also by Edouard Schuré, one of the leading French Wagnerites: "To keep looking at Wagner's head," he said, "was to see at one moment the front face of Faust and at the next the profile of Mephistopheles." Juliette Lamber (later renowned under the name of Madame Adam) who knew Wagner

in Paris in 1861 has left us this vivid description of his countenance:

> His head was enormous and not lacking in character. His
> forehead was broad and high. His questioning eyes were now
> tender, now hard; but his ugly mouth, with its sarcastic expres-
> sion, seemed to press back his cheeks and like nut-crackers to
> bring together an authoritative chin and an arrogant nose.[37]

To return to King Ludwig II, so great was his veneration for
Wagner that he tended to regard him as a kind of saviour. In partial
explanation of this attitude it should be said that if there ever
existed a truly fanatical idolater of theatrical art this was Ludwig
II of Bavaria. Needless to add it was not the ordinary theatre he
had in mind: for that he had as much contempt as Wagner had.
What he envisaged was far more grandiose: a pretentious mixture
of art and religion along the lines propagated by Wagner in his *Art-
Work of the Future* and *Music of the Future* both of which made a
tremendous impact on the King. Of Wagner's early operas,
Lohengrin, which is set in the Antwerp of the tenth century,
strongly appealed to his nostalgia for the medieval past. An even
more powerful chord was struck in Ludwig's troubled soul by the
wild, unmitigated *Weltschmerz* of *Tristan und Isolde*, which was
first performed in Munich in 1865. For all these reasons the King
could hardly bear to wait for the completion of the 'music drama'
of *Der Ring*. This is not the place to relate in detail the dramatic
up and downs in the King's friendship with the composer. All
that matters here is that the most liberal hospitality was extended
to Wagner as well as to his artistic collaborators, whom he brought
with him to Bavaria. The temptation proved too great. Soon
Wagner overplayed his hand and began to indulge in an ostenta-
tious and sybaritic mode of life that necessitated ever-growing demands on the Bavarian exchequer. Between May 1864 and the
end of 1865 Wagner personally cost the State something like
100,000 florins. To make matters worse, he attempted, by fair
means and foul, to increase his hold over the King, and even engaged in large-scale intrigues against Bavarian statesmen. When
he had had his first audience with Ludwig II, the King had
begged him to stay 'for ever'. Seventeen months later, the many

enemies Wagner had made in the meantime prevailed upon the King to send him once more into exile. Though by now disillusioned with regard to Wagner's person, the King continued his generous support of the artist and his ambitious schemes. Thus Wagner was enabled to find a new haven at Triebschen: a spacious villa that overlooked Lake Lucerne. He lived there from 1866 to 1872, and during that period finished his second masterpiece, *Die Meistersinger von Nürnberg*, and also *Siegfried* and the best part of *Die Götterdämmerung*. At the request of the King he dictated to Cosima *Mein Leben*, which turned out to be a singularly unreliable autobiography in some 870 pages. It was at Triebschen that Nietzsche, then professor at Basle, became Wagner's enthusiastic apostle. After Bülow had obtained a divorce, Wagner and Cosima were married in 1870. Two years later, on Reformation Day, (31 October) 1872, Cosima—to the mortification of her father—was formally received into the Protestant Church.

The deeper reason for King Ludwig's unfailing and magnanimous patronage of Wagner, without which the project of the Festival theatre could never have been realized, lay no doubt in the fact that Wagner's conception of art was peculiarly congenial to Ludwig II. Nowhere did the King feel more at home than in the midst of an artificial world of make-believe, for in that atmosphere he could project himself into the role of a medieval ruler. His fantastical architectural schemes too helped to build up the romance which was denied to him by the stark realities of the nineteenth century. Thus Neuschwanstein, built in 1871, purported to be an inaccessible medieval stronghold perched as it was on a dizzy height of rock. To accentuate the fantastic impression, the emblems that adorned the castle were drawn from German sagas and, significantly, from Wagner's operas. That element of escape from the world as it is was strongly emphasized by Wagner himself when he spoke of "calling a non-existent world into being",[38] or of the beneficial effect of "dissolving reality into illusion (Wahn)".[39] As for his last work, *Parsifal*, its declared aim was "to enable everybody to escape, for a while, from the disgusting and disheartening burden of this world of lying and fraud and hypocrisy and legalized murder".[40]

How did Wagner contrive to conjure up that illusionary world?

Obviously a full answer to this question cannot be attempted here, but two main points must be made, the first briefly, the second at some length. Wagner soon realized that, for the purpose of creating the perfect illusion, the ideal subject matter could not be culled from the pages of history, but rather from those of mythology. Germanic and Celtic sagas and legends form the basis of *The Flying Dutchman*, *Lohengrin*, *Tannhäuser*, *Tristan und Isolde* and *Parsifal*, but the gigantic phantasmagoria of *Der Ring des Nibelungen* reaches even further back into the hazy world of primordial Nordic myths.[41] The choice of this subject also enables Wagner to indulge in his passion for the colossal and over-lifesize. Somewhat incongruously, Siegfried's character is meant to embody the 'purely human' element which is idealized in a manner reminiscent of Rousseau's noble savage.

More important even than the choice of the subject matter was the problem of form. Wagner attempted to create what he called the *Gesamtkunstwerk*, i.e. the fully integrated work of art. The idea itself was not new, for as early as 1813, the year Wagner was born, Jean Paul had stated his view that a "genuine opera" could be hoped for only if an artist stepped forward capable of writing its libretto as well as its music.[42] It is perhaps not without interest to note that, in the lighter genre of the operetta, Jean-Jacques Rousseau's *Devin de Village* (1752) had been praised by Corneille's nephew, the nonagenarian Fontenelle, for the very reason that in this case poet and composer were one and the same person. Fontenelle already believed that a perfect musical drama could never result from the co-operation of two artists. To the Romantics as we have seen, not only poetry and music, but all the arts tended to merge into one. Significantly, both the painter Philipp Otto Runge and Hoffmann, the musician, pondered over analogies between colours and tones. The perfect synthesis of the musical, poetic and plastic arts—contemplated by Vigny, Musset and George Sand—may or may not be feasible, but Wagner certainly aimed at it and to some extent achieved it, notably in *Der Ring des Nibelungen*. By combining the functions of dramatist, composer, scenic designer, not to mention that of the most exacting producer, Wagner may really be said to have consummated Romanticism both in theory and practice. His ego-worship and megalomania, in which this late Romantic again resembled Rousseau, were so highly developed that at times he believed himself to combine the grandeur of Shakespeare and Beethoven. The claim is obviously absurd, but even supposing it could be accepted, the question would surely arise whether we should not prefer to experience supreme music and supreme drama separately. In theory at any rate, Wagner would seem to expect too much of his audience over too long a stretch of time. It was rightly pointed out by Nietzsche that Wagner's *Musikdrama*, if the author's intention is to be followed, necessitates on the part of the audience too complex an attention on the acoustic, optical and intellectual planes. Such simultaneous awareness, Nietzsche thought, was possible only for short periods of time, after which our attention would inevitably oscillate between the music, the drama and the scenery. On this crucial aesthetic question, as on so many other aspects of Wagner's *œuvre*, Nietzsche showed greater insight than most biographers of Wagner or professional music critics.[43] The fact that he had once been an ardent admirer does not invalidate his later judgment, though it helps to explain the acerbity with which it was expressed.

Once our critical sense is aroused it is not difficult to discern flaws in the poetry, if not the music, of the Wagnerian *Musikdrama*. At any rate, two of the greatest masters of German style expressed their disappointment with some of Wagner's libretti. Schopenhauer, to whom the composer had sent the text of *Der Ring*, commented upon Wagner's cavalier treatment of the German tongue, and Nietzsche remarked about the language of *Parsifal* that it read like a translation from a foreign tongue. On the other hand, even the severest critic of Wagner as a poet will admit the excellence of parts of the libretto of *Die Meistersinger von Nürnberg* which incidentally was inspired by E. T. A. Hoffmann's tale *Meister Martin der Küfer*. On the purely musical plane, Wagner's epoch-making contribution to harmony and orchestration—which produced a strong impact on composers such as Anton Bruckner, Richard Strauss, Hugo Wolf, Rimsky-Korsakov and Arnold Schönberg—is in contrast to his comparative poverty in the sphere of melody. Again the delightful score of *Die Meistersinger* forms the exception that proves the rule. Often, however, and especially in parts of the tetralogy the paucity of melody is concealed by the use of an almost unprecedented volume of sound. Only Weber and Berlioz had anticipated Wagner in this respect. After a performance of *Die Götterdämmerung* we may well be tempted to echo Franz Schubert's astonishment on hearing Weber's opera *Euryanthe*:

> What is the point of these large masses of sound? *Der Freischütz* was so tender and intimate, it enchanted by its loveliness; in *Euryanthe* there is little to warm the heart![44]

One more, final, point with regard to Wagner's music: in some sections of *Tristan und Isolde*, and notoriously in *Parsifal*, a line of musical development was started which eventually led to the break-up of tonality and the anarchy of dissonance for dissonance's sake.[45] If it be correct to regard atonal music as one of the symptoms of twentieth-century spiritual nihilism, the latter phenomenon's roots can be traced back to the last stages of the Romantic movement where they first became audible.

It lies in the very nature of Wagner's art that a balanced assessment of it is made extremely difficult. The reason for this is that its total impact is likened to that of a strong drug or intoxicant. Baudelaire already noticed this effect even in the music itself. The *Lohengrin* overture, he said, had produced in him an ecstasis comparable to the state of intoxication produced by an opiate. In passing we may note that George Sand, in one of her novels, compared the effect of music to that produced by hashish.[46] Small wonder that the highly strung, let alone the hysterical, were bowled over by what the Impressionist painter Renoir (who painted Wagner's last portrait) called "the passionate fluid of sound in Wagner's music". Naturally, young people and women were particularly susceptible. After concert performances in Zürich, for example, some ladies had to find relief for their emotions in sobs and weeping.

Yet it should be emphasized that even the most unbridled emotionalism, together with all the other magic elements of Wagner's art, could never have had the same narcotic effect without the admixture of a powerful pseudo-religious ingredient.

Without holding out the enticing prospect of 'redemption' (whatever might have been meant by that term) Wagner would never have gained so enthusiastic a following.

Although Christian *motifs* and symbols occur in several of the operas, it is obvious that they are used for effect rather than for reasons of conviction. Too much can be made of Wagner's youthful impressions of Catholic culture which he first encountered in 1826–7, during his visit to Prague, the "Golden city" of the hundred spires.[47] Of his first successful work, *Rienzi* (based on Bulwer Lytton's novel), where the Pope, several Cardinals and a papal Legate appear, the composer himself remarked that its Catholicism lay more in its costume than in its idea. The same applies to *Lohengrin*, *Tannhäuser*, and above all to his last work *Parsifal*. By now the Catholic backcloth had literally become indispensable: for the setting of the Grail scene sketches were used which Joukovsky had made of the interior of Siena Cathedral. Whereas the original medieval story, Wolfram von Eschenbach's *Parzifal*, is imbued with a truly Christian spirit, the message Wagner's opera is meant to proclaim is not *Rom's Glaube ohne Worte* (Rome's faith without the words) as Nietzsche erroneously believed, but rather a strange hotchpotch of ideas among which the abnegation of erotic passion, some Buddhist sentiments and, oddly enough, vegetarianism figure prominently. Somewhat incongruously, great care was taken to render the chorus of Flower Maidens as seductive as possible. Nor can it be denied that Nietzsche was right when he discerned in the music of *Parsifal* something akin to the song of Circe the enchantress. The religious pretence of Wagner's art had now reached its climax. *Parsifal* was described by the author as a *Bühnenweihfestspiel* (stage dedication drama). It was first produced—one might almost say, celebrated— at the Bayreuth Festival in 1882. The idea that it should ever be produced anywhere else seemed to Wagner nothing short of sacrilege. Bayreuth, which in 1876 had also seen the first complete cycle of *Der Ring*, was clearly intended to become a centre of pilgrimage.

In a treatise on Beethoven, written in 1870, Wagner voiced his trust in the strong healing power both of the Christian religion and of music. There was only one way to overcome the ever-growing *malaise* of modern civilization, and that consisted in a return to the principle of pure Christianity via music. Yet it is hard to avoid the impression that at the bottom of his heart Wagner never really believed in Christ, and that instead of believing in the Christian message of salvation he rather agreed with the atheist Schopenhauer that music is the panacea for all our sufferings.[48] Moreover, so inordinate was Wagner's ego-worship that there were times when he saw himself in the same light as King Ludwig saw him: namely, as "the artist by the grace of God" who "had come to this earth to purify, bless and redeem it".[49]

It almost seems that even for his death, on 13 February 1883, the archdramatist chose the perfect setting: a fifteenth-century palazzo overlooking the Grand Canal in Venice, the city of *Weltschmerz* and melancholy associations. A few days later the funeral was held at Bayreuth. In the course of the ceremony, which to the irritation of some Wagnerites followed the Christian rite, a memorable incident took place. The Munich Wagner Society laid down a wreath at the composer's graveside which bore the inscription Redemption to the Redeemer! (*Erlösung dem Erlöser!*), words taken from the finale to *Parsifal*, where, to a Christian, they must indeed seem blasphemous. However, read as an epitaph they could and clearly should have signified the belief that the soul of Richard Wagner, who on this earth sometimes posed as would-be redeemer, had itself been redeemed by the one and only Redeemer.

In conclusion, what was it that made music the most Romantic of all the arts? Moreover, how could the Romantic religion of music ever have originated? It is to the Romantics themselves that we must turn for an answer to this question.

We have already seen how Hoffmann spoke of music's power to stir up, among other feelings, a hopeless yearning in man's soul. These words provide us with an important clue. We know that the Romantics were desperately searching for absolute values, but also that most of them shrank from finally committing themselves. It is this paradoxical double attitude of a near-nihilism coupled with the most fervent yearning for the conquest of nihilism that lies at the very root of the movement. If Hoffmann's analysis be correct, music through its incomparable appeal to the emotions greatly intensifies that yearning. And yet the soul, though deeply stirred by music, is not compelled by it to commit itself. In his essay on Beethoven's instrumental music, Hoffmann wrote explicitly:

> Music unlocks for man the gateway to an unknown realm, a world which has nothing in common with the eternal world of senses that surrounds him, and in which he leaves behind all definable feelings so as to abandon himself to an ineffable yearning.

The same point is corroborated by Robert Schumann's testimony:

> Music speaks the most common language through which the soul is stimulated in a free and undecided manner.[50]

More eloquently the same idea was expressed a few years later by Lamennais. He started by contrasting music and the plastic arts, especially architecture, which he thought found themselves in an impossible situation because the masses had lost their faith and consequently no one knew to what gods temples ought to be erected. Here Lamennais continued:

> Music is the sole art of our epoch because that which is vague and mysterious in it corresponds to that oscillation of souls and indefinable suffering which we all experience.[51]

In our century, it was stated by Igor Stravinsky that music is the only sphere in which man consciously experiences the present. The remark is typical for the approach of the rationalist: no Romantic would have made it. For the Romantics, who, in general preferred to live as it were in the past or the future, music constituted the sphere in which the present could best be experienced in a kind of enchanting dream.

Wagner (portrait by E. Keitz, 1842)

Nietzsche

Epilogue

NOTHING, perhaps, reveals the essence of Romanticism better than an aside in Nietzsche's *The Birth of Tragedy from the Spirit of Music* (1872). He speaks of the basic dissonance in human nature, and asks "What is Man?" Dissonance, that characteristic of the Romantic movement as a whole, was the keynote of Nietzsche's own personality. Lou von Salomé, his congenial friend and earliest biographer, already noted this trait when she commented upon the inner dichotomy of his character.[1] So marked was that discord in his personality that it somehow seemed to lack a firm centre of gravity. Therefore it is not surprising that his *œuvre* contains a vast number of unresolved contradictions, and, indeed, that Nietzsche took great pride in not having produced anything resembling a systematic philosophy.[2] What he has left us instead might be described as the intellectual echo of the recurrent oscillations of his soul, observed with the utmost sensitivity. Never in the history of thought has anyone of comparable stature shown himself to be more impulsive than Nietzsche.

As the pendulum of his evaluations swung backwards and forwards there were times when he seemed nearer to rationalist Enlightenment than to Romanticism, notably during the late 1870s, when, stimulated by his rationalist friend Paul Rée, he wrote the brilliant collection of aphorisms entitled *Human—All too human*, which he dedicated to the memory of Voltaire. Jacob Burckhardt remarked of this work that it might have been written by one of the great French aphorists and that some of its contents would arouse La Rochefoucauld's envy were he to read it in Hades.[3] In other ways too Nietzsche, the late-comer to Romanticism, attempted to conquer his own Romantic inclinations. The story of his early adoration of, and later apostasy from, Richard Wagner has been told in the preceding chapter of this study. Similarly he came to turn his back on Robert Schumann's music, which he now likened to "a lake full of *limonade gazeuse*". The prevailing preoccupation with history, another legacy of Romanticism, also aroused his criticism, since he feared that it might paralyse spontaneous cultural development.[4] Nor had he anything but scorn for the pretensions of messianic nationalism, especially of the new German brand, which, in his later years, he never ceased to castigate. There was a sense in which he was justified to call himself "the last anti-political German". His caustic remarks about Schleiermacher's and Schelling's metaphysical excesses also point in the anti-Romantic direction.

However, just as Nietzsche unmasked Schelling's "camouflaged theology", we in our turn have to uncover his own camouflaged Romanticism, as long as this term—as in the case of Wagner —is understood in its wider European rather than in its narrower German connotation.[5] For all his protestations Nietzsche may indeed be said to have composed the epilogue to Romanticism, an epilogue in which both grandeur and tragedy of the movement reached symbolical heights.

As with Lord Byron, whom Nietzsche admired, the impact of the personality was even greater than that of the *œuvre*. A generation younger than the youngest Romantics—his father was born in the same year as Wagner—Nietzsche, himself born at Röcken near Leipzig in 1844, amazingly quickly caught up with his elders. Before he was able to complete his classical studies at Leipzig, the venerable University of Basle, early in 1869, appointed him to a professorship in that subject at the unprecedented age of twenty-four. Barely three years later, *The Birth of Tragedy from the Spirit of Music*, which he dedicated to Wagner, received the latter's enthusiastic approval, although academic scholars like Ritschl, whose *protégé* Nietzsche had been, were more reserved in their judgment—and others, notably von Willamowitz-Moellendorf, were openly hostile. By 1912, however, F. M. Cornford, the great British classicist, hailed it as "a work of profound insight which left the scholarship of a generation toiling in the rear".

Already at an early stage the polyphonic nature of Nietzsche's mind revolted against the trend towards over-specialization whereby scholars no longer concerned themselves with the philosophical implications of their own branch of knowledge. Indeed, as early as April 1867, in a characteristic letter to his friend von Gersdorff, he deplored the way in which most philologists lacked that "edifying total view of antiquity because they place themselves too close to the picture and investigate a patch of oil instead of admiring —and enjoying—the great, bold features of the whole painting". At the beginning of 1870, he wrote to his friend Rohde that learning, art and philosophy were coalescing in his mind to such an extent that he would surely one day give birth to a centaur. That centaur, *The Birth of Tragedy*, helped to rediscover the exuberant and 'unclassical' element in the ancient Greek civilization. Nietzsche's strictures on the Romantic approach to the past did not prevent him from feeling a marked nostalgia for the culture of pre-Socratic, i.e. pre-rationalist, Greece, which in typical Romantic fashion he extolled at the expense of Socratic Enlightenment.

Nietzsche's academic career was as short as it was meteoric. Only ten years after his appointment he resigned his post, outwardly for reasons of ill health, but more decisively as a result of a growing conviction that his real vocation lay elsewhere. His decision to leave Basle was made easier by the fact that, a few years back, his attempt to exchange the chair of classics for the then vacant chair of philosophy had proved unsuccessful. Now, in 1879, there began for him a restless decade of supra-Byronic mobility from place to place, through Italy, Southern France and Switzerland, interspersed with occasional journeys to Germany and relieved only by longer and recurring sojourns in Nice, or Genoa, and the Upper Engadine. In the latter region, the village of Sils Maria, situated between the Lakes of Sils and Silvaplana, "a wondrous mixture of the mild, the grandiose and the mysterious", as he rightly called it,[6] became his much loved summer residence where he could indulge in his habit of walking and meditating for hours on end. It was near Sils Maria, on the enchanting wooded peninsula of Chastè—the site of a Roman castellum—that he would have liked to build for himself a wooden hut after Henry David Thoreau's fashion.

Although he appreciated the warmth of human friendship he withdrew more and more into solitude and yet suffered intensely from his isolation. Not that he lacked self-sacrificing friends, among whom the upright and discerning Franz Overbeck, a former colleague at Basle, was outstanding. Equally ambivalent was Nietzsche's attitude to the opposite sex. In his youth he experienced a Manfred-like emotion for his sister Elisabeth, who afterwards was to play a baneful role in his life. To Lou von Salomé, a Russian aristocrat sixteen years his junior, he felt strongly attracted almost from the moment they met in St. Peter's in Rome in the spring of 1882, but by the end of the year, when estrangement had set in owing to his sister's jealousy, his emotion towards Lou turned to hatred, or more precisely oscillated between hatred and love, almost combining those two opposite poles in a manner for which Nietzsche himself coined the term *Hass-Liebe* (love-hatred). However, Lou's bold and original mind, which had impressed and stimulated him during their philosophical discussions at Tautenburg in Thuringia in the summer of 1882, continued to fascinate him. His isolation became more complete when his sister's intrigues temporarily estranged him even from his well-meaning mother. Yet in a deeper sense it was perhaps the nature of his self-imposed iconoclastic task that rendered his isolation inevitable.

The choice of places such as the Riviera or the Engadine was by no means exclusively due to the beauty of their scenery. An even more important factor was the serene climate. For, unlike the sturdy Wordsworth, who enjoyed any kind of weather, Nietzsche, with his hypersensitivity, was excessively affected by atmospheric depressions and humidity: a decisive reason that militated against the choice of Venice, for which he otherwise felt the strongest affection. Significantly, the view from that city on to the grave-yard island of San Michele, with its cypresses and its golden walls, had imprinted itself on his mind. At least three factors, excessive myopia, a squint which in those days could not be corrected, and a state of nervous unbalance, combined to cause him uncommonly violent attacks of migraine and subsequent exhaustion. With some reason he believed that he had suffered even more than Leopardi, whose pathetic longing for painlessness he shared. At the same time he took pride in his suffering, which he regarded as a mark of distinction—though not from a religious point of view. The characteristic Romantic concept of the inevitability of pain and suffering found in him the most eloquent exponent. It was in the same vein that he exposed the shallowness of modern or, for that matter, ancient hedonistic and utilitarian ideals.

The dichotomy of his mind is clearly revealed in his general attitude to life and death. On the one hand, a most gloomy type of *Weltschmerz*, exceeding in his own estimation that of Leopardi and Schopenhauer,[7] manifested itself as an intense feeling of disgust with the world as he found it. Again, it was neither ill-health nor any other form of suffering that lay at the root of that *Weltschmerz*. The fact that Nietzsche himself was clearly aware of this is shown, among other things, by the following entry in one of his post-humously published notebooks:

"Without the Christian faith," said Pascal, "you will become for yourselves, just as nature and history will become, *un monstre et un chaos*." This prophecy we have fulfilled.[8]

Time and again Nietzsche drew horrifying pictures of the spiritual void that must prevail in a world from which the old faith has gone out and in which the sensations of uprootedness, purposelessness and despair hold sway. This was never more poignantly done than in an aphorism from his *Joyful Wisdom* (1882). The crucial passage quoted below may be placed side by side with Lamennais's horrifying vision:[9]

The Madman: Have you ever heard of the madman who on a bright morning lighted a lantern and ran to the market-place calling out unceasingly: "I seek God! I seek God! . . . Where is God gone?" he called out. "I mean to tell you! We have killed him—you and I! We are all his murderers! But how have we done it? How were we able to drink up the sea? Who gave us the sponge to wipe away the whole horizon? What did we do when we loosened this earth from its sun? Whither does it now move? Whither do we move? Away from all suns? Do we not dash on unceasingly? Backwards, sideways, forwards, in all directions? Is there still an above and below? Do we not stray, as through infinite nothingness? Does not empty space breathe upon us? Has it not become colder? Does not night come on continually, darker and darker? Shall we not have to light lanterns in the morning? Do we not hear the voice of the grave-diggers who are burying God? Do we not smell the divine putrefaction?—for even Gods putrefy! God is dead! God remains dead! And we have killed him! How shall we console ourselves, the most murderous of all murderers? The holiest and mightiest that the world has hitherto possessed, has bled to death under our knife,—who will wipe the blood from us? With what water could we cleanse ourselves? What lustrums, what sacred games shall we have to devise? Is not the magnitude of this deed too great for us? Shall we not ourselves have to become Gods, merely to seem worthy of it?''

As regards the future, Nietzsche felt that the next two centuries would be characterized by cataclysmic events, such as great wars and revolutions, as well as a further advance of spiritual nihilism. The dilemma appeared to be complete: without a return to Christianity—which Nietzsche rejected—man's spiritual essence would wither away. And yet the other half of Nietzsche's personality refused to surrender to gloom and despondency. Even though human lives were becoming empty and meaningless, could not Life itself be glorified? If no other Gods remained, Life would have to be declared divine. Life for Nietzsche emphatically meant life on this earth, for he no longer believed in the Christian 'finale' of a life in the hereafter. In a strangely paradoxical manner the apotheosis of life came to be linked in his mind to the fatalistic Pythagorean idea of the Eternal Recurrence. In accepting this principle, he was in all probability also influenced by ancient Indian thought as expounded by his friend Paul Deussen in *Das System der Vedanta* (1883). It is only fair to add that the idea of Eternal Recurrence was presented by Nietzsche in a highly modernized, and indeed *avant-garde* version, which in some important aspects foreshadowed the controversial Steady State theory propounded in our days by Fred Hoyle, Bondi and Gold. Whereas Nietzsche regarded space as finite and non-spherical (an anticipation of Einstein!), he held time to be infinite, i.e. endless, or, for that matter, without a beginning. The notion of creation out of nothing was rejected by him as utterly unintelligible. Energy, which was finite, could only have a number of possible states and combinations, which meant that the universe, at some stage, must reach a total state exactly identical with a previous state. Basing his conclusions on the principle of determinism, which in the 1880s enjoyed a far greater reputation in scientific circles than it does nowadays, Nietzsche inferred that the whole process must of necessity repeat exactly the same course previously followed between the two states, so that, at gigantic intervals, every event re-recurs identically in every detail, and so to all eternity. Nietzsche was clearly aware of the fact that this cosmology, as far as man was concerned, constituted the most extreme form of nihilism, projecting meaninglessness into all eternity.[10] Most paradoxically of all, this grotesque and, one might have thought, disconcerting prospect provided Nietzsche with a strong spiritual uplift which Franz Overbeck had in mind when he called his friend's 'optimism' the optimism of a desperado.[11] Indeed Nietzsche himself voiced his genuine astonishment at his own psychological volte-face:

No! Such a life! And myself being the champion of life![12]

It is clear that the idea of Eternal Recurrence, for all its scientific, physicist trappings, was conceived by Nietzsche in a state of metaphysical auto-intoxication. Here there was a substitute religion if ever there was one. Psychologically linked to it was Nietzsche's second *ersatz* religion, although at first sight the two substitutes might seem to clash with each other. Though he himself, in the words of Lou von Salomé, had to put on a mask in order to appear as the champion of Life, there was nothing to stop him from envisaging some future human being to fit that role more perfectly. That Superman—for that is what Nietzsche calls him[13]—would transcend man as we know him as the latter transcends the most highly developed animal. This might suggest an evolutionalist outlook according to which Superman would evolve by a process of natural selection, especially when we are told that "man is a rope stretched between animal and Superman",[14] but Nietzsche adds significantly: "a rope over an abyss" into which that rope might presumably fall unless superior individuals help to pave the way for the advent of Superman.[15] In *Thus Spake Zarathustra*, a kind of anti-bible couched in biblical style, both ideas, of the Eternal Recurrence as well as of the Superman, are fervently propagated. It is noteworthy that Nietzsche used for his mouthpiece the name of the Persian sage and founder of religion who inspired Leopardi's gruesome *Ode to Arimane*. It goes without saying that Zoroastrianism, and Nietzsche's psuedo-religion have very little in common. Yet another Romantic trait may be noticed: the concern for mankind's distant future, a trait Nietzsche shared with Victor Hugo, whom he otherwise detested.

Indeed, nothing could have been more abhorrent to Nietzsche than Victor Hugo's idolization of the People. Although he does not mention Carlyle in this context, the latter's idolization of geniuses and great men came much closer to Nietzsche's ideal. Napoleon and, more ominously, Cesare Borgia, appeared to him as precursors of the Superman. He hated the French Revolution and deplored the process of social levelling which it had set in motion. Against the tide of the time he stressed the importance of an *élite* and an hierarchic society:

> Every raising up of the type 'man' was hitherto the work of an aristocratic society—and so it will always be: of a society, which believes in a long ladder of class-differentiation and of difference in value between man and man and has need of slavery in some sense or other.[16]

He believed himself—erroneously as it turned out—to be of aristocratic origin. (Equally erroneously he thought that his paternal ancestors had been Poles. In fact they are now believed to have migrated to Saxony from Bohemia, that hot-bed of religious strife, during the sixteenth or seventeenth century. The family name is obviously of Slavonic origin.)

However, Nietzsche's anti-egalitarianism, or Aristocratic Radicalism as Georg Brandes called it, was far more radical than that of the Romantics. He shared with them as a belief that European culture was in process of vulgarization: he went beyond most of them in his denial of the equality of all human beings before God. In point of fact one of his main objections to Christianity lay precisely in the fact that that religion presupposes the equal value of all human souls.[17] Moreover, Christianity, in Nietzsche's view, renders man weak, submissive, humbled and resigned, and thereby prevents the emergence of amoral and uninhibited supermen. Here the attitudes of Rousseau and Nietzsche may be compared. Rousseau, too, feared the effect of the Christian precept of humility, but he did so for the opposite reason. What he feared was lest the Church, siding with the powers that be, might teach humility only to the lower classes and thereby help to perpetuate the social and political inequality which he wished to eradicate. We may note in passing that Mazzini's objections to organized religion ran on similar lines. Conversely, Nietzsche rejected the Christian precept of humility on account of its undesirable levelling effect. It was only logical that, unlike Rousseau or Mazzini, who still could appeal to Christian values in a secularized form, Nietzsche from his point of view had to repudiate a religion whose cornerstone is Charity.

If we are to gauge the extent of Nietzsche's defiance of God we also have to bear in mind that not only his father, whom he lost early in life, but also several of his ancestors on both sides had been Lutheran pastors (one of whom had written a book on the eternal survival of Christianity), and that he was educated at the renowned Protestant gymnasium of Pforta, which had previously been attended by Novalis, Fichte and the brothers Schlegel. At Bonn, his first university, he originally intended to read theology side by side with classics, but even after changing to the exclusive study of the ancient world, he was, according to Paul Deussen, still a fervent defender of the faith. At the age of twenty-one, when he no longer believed in Christ, he still clung to the belief that the human soul was in need of redemption.[18] Some ten years later, at the height of his rationalist phase, he spent a good deal of the winter of 1876-7 at Sorrento studying and pondering the New Testament, and even in Turin in the autumn of 1888, while completing his violent attack on Christianity, *Antichrist: Fluch auf das Christentum* (*Antichrist: A Curse on Christianity*), the serious study of the Gospels was carried on. It is also highly significant that at the beginning of January 1889, at the very moment when his mind began to collapse and the subconscious regions of his personality for the first time emerged unmasked, some of his letters carried the signature "Dionysos" while others were signed "The

Crucified". Clearly, Nietzsche's attitude to Christ may best be characterized by the term 'love-hatred'.

In that complex relationship the element of hatred gradually gained the ascendancy, until in the end it almost stifled the last remnants of love. Already in 1883 Nietzsche described himself in a letter to a friend as one of the most terrible adversaries of Christianity.[19] In the same year he completed the last part of *Zarathustra* which, among other things, contained a travesty of the Sermon on the Mount, Christ's Passion and the Last Supper. So glaring was the blasphemy that at first no publisher could be found for it. The demoniacal element which Lou von Salomé in 1883 began to discern in his writings grew in intensity until Nietzsche's hubristic defiance of God reached unsurpassable dimensions during the last six months before his collapse. At that stage his cult of the Ego degenerated into sheer megalomania when, in some moments, he behaved as though he believed himself to be the dead God's successor—as for example when he decreed that henceforth the chronology of A.D. would have to be replaced by that of *Antichrist*. In a grotesque attempt at the "transvaluation of all values"—which, it is believed, may have been suggested to him by Callicles' speech in Plato's *Gorgias* or by Thucydides' reflections on Corcyra[20]—Nietzsche romanticized evil and openly advocated cruelty, injustice, Machiavellian falsehood and, most ominously of all, castration and ruthless annihilation of millions of misfits, decadents and parasites,[21] in the name of the nebulous ideals of vitality and the Will to Power.

It is ironical to reflect that it was one of the early German Romantics, Novalis, who had drawn attention to the fact that the ideal of brute force often has an æsthetic appeal for persons suffering from acute forms of debility.[22] Psychoanalysis has since confirmed the correlation between neurasthenia on the one hand and perverse cruelty on the other, and has shown that the latter is often confined to the person's imagination. It is therefore not surprising to learn that Nietzsche, despite his fulminations against pity[23] and his sadistic visions, which so sadly disfigure his writings, could not bear the sight of a coach-horse being maltreated in the streets of Turin. In fact, it was that very incident, on 3 January 1889, that triggered off his mental collapse.

Epilogue

The root cause of Nietzsche's tragedy was that his tremendous creative urge far exceeded his creative capability. It is true that his artistic gifts were manifold. At one time he even considered taking up the career of a musician, but although some of his compositions elicited Franz Liszt's praise his achievement in that sphere lacked real originality. I myself had an opportunity of hearing a recital of Nietzsche's attractive sonata *Silvesternacht* for violin and piano, and was struck by its indebtedness to Schumann.[23] As a master of German style he stands very high, but apart from some exquisite poems which have greatly influenced German poetry since Stefan George, Nietzsche's artistic sensibility, as Franz Overbeck rightly observed, was almost entirely of a rhetorical nature—perhaps, we may add, not unlike that of the Abbé de Lamennais. In a certain sense the seductive and scintillating style of *Also sprach Zarathustra* bears resemblance to *Paroles d'un Croyant*. Not satisfied with his unusual double achievement as a penetrating critic of his time and a highly intuitive and anticipating mind, Nietzsche desired to be more than a poet-philosopher in the Romantic sense of the word. What he craved for was the more exalted role of prophet or legislator of values, or, in his own words, an intellect called upon to rule the world (*ein weltregierender Geist*). At the same time he was troubled by secret doubts about his mission which he disclosed to Franz Overbeck's wife Ida. Another significant admission is contained in his letter to Franz Overbeck on 2 July 1885, that is after the completion of *Zarathustra*:

> For me life now consists in the wish that all things turn out to be different from the way I grasp them and that someone might render my 'truths' untrustworthy to myself.

It has also been pointed out that the final part of *Zarathustra*, for all its blasphemous frenzy, also contains passages in which a much softer and mysterious countervoice may be discerned.[25]

Further evidence for the experimental nature of Nietzsche's 'prophecy' lies in a revealing remark to Lou von Salomé:

> Once everything has been run through—whither is one to run then? If all potential permutations were exhausted—what

would follow? Why? Would one not have to come back to faith? Perhaps to a Catholic faith? In any case, going round in a circle would be more probable than standing still.[26]

But although Nietzsche could toy with the idea of a return to the faith, his pride would not allow him to retreat. And yet, even at the height of his revolt against Christ, the inner voice was not mute. The nearer he approached to the precipice of his collapse, the more openly he allowed that voice to be heard. Thus, in a letter to Brandes on 20 November 1888, he warningly called himself a disaster (*ein Verhängnis*) and signed himself "Yours Nietzsche, at present monster (*jetzt Untier*)". It will be generally agreed that this is not the manner in which genuine prophets usually think of themselves.

Nietzsche's powers of self-revelation, in which he exceeded even the most introspective Romantics, were mirrored in a passage entitled 'A Fable' in his *Morgenröte* (Dawn of Day) published in 1881:

> The Don Juan of knowledge—no philosopher has yet succeeded in discovering him. He is wanting in love for the things he apprehends, but he possesses wit, a lust for the hunting after knowledge, and the intrigues in connection with it, and he finds enjoyment in all these, even up to the highest and most distant stars of knowledge—until at last there is nothing left for him to pursue but the absolutely injurious side of knowledge, just as the drunkard who ends by drinking absinthe and aquafortis. That is why last of all he feels a longing for hell, for this is the final knowledge which seduces him. Perhaps even this would disappoint him, as all things apprehended do. And then he would have to stand still for all eternity, a victim to eternal disenchantment, himself transformed into the Stony Guest, with a craving for the Last Supper of knowledge which will never more fall to his share! For the whole world has not a morsel left to offer to this famished man.

All the essential features of Nietzsche's spiritual Odyssey are contained in that Fable: the strange lack of commitment, so characteristic of Romanticism, here expressed in the words, "he is wanting in love for the things he apprehends";[27] the intellectual Don Juan's restless search for new adventures of the mind; the sadistic desire to cause pain; the self-torturing Byronic longing for his own perdition (Zarathustra calls himself "self executioner"); and last but not least disillusionment following in the wake of sin and the subsequent yearning for redemption, of which, the hero of the Fable fears, he will never partake. It is hard to avoid the impression that at this stage psychological introspection and religious remorse have become inextricably interwoven.

Nietzsche's mental collapse has been examined from many different angles. While some have surmised an hereditary factor, others have pointed to Nietzsche's abuse of self-prescribed drugs of all kinds (a factor that seems to have been overrated), while still others have laid the greatest stress on the long-term effects of a syphilitic infection which, as we now know, Nietzsche had contracted in the notorious *Totengässlein* in Basle in 1873:[28] an infection which before Ehrlich's discovery of Salvarsan often entailed grave paralytic symptoms. But although present-day aids for a reliable medical diagnosis were not yet available in the 1880s or 1890s, and a certain measure of doubt must therefore always remain, it should be pointed out that, according to well-informed medical experts, Nietzsche's paralysis was not at all of the typical post-syphilitic kind. Nor does he seem to have shown any sure symptoms of a psychotic disturbance—as distinct from a neurological one—at any time before the summer of 1888.[29] The graphological test, for what it is worth, is negative even for the period right up to the actual collapse.

In these circumstances it is perhaps legitimate to surmise that the decisive factor making for the final collapse was what Sigmund Freud would have called *Flucht in die Krankheit* (escape into malady). Lou von Salomé, who knew Nietzsche as well as anybody, certainly had the impression that he had been craving for such a solution. As soon as it came, the unbearable and ever-mounting tension at which he had been living for so long immediately disappeared, as is shown in his note to Peter Gast which reads:

Sing me a new song: the world is transfigured and all heavens are glad.[30]

The Mind of the European Romantics

Physically Nietzsche survived until 25 August 1900, the last three years at Weimar, which, owing to his fame, became once more a place of pilgrimage.

At the present time, two thirds of a century or so after Nietzsche's death, it is safe to hazard the prognosis that, for good or ill, the repercussions of his thought will continue to be felt for a very long time to come. If publication statistics may serve as a guide, it is noteworthy that the *International Nietzsche Bibliography*, published in North Carolina in 1960 listed very nearly 4,000 significant items of Nietzsche criticism in altogether twenty-seven languages. As regards the adverse effects, Karl Kraus's conclusion in his poem *Der Antichrist* (1921) still holds good:

> Er hat es dem Unwert leicht gemacht,
> die Werte umzuwerten.
>
> An diesem halkyonischen Fest
> wird die Welt noch lange kranken.[31]

His impact hitherto has been greater than that of any other nineteenth-century thinker, with the one exception of Karl Marx. Both modern psychology as well as existentialism have received decisive stimuli through Nietzsche. Not without justification has he been hailed as the greatest psychologist among philosophers of all ages. However, the German tendency to carry everything to extremes—a tendency Goethe had already deplored—showed its disastrous effects even in this respect. True, Nietzsche succeeded in sharpening the tools of psychological analysis, but in the end those tools as wielded by him and his disciples cut at the very roots of the human psyche. When all ideals and beliefs had been analysed and made intellectually suspect, the integrated human personality was in danger of breaking down. Highly fruitful though the mutual penetration of the conscious and subconscious regions of the human mind has proved, there are limits beyond which this process ought not to be extended.[32] At certain times Nietzsche, it seems, was clearly aware of this. His *Human—All too human*, which destroyed so many ideals, contains what was perhaps a prophetic passage, describing the light—feeble and indistinct though it might be—which he saw at the end of the long tunnel of spiritual nihilism:

A Few Rungs Back: A degree of culture, and assuredly a very high one, is attained when man rises above superstitions and religious notions and fears, and, for instance, no longer believes in guardian angels or in original sin, and has also ceased to talk of the salvation of his soul—if he has attained to this degree of freedom, he has still to overcome metaphysics with the greatest exertion of his intelligence. Then, however, a *retrogressive movement* is necessary; he must understand the historical justification as well as the psychological in such representations, he must recognize how the greatest advancement of humanity has come therefrom, and how, without such a retrocursive movement, we should have been robbed of the best achievements of man's existence up to the present age. In philosophical metaphysics, I now see ever-increasing numbers who have attained to the negative goal (that all positive metaphysics is error), but as yet few who climb a few rungs backwards; one ought to look out, perhaps, over the last steps of the ladder, but not to try to stand upon them. The most enlightened only succeed so far as to free themselves from metaphysics and look back upon it with superiority, while it is necessary here, too, as in the hippodrome, to turn round the end of the course.[33]

This thought, with its hopeful glimpse of the future, epitomizes the deep-rooted metaphysical urge so characteristic of the Romantics.

Notes and Sources

INTRODUCTION

1. Several writers have drawn attention to this phenomenon; notably Romano Guardini in a Tübingen lecture on the essence of Romanticism, published in a symposium entitled *Romantik* (1948), and John Heath-Stubbs in *The Darkling Plain. A Study of the Later Fortunes of Romanticism in English Poetry* (London, 1950).

2. The same difficulty applies in the case of other great intellectual movements. Ernst Walser, for example, has shown that the Renaissance cannot be defined simply in terms of the two trends of individualism and sensualism (*Gesammelte Studien zur Geistesgeschichte der Renaissance* [Basel, 1932], p. 102). Cf. also Ernst Cassirer, *The Logic of the Humanities*, translated by C. S. Howe (New Haven, 1961), pp. 137–9.

In 1964 the German *Propyläen-Weltgeschichte* published its sixth volume, entitled *Weltkulturen: Renaissance in Europa*, with a contribution by the Italian historian Eugenio Garin on the civilization of the Renaissance. In their Introduction, the editors, Golo Mann and August Nitschke, touch on the question: what was the essence of the Renaissance? They then go on to say: "Professor Garin would presumably reply that that question can hardly be answered more concisely than has been done in the ... pages [of his contribution]."

3. Kierkegaard protests against the view "that Romanticism can be comprehended in one concept" (*The Journals of Søren Kierkegaard*, ed. Alexander Dru [O.U.P., 1938], p. 25).

4. Cf. G. Temple's inaugural lecture at Oxford, 'The Classic and the Romantic in Natural Philosophy', 1954, p. 7.

5. *Revue de littérature comparée*, XXIV, 1950, p. 138.

6. The first part of this statement was endorsed by Lord Acton: "The history of ideas undermines national treatment; ideas are international, make history international" ('Acton's Notes for a

Romanes Lecture', ed. G. E. Fasnacht, *Contemporary Review* [London, 1952], p. 352). Lord Acton's notes, written just before the turn of the century, bear the striking title *History in the Twentieth Century*.

7. *Blütezeit der Romantik* (1899), *Ausbreitung und Verfall der Romantik* (1902).

8. *La crise de la conscience européenne 1680–1715* (Paris, 1935), *La pensée européenne au XVIIIᵉ siècle: de Montesquieu à Lessing* (Paris, 1946).

9. In this respect, the present study deviates both from Farinelli and van Tieghem.

10. *The Civilization of the Renaissance in Italy*, Introduction.

PART ONE: THE REVOLT AGAINST THE EIGHTEENTH CENTURY

I. THE REACTION AGAINST RATIONALISM

1. Cf. E. R. Dodds, *The Greeks and the Irrational* (Berkeley and Los Angeles, 1951), Chapter VI.

2. Letter to De Sinner, 21 February 1832.

3. *Nineteenth-Century Studies* (London, 1949), p. 1.

4. "Cold reason has never done anything illustrious."

5. "In the long run reason takes the line that the heart dictates."

6. "For us, to exist is to feel; and our sensibility is incontestably prior to our reason."

7. *A Defence of Poetry* (1831).

8. The entry is dated 29 March 1824 (*Franz Schubert: Briefe und Schriften*, ed. Otto Erich Deutsch (Vienna, 1954], p. 76).

9. Shelley, on the other hand, argues differently: "Reason is the enumeration of quantities already known; imagination is the perception of the value of those quantities, both separately and as a whole. Reason respects the difference, and imagination the similitude of things." (*Op. cit.*)

10. *Psychologische Typen* (Zürich, 1921), p. 643. The discovery of the intuitive type, according to Jung, was made by M. Moltzer.

11. Cf. W. J. A. Fuller's article on Morphy, *British Chess Magazine*, 1886. Anderssen, too, was always noted for the rapidity of his play. (Cf. Fred Reinfeld, *The Human Side of Chess* [London, 1953],

p. 27). In 1959 the Russian P. A. Romanovsky published a comprehensive book on *Romanticism in the Art of Chess*.

12. His most formidable opponent was Anderssen. In judging the result of their encounter in a match in Paris, in December 1858, it must be borne in mind that the German master, born in 1818, was then nearly double Morphy's age.

13. 'Was heisst: sich im Denken orientieren?' (1786), *Sämmtliche Werke*, ed. G. Hartenstein (Leipzig, 1867), p. 343. Kant's immediate target was Friedrich Heinrich Jacobi's pre-Romantic 'Glaubensphilosophie' (philosophy of faith).

14. This anti-rational brand of irrationalism is well analysed in Jean F. Neurohr, *Der Mythos vom Dritten Reich* (Stuttgart, 1957).

15. *Erlebtes: Halle und Heidelberg*.

16. To Thomas Poole, 16 October 1797 (*Collected Letters of Samuel Taylor Coleridge*, ed. Earl Leslie Griggs, [O.U.P., 1956], Vol. I, pp. 209–10).

17. *Op. cit.*, p. 660. Cf. also Jung's definition: "The irrational is something outside the province of reason, whose essence, therefore, is not established by reason."

18. Cf. the detailed historical account by Margaret Miller, 'Gericault's Paintings of the Insane', in the *Journal of the Warburg and Courtauld Institutes*, Vol. IV (London, 1940–1).

19. "Dreams are the sweetest and, perhaps, the truest things in life."

II. PROGRESS AND DISENCHANTMENT

1. B. H. G. Wormald, 'Progress and Hope', Third Programme broadcast, *The Listener*, 9 April 1964, p. 581.

2. Cf. H. Vyverberg, *Historical Pessimism in the French Enlightenment* (Cambridge, Mass., 1958).

3. For a fuller elaboration of Rousseau's point of view, cf. John Plamenatz, *Man and Society. A critical examination of some important social and political theories from Machiavelli to Marx* (London, 1963), Vol. II, Chapters 2 and 7.

4. 'Auch eine Philosophie der Geschichte zur Bildung der Menschheit' (1774), *Sämmtliche Werke* (Tübingen, 1806), Vol. II, pp. 186–7. Cf also Erich Kayser, 'Herders Wendung zur Geschichte', in *Herder-Studien* (Würzburg, 1960).

Notes and Sources

5. Madame de Staël-Holstein, *De la littérature considérée dans ses rapports avec les institutions sociales*. Seconde partie: 'De l'état actuel des lumières en France, et de leurs progrès futurs', first published in 1800.

6. The version of 1805–6, Book X, ll. 206–11.

7. For a fuller treatment of the Romantic attitude towards centralization, see my article 'Leviathan and the European Romantics', *Cambridge Journal*, Vol. I (Cambridge, 1948).

8. Two names spring to mind: Goethe and Burke.

9. *Fears in Solitude*, written in April 1798, during the alarm of an invasion, ll. 159–61.

10. 'Signatur des Zeitalters', *Concordia* (Vienna, 1820), p. 9. The doctrine of human perfectibility, about which F. Schlegel had entertained grave doubts ever since 1805, was entirely rejected by him towards the end of his life.

11. Cf. also F. Altheim, *Niedergang der Alten Welt* (Frankfurt am Main, 1952).

12. *Revolt of the Masses*, published two years after the original Spanish edition of 1930. Cf. also Henrik de Man, *Vermassung und Kulturverfall. Eine Diagnose unserer Zeit* (Salzburg, 1951).

13. Walter Muschg, *Tragische Literaturgeschichte*, second revised edition (Bern, 1953), pp. 369–75; J. Droz, *Deutschland und die Französische Revolution* (Wiesbaden, 1955,), p. 29.

14. *Das Erlebnis und die Dichtung*, 7th edition (Leipzig, 1921), pp. 269–70. Friedrich Schlegel had already arrived at a similar conclusion when he remarked: "Der Einzelne kann nie sein Zeitalter ganz verleugnen, doch kann er sich über dasselbe erheben, ist an den Gang seiner Zeit nicht mit unabänderlicher Notwendigkeit gebunden" (*Philosophische Vorlesungen*, 1804–6, ed. Windischmann, II, p. 219).

III. THE EMPHASIS ON SINGULARITY

1. For Coleridge's opinion of planners and constitution-makers cf. also *The Statesman's Manual; or the Bible the best guide to political skill and foresight: a Lay Sermon addressed to the Higher Classes of Society* (London, 1816), p. 41.

2. *Fragmente über die neuere deutsche Literatur*.

3. IV. Teil, 4. Kapital (Riga und Leipzig, 1791).

4. *Paměti*, IV (Prague, 1862), p. 281.

5. Kollár's programmatic treatise of 1836 is entitled *O literárnej vzájemnosti mezi kmeny a nářečími slávskými* (On the Literary Inter-dependence among the Slav Nations and Dialects). Cf. Milada Součková, *The Czech Romantics* (The Hague, 1958), Chapter I: 'Romanticism gives birth to Czech literature.'

6. Cf. Robert Auty, '*Spracherneuerung und Sprachschöpfung im Donauram, 1780–1850*', *Österreichische Osthefte*, Vol. III (Vienna, 1961), pp. 369–70.

7. *Geschichte der slawischen Sprache und Literatur nach allen Mundarten* (Buda, 1826). The book was first published in German for reasons of expediency.

8. Knut Gjerset, *History of Iceland* (London, 1937), pp. 367–72.

9. Cf. Oscar J. Falnes, *National Romanticism in Norway*, dissertation (Columbia, New York, 1933), pp. 189–90, pp. 365–7 and *passim;* and, more recently, Heinz Kloss, *Die Entwicklung neuer germanischer Kultursprachen von 1800 bis 1950* (Munich, 1952), pp. 56–62 and 91–8.

10. As regards the German Romantic poets and philosophers, Ernst Cassirer arrived at the same conclusion: "They were anxious to preserve not to conquer" (*The Myth of the State* [New Haven, 1946], p. 184).

11. *Monologen: Eine Neujahrsgabe*, new edition (Berlin, 1868), p. 31. It is noteworthy that, as regards biological characteristics, modern geneticists have arrived at a similar conclusion. The human 'lottery of heredity', as it has been called, is based on ever-changing permutations of inherited characteristics. With an average rhythm of generations of thirty years, it takes nine million years before all the permutations are exhausted.

12. The full original title is: *Die Menschenerziehung, die Erziehungs-, Unterrichts- und Lehrkunst, angestrebt in der allgemeinen deutschen Erziehungsanstalt zu Keilhau, dargestellt von dem Stifter, Begründer und Vorsteher derselben.*

13. In a letter, written in 1838, to H. von Leonhardi, a disciple of the Romantic philosopher Karl Christian Friedrich Krause (who had also influenced Froebel), the educational reformer described it as one of his main tasks "to develop the love of activity that children show between the first and sixth or seventh year".

14. 'Gespräch über die Poesie', *Athenaeum. Eine Zeitschrift von August Wilhelm Schlegel und Friedrich Schlegel*, Vol. III (Berlin, 1800), p. 58.

15. Cf. Alfred Einstein, *Schubert* (London, 1951), pp. 137–8.

16. 'Recollections of Franz Schubert', *Neues Archiv für Geschichte, Staatenkunde, Literatur und Kunst* (Vienna, 23 February 1829).

17. At times, however, a shadow of doubt arose about the genuineness of some feeling or other, or else the paradoxical coexistence of two irreconcilable sentiments made itself felt too strongly. In such cases, the Romantics, especially in Germany, sometimes took refuge in a literary device which they themselves described as "Romantic irony".

18. For the text of the discourse, cf. Institut de France, *Recueil des discours prononcés dans la séance publique annuelle le jeudi 24 avril 1817* (Paris, 1817). Cf. also Girodet-Trioson, *Œuvres posthumes*, ed. P. A. Coupin (Paris, 1829).

19. 'Questions sur le Beau', 1854; 'Des variations du Beau', 1857.

20. "One says of a man if one wishes to praise him that he is unique: can one not affirm, without appearing paradoxical, that it is this singularity, this personality which enchants in a great poet or a great artist, that this new appearance of things revealed by him astonishes us as much as it captivates us, that it produces in our soul the sensation of beauty, independently of those other aspects of the beautiful that have become the patrimony of the minds of all time, and which are consecrated by time-honoured admiration?" ('Des variations du Beau', *Revue des Deux Mondes* [Paris, 1857], p. 919).

IV. THE QUEST FOR RE-INTEGRATION

1. "This proud age which feeds on empty hopes."

2. *England und Schottland im Jahre 1844* (Berlin, 1845), Vol. II, p. 145.

3. *Life, Letters and Journals of G. Ticknor* (London, 1876), Vol. I, p. 272.

4. Thomas Balston, *John Martin, 1789–1854. His Life and Works*

(London, 1947), p. 235. (The painting is in the Tate Gallery, London.)

5. *The Recluse*. Part First, Book First. 'Home at Grasmere', ll. 593–616.

6. Letter to his brother Carlo, 6 December 1822 (*Epistolario di Giacomo Leopardi* [Florence, 1864], Vol. I, p. 261).

7. Hartley Coleridge to H. N. Coleridge, *Letters*, ed. G. E. and E. L. Griggs (London, 1936), p. 90.

8. Second edition (London, 1808), Vol. I, p. 33.

9. See, for example, Franz Baader's remarkable essay, 'Über das dermalige Missverhältnis der Vermögenslosen oder Proletairs zu den Vermögen besitzenden Classen' (1835), *Sämmtliche Werke*, (Leipzig, 1854), Vol. IV.

10. *The Philosophical Lectures of Samuel Taylor Coleridge*, ed. Kathleen Coburn (London, 1949), lecture VI, p. 210.

11. See, particularly, King Adolf's description of his subjects. (I have used the German translation by H. Neuss, *Die Insel der Glückseligkeit. Sagenspiel in fünf Abenteuern* [Leipzig, 1833].)

12. See, for example, his poem 'Anno 1829'.

13. Cf. W. Schenk, *The Concern for Social Justice in the Puritan Revolution* (London, 1948), p. 164.

14. *Sämmtliche Werke* (Leipzig, 1834), Vol. IV, p. 26.

15. "The rejuvenation of society has never depended on a purely political revolution as the moderns would have liked to believe. It is the religions that rejuvenate peoples; the divine spark that enlivens social man can only come from heaven, and this is the true meaning of the beautiful allegory of Prometheus" (*Mélanges*, Vol. II, p. 50).

16. This aspect of the movement was duly emphasized at the impressive Exhibition of European Romantic Art held in London in the summer of 1959.

17. See his essay 'Entartung der Künste und Wissenschaften' (The degeneration of the arts and sciences), reprinted in *Romantiker*, ed. W. Lindemann (Freiburg i. B., 1871), Vol. II.

18. *A History of Modern Criticism, 1750–1950. The Romantic Age* (London, 1955), pp. 151–7.

19. "Loyally united, we freely endeavoured to gather all the rays

of culture into one whole." (The poem appeared in the periodical *Athenaeum* [Berlin, 1800], Vol. III, p. 236.)

20. *Ausbreitung und Verfall der Romantik* (Leipzig, 1902), p. 4. Ricarda Huch was rebutting Goethe's well-known charge against the Romantics: "Das will Alles umfassen und verliert sich darüber immer ins Elementarische." ("Those people want to encompass all and in doing so they get lost in what is elementary.")

V. FOREBODINGS AND NOSTALGIA FOR THE PAST

1. See *Die prophetische Kraft der menschlichen Seele in Dichtern und Denkern* (Munich, 1858).

2. Cf. Sir Maurice Bowra's illuminating Presidential Address to the English Association (London, 1959), entitled *The Prophetic Element*.

3. *Life, Letters and Journals of George Ticknor* (London, 1876), Vol. I, p. 140. Ticknor spent the evening of 16 June 1817 at Chateaubriand's.

4. *Palinodia. Al Marchese Gino Capponi*, ll. 58–62. ("Now no more will the prodigal generation be able to wash itself clear of the blood of its own kindred, so that Europe and the opposite shore of the Atlantic Ocean will be scarred with bloodshed and slaughter.")

5. *De la religion considérée dans ses rapports avec l'ordre politique et civil* (Paris, 1825).

6. See his pamphlet *Du passé et de l'avenir du peuple* (1841).

7. Translation by H. E. Kennedy, London (no date), Part III.

8. *Le Génie du Christianisme*, IIIᵉ partie, Vᵉ livre, Chapter 6.

9. *Sir Thomas More, or Colloquies on the Progress and Prospects of Society* (London, 1829), Vol. II, p. 413.

10. 'Signatur des Zeitalters', *Concordia* (Vienna, 1820), p. 28.

11. Atterbom to E.G. Geijer, Munich, 22 December 1818 (*Aufzeichnungen des schwedischen Dichters P.D.A. Atterbom über berühmte deutsche Männer und Frauen nebst Reiseerinnerungen aus Deutschland und Italien aus den Jahren 1817–1819* [Berlin, 1867]).

12. 'Signatur des Zeitalters', *Concordia* (Vienna, 1820), p. 32.

13. *Magischer Spiegel. Von der Herrlichkeit unseres Reiches edler deutscher Nation* (*1806*) (Leipzig, 1939), p. 100.

14. See J. Huizinga, *The Waning of the Middle Ages. Life, Thought and Art in France and the Netherlands in the Fourteenth and Fifteenth Centuries*, translated from the Dutch by F. Hopman (London, 1924), p. 6.

15. *Vorlesungen über schöne Literatur und Kunst* (Berlin, 1802–3), p. 45.

16. *Mémoires d'Outre Tombe*, Chapter I.

17. Cf. Georg Lukácz, *Der historische Roman* (Berlin, 1955), pp. 27–8, and David Daiches, *Literary Essays* (London, 1956), p. 88.

18. Cf. Louis Maigron, *Le Roman historique à l'Epoque romantique* (Paris, 1912), livre II.

19. Cf. Manzoni's essay *Del Romanzo Storico, e, in genere, de' componimenti misti di storia e d'invenzione* (1845).

20. '*Selbstbiographie*', *Schriften* (Berlin, 1825), Vol. I, p. 135.

21. Cf. the standard biography, *Pugin: A Medieval Victorian*, by Michael Trappes-Lomax (1932). To my mind, Pugin was a genuine Romantic if ever there was one.

22. *A History of the Gothic Revival* (1872), p. 150.

23. Quoted by H. E. G. Roper, *Pugin* (1935), pp. 7–8.

24. Lenau in a letter to Sophie von Löwenthal, 5 July 1840.

25. J. Aynard, 'Comment définir le romantisme?', *Revue de littérature comparée*, 1925, p. 653.

26. Cf. Giorgio Falco, *La Polemica sul Medio Evo* (Turin, 1933), p. 400.

27. The following passage may serve as a sample of Voltaire's contempt for the Middle Ages: "For 900 years," he writes in the initial chapter of his *Siècle de Louis XIV*, "the French genius has been almost always cramped under a Gothic government, in the midst of divisions and civil wars, without fixed laws or customs. . . . The nobles without discipline, knowing only war and idleness, churchmen living in disorder and ignorance, and the populace without industry stagnating in their idleness."

28. Lecture IX, delivered at the 'Crown and Anchor', Strand, London on 22 February 1819 (*The Philosophical Lectures Hitherto Unpublished*, ed. Kathleen Coburn [London, 1949], p. 265).

29. C. V. Wedgwood, *The Sense of the Past*, the Leslie Stephen Lecture, 1957 (Cambridge University Press), p. 10.

30. Cf. Thierry's *Dix ans d'études historiques* (Paris, 1883), p. 7.

But for *Ivanhoe*, Thierry's *Histoire de la Conquête de l'Angleterre par les Normands* might never have been written.

31. *Histoire du XIXᵉ siècle*, Tome II: 'Le Directoire', préface (1872).

32. This aspect is well brought out in Arnold Gehlen, *Urmensch und Spätkultur* (Bonn, 1956).

33. 'German schools of thought', *Essays of Modern History* (1907), p. 346.

34. Acton, Add MS. 5478, Cambridge University Library. Cf. also the retrospective statement contained in the memoirs of the Norwegian-born Romantic Henrik Steffens: "So immeasurably rich was that period that in it a present that was in continuous motion comprised all the important moments of the past..." (*Was ich erlebte*, IV, pp. 316–17).

35. *Werke* (Vienna, 1846), Vol. XIV, p. 149.

36. *Fragmente des Jahres 1798*, No. 384.

37. Cf. Rose Macaulay, *Pleasure of Ruins* (1953), p. 24.

38. *Armut, Reichtum, Schuld und Busse der Gräfin Dolores* (1810), Kap. IV.

39. "... in die Zusammensetzung des fremden Wesens einzudringen, es zu erkennen, wie es ist, zu belauschen, wie es wurde."

40. 'Impromptus', *Taschenbuch für Damen* (1812).

41. It was Leopold von Ranke who coined the phrase *'irdische Unsterblichkeit'*.

42. *Menschliches, Allzumenschliches. Ein Buch für freie Geister* (1878), Vol. II, Aphorismus 17.

PART TWO: NIHILISM AND YEARNING FOR A FAITH

VI. THE ROMANTIC MALADY OF THE SOUL

1. Cf. Oscar Bloch and W. von Wartburg, *Dictionnaire Etymologique de la langue Française*, 2. ed. (Paris, 1950).

2. Cf. Franz Schultz, *Der Verfasser der Nachtwachen von Bonaventura. Untersuchungen zur deutschen Romantik* (Berlin, 1909). In the most recent monograph of the subject, *Untersuchungen zur Struktur der Nachtwachen von Bonaventura* (Göttingen, 1959), Dorothee Sölle-Nipperdey states: "Up to the present, the author

of the *Nachtwachen* cannot be definitely ascertained." I myself am inclined to think that the *Nachtwachen* were written by Clemens Brentano.

3. "I wish to maintain my stubborn Self,
   Sufficient to myself and imperturbable,
   Nobody's slave and subject,
   I proceed inwards on my path."

4. "I have renounced God
   And Nature in proud hatred.
   Within myself I tried to concentrate myself;
   Oh, what delusion! I cannot endure it.
   My Ego, hollow, sombre and piteous
   Shudders round me like a coffin."

5. Thus far I find myself in agreement with Benedetto Croce who, in his *Storia d'Europa* (1932), suggests that the root of the Romantic malady of the soul must be sought in the borderland between the ancient faith which had collapsed, and a new faith, the faith in new philosophical and liberal ideals which had as yet been only imperfectly and partially digested. However, I part company with Croce when he continues (*op. cit.*, p. 53): "This malady was due, not so much to breaking away from a traditional faith, as to the difficulty of really appropriating to oneself and living the new faith, which, to be lived and put into action, demanded courage and a virile attitude."

6. Jung, in 1933, drew attention to the following revealing facts: "During the past thirty years, people from all the civilised countries of the earth have consulted me. . . . Among all my patients in the second half of life . . . there has not been one whose problem in the last resort was not that of finding a religious outlook on life. It is safe to say that everyone of them fell ill because he had lost that which the religions of every age have given their followers, and not one of them has been really healed who did not regain his religious outlook." (*Modern Man in Search of a Soul*, first published in 1933, here quoted from 1961 edition, p. 264.)

7. Cf. Werner Kohlschmidt, 'Nihilismus der Romantik' in: *Form und Innerlichkeit: Beiträge zur Geschichte und Wirkung der deutschen Klassik und Romantik* (Bern, 1955), pp. 157–76. Also, more recently, Helmut Thielicke, *Nihilism: Its Origin and Nature*

—with a Christian Answer, trans. from the German (1962), Chapters IV–X.

8. Cf. his letter of 8 December 1819 to Pietro Giordani.

9. *Zibaldone* (Florence, 1898), Vol. I, p. 83.

10. "Virtue shines not in forms that have no grace." Marchese Gino Capponi wrote of Leopardi: "He could not bear his physical afflictions, which were indeed very great. No one can imagine the sufferings he endured and those he created for himself, nor how many impediments, both to his work and his affections, entered his soul" (*Lettere di Gino Capponi e di altri a lui*, ed. A. Carraresi, IV, pp. 416–17).

11. Cf. *The Sufferings of Young Werther*, second part, the letter dated 15 November: "I have respect for religion, as you know, I feel that it is a staff for many a weary soul, refreshment for many who are faint. But—can it, must it, then be for everyone? When you look at the great world, you see thousands for whom it has not been, thousands for whom it will not be—preached or not preached —must it then be for me?" (Trans. by William Rose, 1929.)

12. Cf. Iris Origo, *Leopardi: A Biography* (1935), pp. 78–9.

13. *La Quiete dopo la Tempesta*. ("Fortunate indeed if when the pain is gone, you feel relief.")

14. *Amore e morte*. ("Vain hope with which men comfort children and themselves.")

15. "Moon, of what value, pray,
     To the shepherd is his life,
     Your life to you? To what goal are we tending,
     I in brief wanderings, thou
     On thine immortal way?"

('Night-Song of a Nomadic Shepherd of Asia', *The Poems of Leopardi*, trans. Geoffrey Bickersteth [Cambridge, 1923].)

16. 'Ad Arimane', *Scritti vari inediti*, pp. 114–15. Nature's mysterious cruelty is also discussed in the 'Dialogue between Tristan and a Friend'.

17. *A Se Stesso*. ("Bitter is life and dull—that and no more. Earth's but a clod.")

18. André Monglond, *Le Journal Intime d'Oberman*, Paris, n.d., p. 335. Cf. also Irene Schärer, *Oberman: Lettres publiées par E. P. de Senancour* (Zürich, 1955).

19. In his earlier *Rêveries sur la Nature Primitive de l'Homme* (1799), Senancour had described the state of mind "where one no longer knows what to desire, precisely because one has too many desires, nor what to wish for because one wants everything; where nothing seems good because one is looking for the absolute good . . ." (*Quatrième rêverie*. In Joachim Merlant's critical edition [Paris, 1910], the passage occurs in Tome I, pp. 73–4).

20. "C'est dans les sons que la nature a placé la plus forte expression du caractère romantique: et c'est sur-tout au sens de l'ouïe que l'on peut rendre sensible, en peu de traits et d'une manière énergique, les lieux et les choses extraordinaires" (*Oberman*, Tome I, troisième fragment).

21. "La vie que je traîne n'est pas très malheureuse. Chacun de mes jours est supportable, mais leur ensemble m'accable" (*Oberman*, Tome I, lettre XLII).

22. *Oberman*, Tome I, lettre XLI.

VII. THE LURE OF NOTHINGNESS

1. Conversation with Julius Frauenstädt, *Schopenhauers Gespräche und Selbstgespräche*, ed. Eduard Grisebach (Berlin, 1898), p. 38.

2. *Aus Schopenhauers handschriftlichem Nachlass*, ed. Julius Frauenstädt, p. 438.

3. *Die Welt als Wille und Vorstellung*, Vol. I, paragraph 58. The phrase is contained already in the 1819 edition (p. 465). Schopenhauer thus anticipated Ludwig Feuerbach by more than twenty years.

4. Frederick Copleston, S.J., *Arthur Schopenhauer: Philosopher of Pessimism* (1946), p. 212.

5. Schopenhauer himself used the English expression (cf. *Schopenhauers Gespräche und Selbstgespräche*, p. 115).

6. *Die Welt als Wille und Vorstellung*, Vol. II, Chapter 46.

7.   "All that's born to be
Deserves to perish utterly.
Better that nothing should be born."
        (*Faust*, trans. W. H. van der Smissen, 1926.)

8. *Die Welt als Wille und Vorstellung*, Vol. I, paragraph 71.

9. *Schopenhauers Gespräche und Selbstgespräche*, p. 87.

10. The photograph of 1859 appears opposite p. 114 in P. J. Möbius, *Schopenhauer* (Leipzig, 1904).

11. For a more detailed comparison, cf. Helmuth von Glasenapp, *Das Indienbild deutscher Denker* (Stuttgart, 1960), pp. 77–8, 89.

12. Cf. F. D. Klingender, *Goya in the Democratic Tradition* (London, 1948), p. 212.

13. André Malraux, *Saturn: An Essay on Goya* (1957), p. 110.

14. *The Complete Etchings of Goya* (1943), p. 10.

15. See, for example, Delacroix's letter to Varcolier, 7 July 1852, or the letter he sent to his oldest friend Soulier in April 1863, four months before his death.

16. At the end of this poem Leopardi calls the human race happy when death has healed all its sufferings:

> beata
> Se te d'ogni dolor morte risana.

17. Cf. his letter to his brother August Wilhelm, dated 21 November 1792.

18. T. G. Masaryk, in his monograph on 'Suicide as a Mass Phenomenon in Modern Civilization', expressed the view that thousands of suicides may be attributable to the above-mentioned trait in European literature. "Our poets," he wrote, "chant their lamentations and the Frankfort sage (Schopenhauer) declaims the funeral oration" (*Der Selbstmord als sociale Massenerscheinung der modern Civilisation* [Vienna, 1881], p. 172).

19. Vassilchikev's account, quoted in Henri Troyat, *L'étrange destin de Lermontov* (Paris, 1952), p. 261.

20. Cf. Shelley's 'On a Future State', first printed in *The Athenaeum* for 29 September 1832, under the title of 'Death', now in the Julian edition of Shelley's *Works* (1929), Vol. IV, p. 209.

VIII. DEFIANCE OF GOD AND RELIGIOUS FRUSTRATION

1. Pierre Moreau, *Le Romantisme* (Paris, 1957), p. 220.

2. "In view of what one was on earth and what one leaves behind
   Silence alone is great, all the rest is weakness."

3. Cf. Václav Černý, *Essai sur le Titanisme dans la Poésie Romantique Occidentale entre 1815 et 1850* (Prague, 1935).

4. *Journal d'un Poète*, éd. anglaise, p. 90.

5. Vigny intended to elaborate this idea. Cf. 'Poèmes à faire', *Journal d'un Poète*, p. 241.

6. For this was his real name of which the pseudonym under which he wrote retained, apart from the Christian name, only the last five letters.

7. His revulsion was so deep that he wrote to a friend: "America is the veritable land of decadence [*Untergang*]." The passage occurs in his letter to Georg Reinbeck from Lisbon, Ohio, 5 March 1833. Cf. also his other letters from America; also Eduard Castle, 'Amerikamüde. Lenau und Kürnberger', *Jahrbuch der Grillparzer-Gesellschaft*, XII (Vienna, 1902).

8. By an uncanny coincidence, the date of Lenau's collapse, 15 October 1844, happened to be the day Friedrich Nietzsche was born. From a medical point of view, Nietzsche's mental collapse, which took place at the beginning of 1889, seems to have had an analogous cause.

9. 'Ueber Leopardis and Lenaus Pessimismus', in: *Aufsätze, Reden und Charakteristiken zur Weltliteratur* (Bonn and Leipzig, 1925).

10. H. L. Martensen, *Aus meinem Leben*, translated from the Danish (Karlsruhe and Leipzig, 1883), p. 218. In the dramatic poem *Faust* (1834) which, as Martensen has shown, is in spite of its defiance of God still cast in the Christian mould, the hero ponders over the problem whether the devil to whom he has sold his soul, was perhaps but "a shadow on his God-consciousness" ('*des Gott-bewusstseins Trübung*').

11. Cf. Eduard Castle, *Lenau und die Familie Löwenthal. Briefe und Gespräche, Gedichte und Entwürfe* (Leipzig, 1906).

12. "Hast thou ever found thyself alone on a heath
    Loveless and without God."

13. "The whole world is sad to the point of despair."

14. Musset's three main self-characterizations, Octave in *La Confession d'un Enfant du Siècle*, Jacques Rolla, and Hassan in the poem 'Namouna', all exhibit that fateful unevenness.

15. *La Confession d'un Enfant du Siècle*, Book IV, Chapter I.

16. *La Confession d'un Enfant du Siècle*, Book V, Chapter VI. Cf. also the poems 'Lettre à Lamartine' and 'L'Espoir en Dieu'.

17.   "I do not believe, oh Christ, in Thy holy word:
        I have come too late to a world too old."

18. "Thy glory is dead, oh Christ! and on our ebony crosses
    Thy heavenly corpse has crumbled to dust.

    "Well then! May the most unbelieving child
    Of this godless age be allowed to kiss that dust,
    And weep, oh Christ! on this cold earth
    That drew life from Thy death, and will die without Thee."

19. Cf. these lines from Musset's 'L'Espoir en Dieu':
            Ma raison revoltée
    Essaye en vain de croire et mon cœur de douter.

20. Cf. Georg Simmel, *Schopenhauer und Nietzsche. Ein Vortragszyklus* (Leipzig, 1907), p. 4.

PART THREE: CHRISTIAN REVIVAL: PROMISE AND UNFULFILMENT

IX. THE ASSAULT ON UNBELIEF

1. Christian Maréchal, *La Jeunesse de Lamennais* (Paris, 1913), p. 38.

2. Lundi, 7 September 1868. (Reprinted in *Les grands écrivains français. XIXᵉ siècle. Philosophes et essayistes* (Paris, 1930), Vol. II, pp. 98–9.

3. *Œuvres inédites*, ed. A. Blaize, Vol. I, *Correspondance*, 1866, p. 213. The letter is dated 5 August 1815.

4. Letter to his brother, December 1810 (*Œuvres inédites*, Vol. I, pp. 94–4).

5. Letter to his brother, 25 June 1816, *op. cit.*, p. 263.

6. *Œuvres inédites*, Vol. I, p. 113.

7. Cf. A. Roussel, *Lamennais d'après des documents inédits*, Tome I (Rennes, 1892), p. 101.

8. Paguelle de Follenoy, *M. Teysseyre*, Chapter XV.

9. To this may be added Henri Bremond's general comment on the dichotomy between the inner life and the philosophy of Lamennais: "I have not been able to establish a necessary link between the

inner life and the philosophy of Lamennais. One always feels oneself to be in the presence of two people, or rather of a man and a system. True, the various books where that system is elaborated carry the name of this man. They are the thoughts which he has collected and for which he has fought, or by means of which he has sought to give expression to his profound soul, and nevertheless one asks oneself: is that thought really he himself?" ('La détresse de Lamennais', *L'Inquiétude Religieuse*, deuxième série [Paris, 1909), pp. 79–80.]

10. Bremond, *op. cit.*, p. 62; cf. also Henri Guillemin's excellent Introduction to the selection of Lamennais's *Œuvres* (Geneva, n.d.), p. 20.

11. I am thinking of the description of Ivan Karamazov's mind in *The Brothers Karamazov*.

12. E.g. *Die fröhliche Wissenschaft*, Aphorismus 125.

13. *Essai sur l'indifférence en matière de religion*, Tome I, Chapter X.

14. *Recollections of The Last Four Popes and of Rome in Their Times* (1858), pp. 337–8.

X. REAFFIRMATION OF THE SUPERNATURAL

1. For Novalis's original contributions as a thinker, cf. Theodor Haering, *Novalis als Philosoph*, Stuttgart, 1954. Cf. also the older monograph by Käte Hamburger, *Novalis und die Mathematik. Zur Erkenntnistheorie der Romantik*, in 'Romantikforschungen' (Deutsche Vierteljahrsschrift für Literaturwissenschaft und Geistesgeschichte, ed. Paul Kluckhohn and Erich Rothacker, Buchreihe, 16 Band, Halle a.d. Saale, 1929).

2. Cf. Fritz Strich, *Deutsche Klassik und Romantik, oder Vollendung und Unendlichkeit. Ein Vergleich* (1922), *passim*.

3. E.g. by Watts-Dunton. Another example of it can be found in Victor Hugo's 'Préface Philosophique' to his novel *Les Misérables*.

4. The entry is dated Weissenfels, 16 April 1800.

5. Novalis originally intended to call them *Christliche Lieder*. After his death his friends altered the title to *Geistliche Lieder*.

6. "Among a thousand glad hours that I have found in my life, there is but one that has remained faithful to me; it is the one when

in a thousand pains I discovered in my heart who has died for us"
(*Geistliche Lieder*, IV).

7. "Suddenly as it were the tombstone was lifted from above and
my inner self revealed" (*op. cit.*).

8. Cf. H. A. Korff, *Geist der Goethezeit* (Leipzig, 1949), Vol. III,
p. 579.

9. It is interesting to note that Herder, in 1801, spoke of "men
who seem to have come from another world and to belong to
another world" and added: "One calls these rarities of nature
Romantic characters" (*Beilage zur Adrastea*, Erstes Stück, Werke,
ed. Suphan, Band XXIII, p. 175).

10. "Take heart, life is moving towards eternal life" (V, *Hymne
an die Nacht*).

XI. THE RETURN TO CATHOLICISM

1. The peculiar problem of the relationship between Romanticism and the Oxford Movement does not concern us here. H. N.
Fairchild, in his article on 'Romanticism and the religious revival
in England' in the *Journal of the History of Ideas* (1941) is right
when he points out that "the movement was by no means a child
of Romantic poetry" (*op. cit.*, p. 330). So is D. G. James, who declares that "the theology of the Oxford Movement would have been
abhorrent to Coleridge" (*The Romantic Comedy* [1963], p. 226).
Nevertheless, in several of its aspects the Oxford Movement could
still have been, and probably was, a symptom of Romanticism, so
long as the latter is understood as a temper characteristic of a
whole epoch.

2. See Ronald Chapman, *Father Faber* (1961).

3. *Die Romantik*, Vol. II, p. 238.

4. *Dichtung und Wahrheit*, Book VII.

5. Cf. Georges Bonnefoy, *La Pensée Religieuse et Morale
d'Alfred de Vigny*, p. 370.

6. *Mémoires d'Outre-Tombe*, Part IV, Book III, Chapter 4.

7. "And the Church without faith, this sad framework of stone
which in past ages had prayer for its soul, that church is indeed
fortunate that nowadays the Levites of art come to pray for it.'
'L'Orgue', an unfinished poem (*Journal d'un Poète* [Paris, 1942],
p. 245).

8. Attilio Momigliano, *Alessandro Manzoni*, 5. ed. (Milan, 1948) p. 19.

9. Notably F. Ruffini, *La vita religiosa di Alessandro Manzoni*, 2 vols. (Bari, 1931). It has justly been remarked that the book's only fault lies in the title. "What Ruffini has dealt with is Jansenism, and not the religious life of Alessandro Manzoni" (A. Zottoli, 'Perchè il Manzoni si convertì' in *Umili e potenti nella poetica di A. Manzoni* [Milan, 1931], p. 346).

10. 'Alessandro Manzoni', Annual Italian Lecture of the British Academy, 1949, p. 31.

11. Marcel Brion, *Romantic Art* (1960), p. 134.

XII. OECUMENICAL TRENDS

1. For the ideological and diplomatic history of the Holy Alliance Treaty, I may perhaps refer the reader to the first two chapters of my study *The Aftermath of the Napoleonic Wars. The Concert of Europe—an Experiment* (1947).

2. Cf. Peter von Goetze, *Fürst Alexander Nikolajewitsch Galitzin und seine Zeit* (Leipzig, 1882), pp. 86–106.

3. Cf. Ernst Benz, 'Die abendländische Sendung der östlich-orthodoxen Kirche. Die russische Kirche und das abendländische Christentum im Zeitalter der Heiligen Allianz', Akademie der Wissenschaften und der Literatur, Abhandlungen der geistes- und sozialwissenschaftlichen Klasse (Mainz, 1950), pp. 42–3.

4. The French text is reprinted in Baader's *Sämmtliche Werke*, Band X, pp. 204–18. Cf. also Baader's comments, *op. cit.*, pp. 219–54.

5. Eugène Susini, *Lettres inédites de Franz von Baader*, 1942, pp. 451–61, reprints three letters addressed by Baader to Uvarov at the beginning of 1841.

6. *Souvenirs de Jeunesse (1828–1835)* (Paris, 1911), p. 266.

XIII. EMOTIONAL CHRISTIANITY

1. The title has been freely translated as *Religion: Addresses to its Cultured Despisers*.

2. The letter is dated 27 August 1798.

3. Cf. H. A. Korff, *Geist der Goethezeit*, Band III, p. 334.

4. The disintegration in question is well analysed in the

Memoirs of the Norwegian Romantic Henrik Steffens, *Was ich erlebte. Aus der Erinnerung niedergeschrieben* (Berlin, 1840), Bd. I pp. 259–60.

5. Cf. *5. Rede.*

6. Nor was this to be understood in the accepted Christian sense according to which people outside the Church who have lived a Christian life should be held to have received what the Church calls "the baptism of desire".

7. Volume X, pp. 143–4.

8. *Die protestantische Theologie im neunzehnten Jahrhundert* (Zürich, 1947), p. 424.

9. All three quotations are from the 2nd *Rede.*

10. *Deutsche Geschichte im neunzehnten Jahrhundert* (Freiburg, 1951), Bd. IV, p. 308.

XIV. UNFULFILMENT

1. Charles Boutard, *Lamennais: sa vie et ses doctrines* (Paris, 1905–13); F. Duine, *La Mennais. Sa vie, ses idées, ses ouvrages* (Paris, 1922); Alec R. Vidler, *Prophecy and Papacy. A Study of Lamennais, the Church and the Revolution* (1954).

2. Louis Veuillot, in a letter dated 22 May 1846, to Desiré Carrière (*Correspondance de Louis Veuillot*, ed. F. Veuillot [1931], Vol. II, p. 174 f.).

3. Cf. *L'Avenir*, 16 October 1830.

4. Cf. the Archbishop's words to Charles X, quoted in Vidler, *op. cit.*, pp. 154–5.

5. *Delle Cinque Piaghe della Santa Chiesa* was not published until 1849.

6. Cf. Sean O'Faolain, *The Irish* (1947), p. 98.

7. On Charles de Coux, cf. J.-B. Duroselle, *Les Débuts du Catholicisme Social en France (1820–1870)* (Paris, 1951), *passim.*

8. For the whole question, cf. the well balanced article by Conrad Bonacina, 'The Catholic Church and Modern Democracy', in the periodical *The Wind and the Rain*, Vol. VII, 1951, pp. 105–20.

9. It may be worth noting that Lamennais and his friends received reports from Rome itself to the effect that the encyclical *Mirari vos* was regarded there by some of the highest dignitaries of

the Church as a deplorable document. See Paul Dudon, *Lamennais et le Saint-Siège, 1820–1834* (1911), pp. 221 f. Dudon refers to a letter of 4 September 1832, to be found in the Dossier Lamennais in the Archivum Vaticanum.

10. The last-mentioned article appeared in the 'Festgabe zur Hundert-Jahr-Feier des Instituts', in *Mitteilungen des Instituts für österreichische Geschichtsforschung*, Band LXII, 1954, pp. 490–516.

11. Cf. Josef Schmidlin, *Papstgeschichte der neuesten Zeit*, (Munich, 1933), Bd. I, p. 565.

PART FOUR: ROMANTIC ENCHANTMENT

XV. THE CULT OF THE EGO

1. The full title is *Essai historique, politique et moral sur les Révolutions anciennes et modernes considérées dans leurs rapports avec la révolution française de nos jours.*

2. Pierre Moreau, *Chateaubriand. L'homme et l'œuvre* (Paris, 1956), p. 28.

3. *Mémoires d'Outre-Tomb*, Part I, Book V, Ch. 15.

4. *Mémoires d'Outre-Tombe*, Part II, Book I, Ch. 12.

5. *Mercure*, 18 nivôse, an XI (8 January 1803).

6. *Mémoires d'Outre-Tombe*, Part I, Book IV, Ch. 2.

7. *René ou la Vie de Chateaubriand* (Paris, 1935), p. 461. Indeed, Chateaubriand himself confessed: "Je crois en Dieu aussi fermement qu'en ma propre existence. Je crois au christianisme comme grande vérité toujours, comme religion tant que je puis. J'y crois vingt-quatre heures, mais le diable revient, qui me plonge dans un grand doute, que je suis tout occupé à débrouiller à l'approche de la mort" (Quoted by A. Maurois, *René ou la vie de Chateaubriand* [Paris, 1938], p. 454).

8. Faguet, *Dix-neuvième Siècle*. Etudes Littéraires, Paris, n.d., p. 71.

9. *Mémoires d'Outre-Tombe*, Vol. I, III, 13.

10. The question as to when this particular plan was conceived has never been clarified. In contradiction to Chateaubriand's own assertion it has been suggested that the idea may not have occurred to him until after his return to Europe (cf. Pierre Martino, 'Le

Voyage de Chateaubriand en Amérique. Essai de Mise au Point 1952', *Revue d'Histoire littéraire de la France*, Vol. LII, 1952, p. 161).

11. *Jenseits von Gut und Böse* (*Beyond Good and Evil*), aphorism 224.

12. *Op. cit.*, Part I, Book I, Ch. 2.

13. *Op. cit.*, Part IV, Book XII, Ch. 3 and 6.

14. Funeral oration for Henriette-Marie, widow of King Charles I of England, 16 November 1669.

15. *Op. cit.*, Vol. IV, XII, 7.

16. *Op. cit.*, Vol. IV, XII, 6.

17. *Op. cit.*, Vol. IV, XII, 8.

18. The letter is dated 11 July 1831.

19. *Mémoires d'Outre-Tombe*, ed. M. Levaillant, Part I, p. 514.

20. The two volumes by Marian Zdziechowski were published in 1894–7.

21. Thomas Moore, *Letters and Journals of Lord Byron, with Notices of His Life* (1830), Vol. I. p. 357.

22. *The Deformed Transformed*, Part I, Scene I, ll. 331–2.

23. In conversation with Dr. James Alexander at Genoa (cf. Aaron Watson, 'Byron at First Hand, A talk with his Doctor', *Daily Telegraph*, 19 April 1924).

24. Thomas Medwin, *Conversations of Lord Byron: noted during a residence with his Lordship at Pisa in the years 1821 and 1822* (1824), p. 76.

25. *The Works of Lord Byron. Letters and Journals*, edited by Roland E. Prothero (1901), Vol. V, p. 450.

26. Canto I, stanza IV.

27. Cf. Terence Spencer, *Fair Greece. Sad Relic* (1954), p. 288.

28. Diary, 5 December 1813. (*Letters and Journals*, ed. Prothero, Vol. II, pp. 361–2.)

29. *Sardanapalus*, Act IV, Scene I.

30. All but conclusive evidence is to be found in *Astarte: A Fragment of Truth Concerning George Gordon Byron*, Sixth Lord Byron, recorded by his grandson Ralph Milbanke, Earl of Lovelace (1921), p. 82. Leslie Marchand, author of the most comprehensive biography of Byron, arrives at the same conclusion (cf. *Byron: A Biography* [1957], Vol. I, p. 404, n. 4).

31. *Conversations of Lord Byron with the Countess of Blessington* (1834), p. 364.

32. Lord Broughton (John Cam Hobhouse), *Recollections of a Long Life* (1910), Vol. III, p. 360. According to John Murray, the manuscript had also been read by Mr Gifford, who declared that if it were published it would render Byron's name eternally infamous (Hobhouse diary, entry of 17 May 1824, quoted by Leslie A. Marchand, *op. cit.*, p. 1249). More recently, Doris Langley Moore, *The Late Lord Byron: Posthumous Dramas* (1961), Ch. I, presents the story of the motives behind the burning of the Memoirs in a different light, though to my mind not convincingly.

33. *Lara*, Canto I, stanza XVIII.

34. *Manfred*, Act III, Scene I.

35. *The Island, or Christian and His Comrades*, Canto I, stanza VI.

36. *Manfred*, Act I, Scene I. It should be noted that it is uncertain whom Byron had in mind when he wrote the incantation. This does not, however, affect my argument. Since I finished this chapter, I find that Leslie A. Marchand, *op. cit.*, p. 656, interprets the crucial passage in the same way as I do.

37. Johann Peter Eckermann, *Gespräche mit Goethe in den letzten Jahren seines Lebens*. The date of the conversation is 5 July 1827.

38. 'Lord Byron en Italie', *Revue de Paris*, March 1830.

39. 'Detached Thoughts', Ravenna notebook (1821), reprinted in *Letters and Journals*, ed. R. E. Prothero, Vol. V, pp. 408–10.

40. *A History of English Literature*, by Emile Legouis and Louis Cazamian, revised edition (1947), p. 996.

41. This point is well made in J. O. E. Donner, 'Lord Byrons Weltanschauung', *Acta Societatis Scientiarum Fennicae*, Vol. XXII, No. 4, Helsingfors, 1897, pp. 55–6. The same critic also noted that Byron's Cain bemoans death as the greatest evil.

42. *Op. cit.*, p. 105.

43. Cf. Dr. James Kennedy, *Conversations on Religion with Lord Byron and others, held in Cephalonia, a short time previous to his Lordship's death* (posthumously published in 1830).

44. Quoted in Harriet Beecher Stowe, *Lady Byron Vindicated. A History of the Byron Controversy from Its Beginning in 1816 to the Present Time* (1870), p. 302.

45. Cf. H. N. Fairchild, *Religious Trends in English Poetry* (New York, 1949), Vol. III, p. 437.

46. H. N. Fairchild, *op. cit.*, p. 414.

47. *Julian and Maddalo: A Conversation*, ll. 50–2. It is clear from the preface that the protagonists are meant to stand for Shelley and Byron.

48. *Op. cit.*, preface.

49. From Canto XVII of *Don Juan*, found by Edward John Trelawny in Byron's room at Missolonghi.

50. *Childe Harold's Pilgrimage*, Canto III, stanza LXX.

51. Iris Origo, *The Last Attachment* (1949), p. 13.

52. 'Byron', in *From Anne to Victoria*, ed. B. Dobrée (1937), p. 617.

53. In *Beppo. A Venetian Story* (Stanza LII) Byron says:
    I've half a mind to tumble down to prose,
    But verse is more in fashion—so here goes.

54. *Praeterita*, Chapter VIII.

55. New York, 1954. The editor, Ernest J. Lovell, Jr., has contributed a well-balanced critical summary.

56. *Julian and Maddalo*, preface.

57. *Letters and Journals*, ed. Prothero, Vol. V, pp. 405–6.

58. *Correspondence*, ed. John Murray (London, 1922), Vol. II, p. 148.

59. *Don Juan*, Canto I, stanza CCXIII.

60. Iris Origo, *The Last Attachment. The story of Byron and Teresa Guiccioli as told in their unpublished letters and other family papers* (1949), p. 351.

61. The final stanzas of the poem entitled 'On This Day I Complete My Thirty-Sixth Year'.

62. According to Dr. Millingen, a physician, who had several conversations with him in Metaxata in November and December 1823. (*His Very Self and Voice*, ed. E. J. Lovell, Jr., p. 465.)

63. *Childe Harold's Pilgrimage*, Canto I, 'To Inez', stanza 6.

64. Cf. Edmond Estève, *Byron et le Romanticisme français* (Paris, 1907), p. 37.

65. Goethe's *Faust* was not unknown to Byron. In Geneva in 1817, 'Monk' Lewis translated to him passages from this drama.

66. 'Byron e Goethe', reprinted in *Scritti scelti di Giuseppe Mazzini* (Florence, 1916), p. 143.

67. Translated by C. M. Bowra in *A Book of Russian Verse*, translated into English by various hands and edited by C. M. Bowra (1943).

68. *Passages from Correspondence with my Friends.*

69. Translated by C. M. Bowra in *A Book of Russian Verse* (1943), p. 39.

70. The Verdict is Prince Svyatopolk Mirsky's. Cf. his *History of Russian Literature* (1949), p. 156.

71. Lermontov's Russian-born biographer Henri Troyat also emphasizes the autobiographical character of *A Hero of Our Time* (*L'étrange destin de Lermontov* [Paris, 1952], p. 278).

XVI. ROMANTIC LOVE AND FRIENDSHIP

1. Cf. F. Schlegel, *Über die Philosophie. An Dorothea.*

2. Letter to Sophie von Löwenthal, 30 June 1839.

3. *Die Welt als Wille und Vorstellung.* Zweiter Teil. Viertes Buch, Kapitel 44.

4. The two leading ladies of German Romanticism, Karoline and Dorothea, married—at one stage or another—to August Wilhelm Schlegel and his brother Friedrich respectively, spring to mind. So does the poetess Caroline von Günderode, significantly addressed in letters by her lover Friedrich Creuzer as "Freund" (and not 'Freundin'). It is noteworthy that a similar development took place during the Renaissance. According to Jacob Burckhardt, "the greatest possible praise which could be given to the Italian women celebrities of the time was to say that they had the mind and the courage of men" (*The Civilization of the Renaissance* [Oxford, 1944], p. 241).

5. Quoted in M. Jastrun, *Mickiewicz*, translated from the Polish (Berlin, 1953), p. 254.

6. E.g. Schopenhauer, *Die Welt als Wille und Vorstellung*, Zweiter Teil, Viertes Buch, Par. 44.

7. Cf. Schelling, *Clara oder über den Zusammenhang der Natur mit der Geisterwelt. Ein Gespräch*, first published posthumously in 1861 in Vol. IX of Schelling's *Sämtliche Werke*. Cf. also Schelling's

letter to Georgii on 19 March 1811. Schelling's ideas were based on speculations conceived by the Swedish mystic Emanuel Swedenborg.

8. Letter of 12 May 1841.

9. C. S. Lewis, *The Allegory of Love: A Study in Medieval Tradition* (Oxford, 1938); M. C. D'Arcy, *The Mind and Heart of Love*, revised edition (1954); Denis de Rougemont, *L'Amour et l'Occident* (Paris, 1939).

10. Cf. Christopher Dawson, 'The Romantic Tradition', in *Medieval Essays* (1953), p. 227. Another interesting parallel to the Romantic period: according to Dawson, "the Troubadour is absorbed in the study of his own emotions and has already acquired a passion for psychological analysis" (*op. cit.*, p. 217).

11. Max Scheler, *Die Sinngesetze des emotionalen Lebens*, I. Band: *Wesen und Formen der Sympathie* (Bonn, 1931), pp. 111–12. Cf. also Ortega y Gasset's perceptive remark about the different "soul-temperatures" among the great historical nations (*On Love: Aspects of a Single Theme*, translated from the Spanish [London, 1959], p. 17).

12. Letter of 28 February 1837, reprinted in *The Intimate Journal of George Sand* (1929), p. 165.

13. *Notes to Queen Mab* (1810).

14. This and the following quotations are from the *Notes to Queen Mab*.

15. "Are we our own masters where love is concerned? Why do two beings love each other? Ask the water that flows, the air that speeds away, the gnat that flies into the night's flame, the ray of gold that comes to kiss the ripe bunch of grapes! Ask that which sings, calls, waits, murmurs! Ask the deep nests where April has spread confusion! The bewildered heart cries: Do I know why?"

16. The passages quoted occur in the above-mentioned letter to Lamennais, dated 28 February 1837.

17. *Die Hauptströmungen der Litteratur des neunzehnten Jahrhunderts*. V. Band: *Die romantische Schule in Frankreich* (Charlottenburg, 1900), pp. 121–2.

18. A photograph of the portrait painted by Ph.O. Runge of his brother, himself and his wife is to be found in the appendix to

Klaus Lankheit's book *Das Freundschaftsbild der Romantik* (Heidelberg, 1952). The painting itself perished in a fire in 1931.

19. Cf. André Merland, *Jean-Marie de la Mennais. La Renaissance d'une Chrétienté* (Paris, 1960).

20. *Prelude* (1805), Book VI, ll. 251–6.

21. 'The art of conversation', in: *Wordsworthian and Other Studies* (1947), p. 187.

XVII. NATURE MYSTICISM

1. *Deutsche Klassik und Romantik oder Vollendung und Unendlichkeit. Ein Vergleich* (Bern, 1949), p. 82. Among German Romantic poets, Eichendorff is the most characteristic 'Wanderer'. Cf. his poem *Allgemeines Wandern* and the delightful novel *Aus dem Leben eines Taugenichts*.

2. Letter to his brother-in-law Anton Schurz, from Ischl, 28 July 1839.

3. Cf. H. D. Rawnsley, 'Reminiscences of Wordsworth among the Peasantry of Westmorland', in: *Wordsworthiana: A Selection from Papers read to the Wordsworth Society* (1889), p. 92.

4. Book XIII, ll. 1–4.

5. *L'Idée Romantique de la Poésie en Angleterre. Etudes sur la théorie de la poésie chez Coleridge, Wordsworth, Keats and Shelley* (Paris, 1955), p. 72.

6. Cf. Anton Schindler, *Biographie von Ludwig van Beethoven*, 3rd edition (Münster, 1860), Vol. I, p. 154.

7. Gustav Nottebohm, *Zweite Beethoveniana* (Leipzig, 1887), p. 375.

8. George Grove, *Beethoven, and His Nine Symphonies* (London and New York, 1896), pp. 185–6.

9. Foreign translations of Sturm's work soon appeared; the earliest English one of 1791–2 was entitled *Reflections on the Works of God and Providence*.

10. Cf. Helen Darbishire, 'Wordsworth and the Weather', *A Review of English Literature*, July 1960, p. 40.

11. *The Excursion*, Book IV, ll. 509–39.

12. *The Prelude* (1805), Book III, ll. 124–9.

13. Book II, ll. 450–7; Book VIII, l. 627.

14. Cf. N. P. Stallknecht, *Strange Seas of Thought. Studies in William Wordsworth's Philosophy of Nature* (Durham, 1945), pp. 79–80.

15. Cf. A. N. Whitehead, *Science and the Modern World* (Cambridge, 1927), p. 106.

16. Book III, ll. 420–7.

17. Cf. Katherine Chorley, 'Wordsworth and Nature Mysticism', *The Month* (London, 1953), p. 350.

18. 1805 version, Book I, ll. 21–5. A like thought is expressed in the poem *Lines composed a few miles above Tintern Abbey*.

19. Allsop, *Letters, Conversations, and Recollections of Samuel Taylor Coleridge*, Vol. I (1836), p. 107.

20. Cf. Henry Crabb Robinson's entry in his diary on 19 April 1824 (*Diary, Reminiscences, and Correspondence*, ed. Thomas Sadler [1872], Vol. I, p. 406).

21. *Christianity Past and Present* (Cambridge, 1952), p. 101.

22. 'Walking' (1862), *Essays and Other Writings*, ed. W. H. Dircks, p. 1.

23. Ralph Waldo Emerson's posthumous biographical sketch, reprinted in Thoreau, *Life without Principle* (1902), p. 6.

24. *Walden*, conclusion.

25. Cf. J. Wood Krutch, *Henry David Thoreau* (1949), *passim*.

26. For similar reasons, Senancour, for a time, took refuge in Switzerland. He says in *Oberman*: "I went to live in what is perhaps the only country in Europe where, in a rather favourable climate, one may still find the stark beauty of a natural landscape" (Tome I, 2nd letter).

27. Cf. Lenau's poem *Der Indianerzug*, written during his sojourn in America.

28. Here again there is a parallel between Thoreau and Senancour. Cf. the latter's *Rêveries sur la nature primitive de l'homme* (1799), 17. rêverie. The idea can, of course, be traced back to Rousseau.

Notes and Sources

XVIII. METAPHYSICAL INTOXICATION

1. *Antichrist*, aphorism 10 (Musarion edition, XVII, p. 178).

2. Alexander Rüstow, *Ortsbestimmung der Gegenwart*, Vol. II, p. 460.

3. Cf. R. Kroner's Introduction to *Hegel's Early Theological Writings*, ed. T. M. Knox (Chicago, 1948), p. 16.

4. These analogies have been made the subject of a monograph by E. D. Hirsch, Jr., *Wordsworth and Schelling: A typological study of Romanticism* (New Haven, Connecticut, 1960).

5. Cf. Goethe's letter to Schelling of 27 September 1800.

6. For the impact on his audience, cf. G. H. Schubert, *Selbstbiographie*, Vol. I, pp. 388 ff.

7. *The Limits of Science. Outline of Logic and the Mathematics of the Exact Sciences* (1948), pp. 15–16.

8. Cf. Helmholtz's paper, delivered in 1877, on 'Das Denken in der Medizin'. Heinrich Hertz's retrospect, in its turn, was written on the occasion of Helmholtz's seventieth birthday in 1891. Cf. also, more recently, Walter Gerlach, 'Fortschritte der Naturwissenschaft im neunzehnten Jahrhundert', *Propyläen-Weltgeschichte*, Vol. VIII (1960), p. 238; and Wolfgang Bargmann, 'Der Weg der Medizin seit dem 19. Jahrhundert', *op. cit.*, Vol. IX (1960), pp. 530–1, 542. It is only fair to add that some exponents of *Naturphilosophie* were among the first to make the highly fruitful suggestion that psychological and physiological studies be brought into closer contact with each other. (E.g., Carl Gustav Carus, *Symbolik der menschlichen Gestalt* [Leipzig, 1853].)

9. Cf. Horst Fuhrmans, *Schellings Philosophie der Weltalter. Schellings Philosophie in den Jahren 1806–1821* (Düsseldorf, 1954), pp. 202–3.

10. Letter to Gottfried Kinkel, 13 June 1842 (*Briefe*, Vol. I [Basel, 1949], p. 202).

11. *Schelling: Grösse und Verhängnis* [Greatness and Disaster] (Munich, 1955), p. 273.

12. Quoted from Willibald Beyschlag, *Aus meinem Leben: Erinnerungen und Erfahrungen der jüngeren Jahre*, Vol. I (Halle, 1896), pp. 144–5.

13. E.g. in a letter to Chalmers of 20 February 1847.

14. The idea occurs in the third of Fichte's lectures delivered in Berlin in 1800.

15. Cf. Basil Willey, *Nineteenth Century Studies* (1949), p. 102.

16. *The Myth of the State* (New Haven, Connecticut, 1946)' Chapter XV.

17. I find myself in agreement with Pieter Geyl when he writes, " . . . this looking for the pioneers of National Socialism among generations which had not the remotest notion of that evil thing is a dangerous game" (*Debates with Historians* [Groningen and The Hague, 1955], p. 17).

XIX. NATIONAL MESSIANISM

1. Oddly enough, Fichte based these claims mainly on the alleged purity of the German language (cf. his *Reden an die Deutsche Nation*, Vierte *Rede* [1808], *passim*).

2. Mickiewicz may have had in mind the Constitution of 3 May 1791, which reformed and modernized the obsolete system of government in Poland, though the neighbouring powers would not allow the Constitution to come into effect. More likely still, Mickiewicz thought of the far more ancient Polish–Lithuanian Union, which had developed from an association of independent countries, and could therefore serve as a model for the world to follow.

3. Cf. Mateusz W. Mieses, *Polacy chrześcijane pochodzenia żydowskiego* (Warsaw, 1938), Vol. I, pp. 83–92. Juliusz Kleiner, in his monograph on Mickiewicz (Lublin, 1948) summarized the result of his investigations as follows: "There is no foundation to the thesis that Mickiewicz's mother was a Jewess, or a daughter of Jews, but the supposition that a person of Jewish blood existed among more remote ancestors of Mickiewicz's mother is justified" (*Op. cit.*, p. 913).

4. It is now believed that Mickiewicz under the influence of Tovianism—where Israel's importance was stressed and held in high esteem—chose to present himself as a half-Jew, even though this involved a certain mystification.

5. 'Daily Conversations with the Very Learned and Highly Skilled Doctor Piffoël', written in 1837, published in the *Intimate Journal*, 1929, pp. 100–1.

XX. THE NEW RELIGION OF PROGRESS

1. A. Rambaud, *Histoire de la civilisation contemporaine en France*, 9. éd. (Paris, 1912), p. 136.

2. "The immense heart of the world beats in his breast."

3. "I am almost a prophet and almost an apostle."

4. "To dream a rêverie is good, to dream utopia is better."

5. Denis Saurat in his Introduction to the Everyman edition of *Les Misérables*.

6. Daniel Halévy, *La Vie de Proudhon* (Paris, 1948), p. 444. The passages quoted are taken from one of two hitherto unpublished fragments left by Proudhon.

7. Pierre Moreau, *Le Romantisme* (Paris, 1957), p. 400.

8. *La Légende des Siècles*, LVIII: 'Vingtième Siècle', II: 'Plein Ciel', Pleiade éd. (Paris, 1950), pp. 728–9. "Where is this ship going? Clothed in sunlight it is travelling to a future divine and pure, towards virtue, towards science which one sees shining, towards the extinction of scourges, towards generous forgiveness, towards abundance, tranquillity, laughter and the happy man. It is going, that glorious ship, towards righteousness, reason and fraternity, towards religious and holy truth without imposture and without a veil, towards love as it ties hearts together in sweet bonds, towards the just, the great, the good, the beautiful. . . . You see very well that, indeed, it is rising to the Stars."

9. Edmond et Jules de Goncourt, *Journal: Mémoires de la vie littéraire* (Paris), n.d., Tome V, p. 36.

10. *Augsburger Allgemeine Zeitung*, 15 June 1834, reprinted under the title *Lutetia* (Hamburg, 1854).

11. *Roman*, ed. Ollendorff, Vol. IV, p. 554.

XXI. REDEMPTION THROUGH MUSIC

1. *Consuelo*, Chapter LV.

2. My late brother, Wilhelm Schenk, dealt with this phenomenon in an essay entitled 'The Religion of Music', *Humanitas* (Manchester, 1948–9).

3. Beethovens Symphonie in C-Moll.

4. *Kreisleriana*.

5. *Alte und neue Kirchenmusik. Gespräche der Serapionsbrüder.*

6. 'E. T. A. Hoffmann', in *Deutsche Biographie*, Vol. III, p. 60.

7. In conversation with Max Löwenthal, on 19 April 1842.

8. *Briefe an eine Freundin*, p. 108. Cf. also a similar passage in L. Vitet's article in *Le Globe* of 15 January 1825.

9. Marie von Bülow, *Hans von Bülow in Leben und Wort* (Stuttgart, 1925), p. 69.

10. Alfred Einstein, *Music in the Romantic Era* (1947), p. 100.

11. Amy Fay, *Music-Study in Germany* (Leipzig, 1886), pp. 187–8.

12. *Roman Journal*, 7 May 1862.

13. Cf., for example, Paul Arthur Loos, *Richard Wagner. Volendung und Tragik der deutschen Romantik* (Bern, 1952).

14. The vexed question of Wagner's paternity is discussed in each of the four volumes of Newman's *magnum opus*. In an appendix to Volume III (1945) the author concludes: "It certainly looks now . . . as if the gallant opponents of the theory of the Geyer paternity have been defending a lost cause." Cf. also the remarkable facts related in Vol. IV (1947), p. 597, n. 9.

15. Cf. Ernest Newman, *op. cit.*, Vol. I, p. 36, and Vol. II, pp. 564–70.

16. Ernest Newman, *op. cit.*, Vol. I, p. 289.

17. Ernest Newman, *op. cit.*, Vol. I, p. 476.

18. Cf. Chapter VIII of this study.

19. Letter to Röckel, 23 August 1856.

20. Though the music to *Der Ring des Nibelungen* was not completed until 1874, the text appeared as early as 1853. In the second scene of act II of *Die Walküre*, Wotan exclaims:

> Auf geb' ich mein Werk;
> Eines nur will ich noch:
> das Ende — —
> das Ende!

21. Letter to Liszt, 15 January 1854.

22. *Briefwechsel zwischen Wagner und Liszt*, ed. Erich Kloss (Leipzig, 1910), p. 42.

23. *Literary Notebooks*, ed. H. Eichner (1957), no. 1297.

24. Letter from Paris, 7 October 1859 (Richard Wagner, *Briefe*

an Hans von Bülow [Jena, 1916], pp. 125–6). However, Wagner did not wish the public to know about his indebtedness to Liszt.

25. *Op. cit.* (Zürich, 1948), p. 84.

26. Nietzsche rightly remarked: "The connoisseur of European cultural trends knows for certain that French Romanticism and Richard Wagner are intimately bound up with each other" (*Nietzsche contra Wagner*, Musarionausgabe [Munich, 1926], Vol. XVII, p. 288; cf. also Nachlass, Vol. XVII, p. 313).

27. The first of the articles on *German Art and German Politics*.

28. Fritz Friedrich, *Studien über Gobineau* (Leipzig, 1906). Cf. also Friedrich Hertz, *Race and Civilization* (1928), pp. 158–62.

29. This is not the place to enter into a discussion of this grossly misused term. In 1952, the leading German encyclopedia, *Der Grosse Brockhaus* (Vol. I) summarized the position as follows: "The use of the term Aryan in the racial sense is unscientific." A sound entry, if somewhat laconic after all that had gone before.

30. 'Religion und Kunst', *Bayreuther Blätter*, October 1860.

31. Entry of September 1865. The Journal was intended for the political education of King Ludwig II.

32. In 1911 the book appeared in English under the title *The Foundations of the Nineteenth Century*.

33. Felix Weingartner, *Lebenserinnerungen*, 2nd ed. (Zürich, and Leipzig, 1928), Vol. I, p. 266.

34. Cosima herself thus had as much Jewish blood as Adolf Hitler is now believed to have had (cf. Franz Jetzinger, *Hitlers Jugend* [Vienna, 1956], pp. 31, 33).

35. On this point I find myself in entire agreement with the view put forward by Judith N. Shklar, *After Utopia: The Decline of Political Faith* (Princeton, 1957), p. 107.

36. Cf. Woldemar Lippert, *Wagner in Exile 1849–62*, transl. by Paul Englund (1930), pp. 59 ff.

37. Winifred Stephens, *Madame Adam from Louis Philippe until 1917* (1918), p. 73.

38. Letter to Liszt, 15 January 1854.

39. *Werke*, Vol. VIII, p. 29. Cf. also 'Ueber Staat und Religion' (1864), *Gesammelte Schriften und Dichtungen* (Leipzig, 1873), Vol. VII, pp. 36–7.

40. 'Das Bühnenweihfestspiel in Bayreuth', in *Bayreuther Blätter*, November–December, 1882.

41. Cf. the recent monograph by Robert Donington, *Wagner's 'Ring' and its Symbols: The Music and the Myth* (1963).

42. Cf. also the interesting article from the German Romantic periodical *Orpheus*, reprinted in Alfred Wiese, *Die Entwicklung des Fühlens und Denkens der Romantik, auf Grund der romantischen Zeitschriften* (Leipzig, 1912), pp. 179–80.

43. Both Ernest Newman (*op. cit.*, Vol. IV, pp. 475–520) and more recently Curt von Westernhagen (*Richard Wagner. Sein Werk. Sein Wesen. Seine Welt* [Zürich, 1956], pp. 509–31) make laborious but, to my mind, unconvincing attempts to rebut Nietzsche's criticisms.

44. Helmina von Chézy, *Denkwürdigkeiten aus dem Leben von Helmina von Chézy* (Leipzig, 1858), pp. 259 ff.

45. Cf. Robert L. Jacobs, *Wagner* (1935), p. 180. It may be noteworthy in this context that Colet in his *Panharmonie musicale* (1839) had laid down rules for the use of consecutive dissonances which were meant to portray the chaos of the passions.

46. Th. Marix-Spire, *Le Romantisme et la Musique: Le Cas George Sand*, p. 596.

47. Cf. Paul Arthur Loos, *op. cit.*, p. 206.

48. *Die Welt als Wille und Vorstellung*, Drittes Buch, par. 52.

49. Ernest Newman, *op. cit.*, Vol. IV, p. 466.

50. *Gesammelte Schriften über Musik und Musiker*, 2nd edition (Leipzig, 1875), Vol. I, p. 17. (The essay in question, which was written in 1834, is entitled 'Aus Meister Raro's, Florestan's und Eusebius' Denk- und Dicht Büchlein'.)

51. Lamennais's dictum is quoted in Comtesse d'Agoult's letter to Liszt, dated 11 December 1840 (*Correspondance de Liszt et de Madame d'Agoult* [Paris, 1934], Vol. II, pp. 73–4). Cf. also Lenau's utterance of 1839: "Jetzt gilt nur mehr die Musik etwas. Das Gehör ist der letzte Sinn, der dem Sterbenden vergeht."

Notes and Sources

EPILOGUE

1. *Friedrich Nietzsche in seinen Werken* (Vienna, 1894), p. 35.

2. Cf. *Götzendämmerung. Sprüche und Pfeile*, No. 26: "I distrust all systematizers and avoid them. The will to a system shows a lack of honesty."

3. Burckhardt's letter to Nietzsche, Basel, 5 April 1879 (Jacob Burckhardt, *Briefe*, ed. Fritz Kaphahn [Leipzig, 1935], p. 427).

4. Cf. *Vom Nutzen und Nachteil der Historie für das Leben [Unzeitgemässe Betrachtungen. Zweites Stück]* (Leipzig, 1874), preface and *passim*.

5. For the classification of Nietzsche as a Romantic, cf. Karl Joël, *Nietzsche und die Romantik*, 2nd ed. (Jena, 1923) [in my opinion Joël overemphasizes the analogies between Nietzsche and German as distinct from European Romantics]; Thomas Mann, *Nietzsche Philosophie im Lichte unserer Erfahrung* (Stockholm, 1948), p. 37; and Victor von Seckendorff, 'Nietzsche et le Romantisme tardif', in *Nietzsche 1844–1900. Etudes et témoignages de cinquantenaire* (Paris, 1950). Walter A. Kaufmann, on the other hand, rejects the 'cliché' of Nietzsche's Romanticism, but even he admits that it is possible to define the notoriously equivocal word in a sense which would permit its application to Nietzsche (*Nietzsche. Philosopher, Psychologist, Antichrist* [Princeton, 1950], pp. VII, 14).

6. Letter to Peter Gast from Sils Maria, 25 July 1884.

7. Letter to Peter Gast from Sils Maria, 3 September 1883.

8. 'Aus dem Nachlass der Achtzigerjahre', *Werke in drei Bänden*, ed. K. Schlechta (Munich, 1956), Vol. III, p. 509.

9. The latter is quoted above in Chapter IX of this study.

10. *Werke*, Taschenausgabe, Vol. IX, pp. 47–53.

11. C. Bernouilli, *Franz Overbeck und Friedrich Nietzsche. Eine Freundschaft* (Jena, 1908), Vol. I, pp. 288, 325.

12. Letter to Overbeck from Rapallo, 22 February 1883.

13. The term *Uebermensch* goes back to the sixteenth century. Goethe, in *Faust*, Part One, l. 489, still uses it to denote a human being full of overweening pride.

14. 'Also Sprach Zarathustra', Vorrede, *Werke*, ed. K. Schlechta, Vol. II, p. 281.

15. Cf. Frederick Copleston, S.J., *A History of Philosophy*, Vol. VII, 1963, pp. 413–14.

16. *Beyond Good and Evil*, aphorism 257.

17. Cf. Georg Simmel, *Schopenhauer und Nietzsche. Ein Vortragszyklus*, 2nd edition (Munich–Leipzig, 1920), pp. 215–16.

18. Cf. his letter to von Gersdorff from Naumburg, 7 April 1866.

19. To Peter Gast, from Sils Maria, 26 August 1883.

20. Thucydides Book 3, 82. Cf. E. R. Dodds, *Plato, Gorgias* (Oxford, 1959), Appendix, pp. 387–91.

21. *Ecce Homo*, Werke, ed. K. Schlechta, Vol. II, p. 1111. As for castration cf. *Nachlass*, Werke III, p. 913.

22. 'Fragmente des Jahres 1798', No. 1007. In *Gesammelte Werke*, ed. Carl Seelig (Zürich, 1946), Vol. III, p. 77.

23. E.g., "on the whole pity thwarts the law of development which is the law of selection. It preserves that which is ripe for death, it fights in favour of the disinherited and the condemned of life." (*Antichrist*, pp. 131–2.) Although Jacob Burckhardt no longer regarded himself as a Christian, he was repelled by Nietzsche's attack on human compassion. (Cf. Heinrich Wölfflin's letter to Edgar Salin, 14 April 1938, referring to conversations with Burckhardt. Cf. Salin, *Vom deutschen Verhängnis. Gespräch an der Zeitenwende: Burckhardt–Nietzsche* [Hamburg, 1959], p. 132, n. 1.)

24. The recital took place at Sils Maria on 25 August 1960, on the sixtieth anniversary of Nietzsche's death. On the same day the Nietzsche-Haus was officially opened as a foundation.

25. Cf. Karl Schlechta, 'Nachwort', in Friedrich Nietzsche, *Werke in drei Bänden*, Vol. III, pp. 1451–2.

26. Lou Andreas Salomé, *Friedrich Nietzsche in seinen Werken* (Vienna, 1894), pp. 50, 155.

27. Elsewhere in *Dawn of Day* he admits that truth sometimes bores him, and that, from time to time, one must be able to find relief in untruth.

28. Cf. Theo Baeschlin-Osse's letter to Edgar Salin, 22 July 1957, reprinted in Salin, *op. cit.*, pp. 168–9.

29. Cf. Georges Codino, 'Nietzsche. Maladie, Orgueil et Génie', in *Nietzsche. Cinquantenaire* (Paris, 1950), pp. 94–6.

30. The date of the postmark, Turin, 4 a.m., 4 January 1889.

Seventeen months later, while he was living under his mother's care at her native town of Naumburg, she noticed that he often played chorales for himself on the piano. Altogether she had the impression that his soul was finding its way back to God. (Cf. her letter to Overbeck, for the first time quoted in full in Erich F. Podach, *Gestalten um Nietzsche* [Weimar, 1932], pp. 29–31.)

31. "He has made it easy for the worthless to transvaluate values. For a long time to come the world will feel the ill effects of this halcyonic feast."

32. Carl Gustav Carus realized this already over a hundred years ago. (Cf. *Psyche. Zur Entwicklungsgeschichte der Seele* [Pforzheim. 1846], preface, p. V.)

33. *Menschliches, Allzumenschliches*, Band I, aphorism 20. Cf. also aphorism 251, where the idea is further elaborated.

Index

Index

Index

Index

288

Index

Index

Index

Index

Index

Index

Index

McDonnell, Alexander, 6
Mácha, Karel Hynek, 65, 148
Maclure, J. Stuart, 187
Macpherson, James, 42
Madame Adam from Louis Philippe until 1917, 280
Madrid, 61
Magischer Spiegel, 32, 255
Mahomet, 186
Maigron, Louis, 256
Main Currents in Nineteenth-century Literature, xxii
Maistre, Joseph de, 14, 106–7
Maitland, F. W., xxiii
Máj, 148
Mal de siècle. See Weltschmerz
Malady of the Soul. *See Weltschmerz*
Malebranche, Nicolas, 84
Malouet, Pierre-Victor, Baron, 131
Malraux, André, 261
Malta, Order of, 125
Malvern, 39
Man and Society, 250
Man, Henrik de, 251
Manchester, 22
Manfred, 135, 139–40, 142, 148, 149, 270
Mangan, James Clarence, 33
Mann, Golo, 248
Mann, Thomas, 282
Manners, Customs and Conditions of the North American Indians, The, 175
Manon Lescaut, 155
Manzoni, Alessandro, xix, 13, 35–6, 40, 53, 65, 93, 96–102, 117, 256, 265–6; on Christianity, 98–9
Manzoni, Donna Giulia, 97
Manzoni, Henriette, 97, 102
Manzoni, Pietro, 102
Marchand, Leslie A., 269, 270
Maréchal, Christian, 263
Marie Tudor, 197
Marix-Spire, Th., 281
Marquise, La, 157
Marriage, 155, 156–8
Martensen, H. L., 72, 262
Martha, 215
Martin, John, 33; on the Black Country, 22–3
Martino, Pierre, 268–9
Martyrs de Dioclétien, Les, 133
Marx, Karl, 25, 26, 58, 246
Masaryk, T. G., 261
Masked Ball, The, 148
Mass civilization, reaction to, 175, 176
Materialism, 169, 170, 189, 214
Maurois, André, 129, 268
Maximilian I, 224
Mayrhofer, Johann, 20

Mazzini, Giuseppe, 26, 120, 148, 198, 241
Mechanization, Romantic view of, 22–7
Médecin de Campagne, Le, 99
Medicine, 180–1
Medieval Essays, 273
Medievalism, 38–40
Medwin, Thomas, 138, 143, 269
Megalomania, 227–8
'Mein Gebet', 65
Mein Kampf, 221
Mein Leben (Wagner), 226
Meister Floh, 205
Meister Martin der Küfer, 228
Meistersinger von Nürnberg, Die, 223, 226, 228
Mélanges, 254
Memel, 107
Mémoires d'Outre-Tombe, 126, 128, 129, 130, 131, 132, 133, 256, 265, 268, 269
Mendelssohn, Felix, 65, 219
Mendelssohn, Moses, 93
Mennais, Abbé Jean-Marie de la, 82–3
Menschenerziehung, Die, 252
Menschliches, 284
Mephisto Waltz, 211
Mer de Glace, 172
Mercier, L. S., 49
Mercure, 268
Mérimée, Prosper, 38, 158
Merland, André, 274
Meshchersky, Prince E. P., 108
Messianism, French national, 195–201; national, 234; Polish national, 187–94, 196
Metaphysical speculation, 29
Metaphysics, 177–87, 247
Metaxata, 271
Metternich, Prince, 107, 119
Meyendorff, Baroness, 210
Michelet, Jules, xx, 41, 43, 100, 196, 198, 200
Mickiewicz, Adam, xx, 4, 13, 34, 36, 41–2, 64, 69, 153, 187–94, 197, 198, 277; George Sand on, 192
Mickiewicz (Jastrun), 272
Mickiewicz, Celina, 191, 192–3
Middle Ages, the, 36–40, 96, 103, 154, 173, 185, 225, 256; adoration of, 36–40; Voltaire on, 256
Mieses, Mateusz W., 277
Mill, J. S., 29
Millingen, Dr., 271
Mind and Heart of Love, The, 273
Minnedienst, 155
Mirari vos, 118, 267

Index

Index

Index

Index

Index

Index

Index

Index